Quaker Records

of

CEDAR CREEK
MONTHLY MEETING
Virginia

1739–1793

Mary Marshall Brewer

HERITAGE BOOKS
2019

HERITAGE BOOKS

AN IMPRINT OF HERITAGE BOOKS, INC.

Books, CDs, and more—Worldwide

For our listing of thousands of titles see our website
at
www.HeritageBooks.com

Published 2019 by
HERITAGE BOOKS, INC.
Publishing Division
5810 Ruatan Street
Berwyn Heights, Md. 20740

International Standard Book Number
Paperbound: 978-1-68034-981-8

CONTENTS

Introduction v

Quaker Records of Cedar Creek Monthly Meeting 1

Index 183

iv

INTRODUCTION

Cedar Creek Monthly Meeting

Friends of the Upper James River, under the care of Henrico Monthly Meeting, settled a meeting by Cedar Creek in Hanover County before 1722. In that year, Edward Mosby of Henrico was charged with the erection of a meeting house near the creek. In 1739 the Cedar Creek Particular Meeting and the Particular Meeting held in Caroline County were united to form a separate monthly meeting, known as Cedar Creek Monthly Meeting. It soon encompassed Friends living in the counties of Albemarle, Amelia, Bedford, Campbell, Caroline, Charles City (part) Goochland, Halifax, Hanover, Henrico, Louisa and Orange counties and Richmond City.

Henrico Monthly Meeting[1]

Prior to the formation of Cedar Creek Monthly Meeting Quakers of this region were considered within the "compass" of Henrico Monthly Meeting. This meeting has been called Henrico, Curles, New Kent, Upper, Upland, White Oak Swamp, and Wayn Oak (or Weyanoke Monthly Meeting). This meeting was initially established as Curles prior to 1699, when its records begin. A decision was made that year not to repair the meeting house at Curles, but to build a new one. Despite the completion of the meeting house in 1704, it continued to meet at the house of William Porter, Jr. who lived by the James River in Henrico County. In 1717 the monthly meeting was held at Curles and in 1718 it met at Edward Mosby's in Henrico County. In 1719 it met among three of the Particular Meetings: Curles in Henrico County, Black Creek in New Kent County, and Wayne Oak in Charles City County. Subsequently it met at Mosby's, the Swamp, Cedar Creek, Widow Bullar's at Appomattox and Robert Hunnicutt's Meeting House called Burley. With the completion of a new meeting house in 1723 it was commonly called thereafter the "Monthly Meeting held at White Oak Swamp." By 1781, the particular meetings belonging to the Henrico Monthly Meeting ("the Monthly Meeting held at White Oak Swamp") were Wayne Oak, Curles, White Oak, Skimono and Black Creek. In 1795 Richmond became an indulged meeting under the care of Henrico Monthly Meeting.

The records of Henrico Monthly Meeting are contained in *Records of*

---

1. For a full coverage of the history of Henrico Monthly Meeting and Cedar Creek Monthly Meeting, see the description given by Douglas Summers Brown in William Wade Hinshaw's *Encyclopedia of American Quaker Genealogy*, Volume VI: Virginia (1950). See also *Quaker Records in Maryland* by Phebe R Jacobsen (1966) which also treats these two monthly meetings..

Henrico Monthly Meeting, Virginia 1699-1805, recently published by Colonial Roots.

F. Edward Wright
Lewes, Delaware
2002

SPECIAL MEANINGS AND ABBREVIATIONS

Certificates (of removal) - statements sent to another monthly meeting indicating that the person or family is transferring to the area of that monthly meeting, certifying their previous attendance of religious meeting, behavior, and in the case of single persons, their clearness from marriage engagements.

Clearness - refers to clearness from marriage engagements.

Come under the care of friends - become a member of the Society of Friends

Disowned - dismissed as a member. One of the prevalent reasons for disownment was marriage to a person who was not a member of the Society.

Excepted - The clerk of Cedar Creek Monthly Meeting commonly misuses this word for accepted.

Friends - Society of Friends or Quakers.

Hireling priest - Any minister of some other denomination, referring to the fact that ministers outside the Society of Friends were paid.

Monthly Meeting - The second level up from a preparative or weekly meeting. The records of marriages, births, and sometimes deaths were maintained by the monthly meeting. It encompassed one or more preparative or weekly meetings.

Preparative Meeting - A business meeting, representing a single congregation within the bounds of the monthly meeting of which it is a subordinate part. Minutes of preparative meetings were recorded.

Quarterly Meeting - The next level up from a monthly meeting

Sufferings - loss of property confiscated by the county officials to support the Anglican Church or the war effort.

ABBREVIATIONS

abt - about
b. - born
Co - County
d. - died
da - day
MD - Maryland
mo(s) - month(s)

NC - North Carolina
NJ - New Jersey
PA - Pennsylvania
Richd - Richard
Thos - Thomas
VA - Virginia

MONTHLY MEETINGS MENTIONED IN THESE RECORDS

Amelia Meeting (Johnson's) - Amelia County, Virginia

Bedford Meeting (South River) - Campbell County, Virginia

Blackwater Meeting (Surry) - Surry County, Virginia

Bradford Monthly Meeting - Chester County, Pennsylvania

Burleigh Meting - Prince George County, Virginia

Burlington Monthly Meeting - Burlington, New Jersey

Camp Creek Meeting - Louisa County, Virginia

Cane (Cain) Creek Meeting - Snow Camp, Orange (now Alamance) County, North Carolina

Caroline Meeting - Caroline County, Virginia

Deep River - Guilford County, North Carolina

Deer (Dear) Creek Meeting - Darlington, Harford County, Maryland

Fairfax Meeting (Waterford) - Loudoun County, Virginia

Fine Creek Meeting - Cumberland County, North Carolina

Fork Creek Meeting - Louisa County, Virginia

Genito Meeting - Fluvanna County, Virginia

Goose Creek Monthly Meeting - Loudoun County, Virginia

Goose Creek Monthly Meeting - Bedford County, Virginia

Green Spring Meeting - Louisa County, Virginia

Guinedd (Gwynedd) Monthly Meeting - Montgomery County, Pennsylvania

Henrico Monthly Meeting (Curles, White Oak Swamp, Weyanoke) - Henrico County, Virginia

Hopewell Meeting (Opeckon) - Clearbrook, Frederick County, Virginia

Indian Spring Meeting - Anne Arundel County, Maryland

Jenito Meeting. See Genato.

Muddy Creek Meeting - Surry County, North Carolina

Nansemond (Chuckatuck) Monthly Meeting) - Nansemond County, Virginia

New Garden Monthly Meeting - Chester County, Pennsylvania

New Garden Monthly Meeting - Guilford County, North Carolina

Orange Meeting (Douglas) - Orange County, Virginia

Pipe Creek Monthly Meeting - Carroll County, Maryland

Pequimans Monthly Meeeting - Pequimans County, North Carolina

Pasquotank Meeting - Pasquotank County, North Carolina

Philadelphia Meeting - Philadelphia, Pennsylvania

Redstone Quarterly Meeting - Fayette County, Pennsylvania

Rich Square Monthly Meeting - North Carolina

South River Monthly Meeting (near Lynchburg) - Bedford and Campbell counties, Virginia

Western Branch Meeting - Nansemond County, Virginia

West River Meeting, Anne Arundel County, Maryland

White Oak Swamp (Curles, Henrico) Monthly Meeting - Henrico County, Virginia

Wrights Borough Monthly Meeting - McDuffie, Georgia

Menoah and Anne Chiles, Caroline Co. Their children: John, b. 3/5/1747; Anne, b. 6/9/1750; Henry, b. 11/6/1752; Patty, b. 3/9/1757; Samuel, b. 30/12/1759.

Daniel and [blank] Harris, Hanover Co. Their children: John, b. 11/1/1731; Edith, b. 20/12/1733; Moses, b. 31/3/1738; Mary, b. 20/10/1740.

Joseph and Agnes Crew. Their children: Armesby, b. 31/8/1745; Mary, b. 26/1/1749; Macajah, b. 22/7/1750; Aggy, b. 10/3/1753; Sucky, b. 16/7/1756.

David and Mary Garland. Their children: Elizabeth, b. 31/9/1745.

Thomas and Judith Cheadle, Caroline Co. Their children: Molly, b. 13/8/1748; John, b. 27/8/1749; George, b. 19/10/1750; Thomas, b. 7/10/1753.

Nathaniel and Jemimah Winston, Caroline Co. Their children: Mary, b. 28/7/1750; Samuel, b. 19/9/1752; Rebeccah, b. 28/2/1755; Anthony, b. 1/4/1757; George, b. 7/12/1759.

Samuel and Martha Hargrave, Caroline Co. Their children: Jesse, b. 8/7/1752; Elizabeth, b. 28/12/1756; Mary, b. 7/3/1759; Martha, b. 10/8/1761; Sarah, b. 13/10/176-; Thomas, b. 31/1/1766; John, b. 21/8/1768.

Maddox and Hulday Stanley. Their children: John, b. 23/1/1747/8; Elizabeth, b. 15/5/1749; William, b. 22/7/1750; Obediah, b. 27/4/17/1751; Mary, b. 17/10/1753; Rachael, b. 6/6/1757; Hulday, b. 9/2/1759; Maddox, b. 15/3/1761.

Ashly and Agatha Johnson, Amelia Co. Their children: John, b. 19/10/1747. By second wife Mary. Their children: Elizabeth, b. 14/5/1752; Mary, b. 18/12/1753; Jane, b. 29/5/1755; Gerard, b. 26/1/1757; Benjamin, 10/7/1758; Drusylla, b. 25/4/1761; Anne, b. 15/1/1763; Ashly, b. 4/5/1766; Edith, b. 11/9/1769; Thomas Watkins, b. 23/11/1771.

Jesse and Elizabeth Johnson, Amelia Co. Their children: Benjamin, b. 21/10/1752; John, b. 31/1/1754; Jesse, b. 7/9/1755; William, b. 8/5/1757; Sarah, b. 10/4/1759; Thomas, b. 1/12/1760; Elizabeth, b. 7/9/1763; Jane, b. 19/4/1766; Agatha, b. 8/10/1768; Watkins, b. 15/4/1770.

William and Elizabeth Stanley. Their children: Samuel, b. 21/9/1759; Hannah, b. 2/1/1762.

Richard and Ann Bloxom, Louisa Co. Their children: Sarah, b. 14/12/1764; William, b. 24/8/1766; Richard, b. 18/12/1767; Obediah, b. 10/4/1770; Gregory, b. 17/10/1771; Gideon, b. 17/9/1772; Ann, b. 17/11/1774; Mary, b. 7/9/1776; Elizabeth, b. 15/11/1779.

William and Mary Ballard. Their children: Thomas, b. 12/11/1735; Frances, b. 12/12/1737; Byram, b. 27/2/1740; Delphin, b. 1/5/1742; David, b. 9/4/1750; Moorman, b. 16/3/1747.

George and Cicily Bell, Louisa Co. Their children: Robert, b. 16/2/1764; George, b. 13/7/1767; Nathan, b. 5/4/1769; Ashley, b. 2/12/1770; Anthony, b. 22/7/1773; Pleasants, b. 21/12/1777.

Byrom and Eleanor Ballard, Albemarle Co. Their children: Mary, b. 16/6/1764; Betty, b. 1/11/1765; William, b. 20/7/1767; Byrom, b. 14/5/1769, d. 14/12/1769; Amos, b. 15/11/1770; Byrom, b. 9/6/1773, d. 9/11/1774; Mouring, b. 14/5/1775; Judith, b. 10/12/1775

Benjamin and Tace Bates (d. 10/3/1810 in her 34th year), Hanover Co. Their children: Lucy, b. 6/5/1795; Macajah, b. 12/6/1797; Martha, b. 17/3/1800; Tace Crew, b. 11/10/1803, d. 19/9/1892 ; William Savery, b. 7/4/1806; Fleming, b. 1/3/1808, d. 8/9/1809.

Micajah and Judith Clark, Camp Creek. Their children: Christopher, b. 20/2/1737; Robert, b. 15/6/1738; Mourning, b. 6/6/1740; Micajah, b. 27/12/1741; John, b. 26/10/1743; Edward, b. 12/10/1745.

Boling and Winifred Clarke. Their children: Christopher, b. 30/2/1743; Elizabeth, b. 21/11/1744.

Francis and Christiana Clarke, Fork Creek (Camp Creek Records). Their children: Molley, b. 17/9/1747; Betty, b. 22/11/1748; Nicholas, b. 6/2/1750; Frances, b. 7/2/1753.

John and Anne Clarke, Fork Creek (Camp Creek Records). Their children: Thomas, b. 30/7/1746; Francis, b. 5/8/1748; John, b. 3/11/1750.

James and Judith Crew, Hanover Co. Their children: Unity, b. 31/8/1760; Littlebury, b. 18/12/1762; Jesse, b. 18/1/1765; Obediah, b. 31/3/1767; Sarah, b. 16/7/1769; Judith, b. 1/2/1772; James, b. 5/1/1774; Dorothy, 27/6/1776; Benjamin, b. 21/5/1779; Marry, b. 20/7/1781.

Micah and Margaret Crew, Hanover Co. Their children: Tace, b. 30/8/1776; Lemuel, b. 5/8/1778; Unity, b. 25/9/1780; Walter, b. 28/12/1784; Tallitha, b. 18/2/1888; Margaret, b. 31/5/1790; Susanna, b. 15/10/1792; Deborah, b. 25/11/1794.

Pleasant and Amy Cobbs, Caroline Co. Their children: Thomas, b. 21/4/1786; Rebecca, b. 20/10/1787; Mary, b. 18/3/1789; Rhoda, b. 30/9/1790; Abigal, b.

28/3/1792; Elizabeth, b. 19/11/1793; Pleasant, b. 13/12/1795; Joseph, b. 21/6/1797; Anselm, b. 16/4/1799; Joanna, b. 17/6/1803; Robert, b. 16/2/1806.

Samuel and Ann Couch, Goochland Co. Their children: Rebecca, b. 26/8/1796.

Littlebury and Huldah Crew, Hanover Co. Their children: James, b. 229/1795; Benjamin, b. 16/11/1799; John, b. 30/4/1801, d. 26/10/1801; Milly, b. 21/9/1802.

James and Charlotte Cowgill, Hanover Co., "from Culpepper." Their children: Rachael, b. 18/10/1794; Abigail, b. 16/10/1796; John, b. 21/8/1798; James, b. 24/5/1801.

John and Judith Douglas. Their children: Charles, b. 29/4/1732; Elizabeth, b. 18/12/1733; Thomas, b. 2/9/1740; Polly, b. 12/6/1744; Judith, b. 18/7/1746; John, b. 8/8/1748; Anne, b. 10/2/1750; ///b. 22/9/1752; ///, b. 9/1/1756.

Micajah and Mary Davis, Louisa Co. Their children: Susanna, b. 29/4/1779; Martha and Mary (twins), b. 6/3/1780.

Daniel and Mary Harris, Hanover Co. Their children: John, b. 11/1/1731; Edith, b. 20/12/1733; Cornelius, b. 11/11/1735; Moses, b. 31/3/1735; Mary, b. 20/10/1740; Daniel; Thomas; Nicholas.

Samuel and Martha Hargrave, Caroline Co. Their children: Jesse, b. 8/7/1752; Samuel, b. 9/9/1754; Elizabeth, b. 28/12/1756; Mary, b. 7/3/1759; Martha, b. 10/8/1761; Sarah, b. 15/10/1763; Thomas, b. 31/1/1766; John, b. 21/8/1768.

Moses and Elizabeth Harris. Their child: Sarah, b. 11/11/1762. By Sopphia his 2nd wife: William Eley, b. 3/12/1763; Sally Lowes and Priscilla Lowes, b. 27/4/1772.

Henry Philips Hart and Mary his wife. Their children: James Philips, b. 20/6/1741; William, b. 13/2/1743; John, b. 18/3/1745; Joseph, b. 3/12/1748; Elizabeth, b. 3/2/1751.

Jeremiah and Ann Harris, Hanover Co. Their children: Sally, b. 7/6/1767; John b. 14/8/1769; Lucy, b. 15/3/1772; Cheadle, b. 9/6/1774; Elizabeth, b. 22/11/1779.

John and Alice Hutchins, Goochland Co. Their children: Jonathan, b. 28/2/1763; Agatha, b. 21/1/1763; Susanna, b. 15/1/1769; Mary, b. 20/1/1771; Elizabeth, b. 1/12/1772; Thomas, b. 23/11/1774; Strangman, b. 15/9/1776; William, b. 14/8/1778; Patrick, b. 3/10/1781

Joseph and Rachael Hargrave, Caroline Co. Their children: Garland, b. 30/1/1793; Lucy, b. 3/2/1797.

Thomas and Chatilda Harris, Hanover Co. Their children: Deborah, b. 17/12/1787; a son, d. —; Rebecca, b. 24/9/1790; Benjamin, b. 24/2/1794; Isabella, b. 2/4/1803; Sarah Ann, b. 15/1/1809.

Benjamin and Sarah Harris. Their child: Thomas, b. 17/3/1760.

James and Rebecca Hunnicutt, Goochland Co. Their children: John Murdaugh, b. 16/12/1773; Ann, b. 6/9/1775; Miriam Murdaugh, b. 21/9/1777; James, b. 12/2/1780; Thomas Pretlow, b. 5/9/1782.

Thomas and Unity Harris, Hanover Co. Their children: Benjamin, b. 10/2/1806.

Benjamin and Mary Johnson. Their children: Thomas, b. 14/11/1749; John, b. 14/1/1751; Andrew, b. 7/4/11/1754; William, b. 12/8/1756.

William (b. 22/8/1739) and Agatha (b. 18/9/1749) Johnson, Amelia Co. Their children: Milley, b. 12/3/1766; Elizabeth, b. 24/10/1768; Zachariah, b. 27/1/1770; William, b. 28/7/1771; Rachael, b. 30/11/1774; Charles, b. 4/3/1777; Pleasants, b. 12/8/1780; Thomas, b. 14/4/1783; Christopher, b. 4/5/1785; Moreman, b. 26/6/1787.

John (b. 20/7/1731) and Lydia (b. 1/1/1736) Johnson, Amelia Co. Their children: Judith, b. 13/8/1755; Susanna, b. 28/3/1757; James, b. 27/8/1758; Samuel, b. 18/2/1761; Joseph, b. 1/10/1763; John, b. 5/2/1766; Thomas, b. 29/12/1769; Jonathan, b. 13/4/1771; Strangeman, 28/9/1772; Benjamin, b. 26/3/1774; Agatha, b. 21/11/1774; Lydia, b. 29/1/1779; Ashly, b. 15/1/1780.

Gerard and Judith Johnson, Amelia Co. Their children: Jane, b. 30/5/1762; Elizabeth, b. -/12/1763; Benjamin, b. 21/10/1765; Judith, b. 11/11/1767; Gerard, b. 4/6/1769; John Watkins, b. 5/3/1771; David, b. 30/9/1772; Elizabeth, b. 3/12/1774; Samuel, b. 16/9/1776.

Robert and Sarah Johnson (Camp Creek Records). Their child: Margaret, b. 5/8/1752.

Benjamin and Agnes Johnson. Their children: Sarah, b. 30/1/1729; Christopher, b. 22/11/1731; William, b. 25/4/1734; Benjamin, b. 24/8/1736; Penelope, b. 27/2/1739; Collings, b. 28/6/1741; Edward, b. 23/2/1744; Agnes, b. 11/12/1746.

Elerah(?) And Betsey Johnson, Louisa Co. Their children: Thomas Garland, b. 22/4/1794; James, b. 12/1/1796; Sally, b. 26/6/1797; Patsey(?), b. 16/2/1801.

John and Dorothy Johnson, Hanover Co. Their children: Benjamin, b. 15/12/1797; Sarah, b. 27/10/1799; Penelope, b. 13/2/1802; Judith, b. 9/5/1804; James, b. 28/5/1807; Deborah, b. 8/11/1809; Unity and Mary, b. 11/4/1811.

Thomas and Rachael Moorman. Their children: Mary, b. 19/12/1730; Zachariah, b. 2/2/1732; Micajah, b. 22/6/1735; Elizabeth, b. 2/2/1738; Thomas, b. 6/6/1740; Mildred, b. 25/11/1742; Pleasant, b. 19/3/1745.

Charles and Mary Moorman, Louisa Co. Their children: Elizabeth, b. 9/2/1737/8; Lucy, b. 20/2/1741; Aggy, b. 26/2/1743; Charles, b. 28/6/1746; Judith or Jude, b. 26/6/1742; Molley, b. 25/9/1751; Robert, b. 16/11/1753; Thomas, b. 25/11/1756.

John Wilson Maddox and Mildred his wife, Hanover Co. Their children: Thomas, b. 2/4/1775; John, b. 16/1/1777; William Griffin, b. 9/3/1779; Wilson, b. 9/4/1781.

John and Sarah Peatross, Caroline Co. Their children: Mary, b. 11/1/1776; Amey, b. 22/1/1778; Anna, b. 5/1/1780; Nelson, b. 25/4/1782; Rhoda, b. 27/6/1784; Elizabeth, b. 9/2/1790.

Samuel and Sarah ....ns, Goochland Co. Removed to Richmond. Their children: Samuel Pleasants (1st son), b. 5/9/1783; Margaret Pleasants (2nd dau.), b. 25/11/1786.

Thomas Snowden and Elizabeth Tucker Pleasants. Their child: Elizabeth Snowden, b. 20/1/1792, d. 31/8/1796.

William Henry and Mary Pleasants, Charley Forest, Goochland. Their children: Thomas Snowden, b. 29/11/1796; Joseph Jordan, b. 19/1/1799.

William and Elizabeth Ratcliff. Their children: Mary, b. 25/3/1760; Harrison, b. 11/3/1762; William, b. 14/1/1764; John, b. 11/11/1766; Gideon, b. 21/5/1769.

James and Elizabeth Stanley. Their child: Caleb, b. 6/8/1758.

Thomas and [blank] Stanley. Their children: maddox, b. 17/8/1715; Elizabeth, b. 29/3/1718. By Elizabeth his 2nd wife: Margery, b. 1/8/1722; Mary, b. 5/6/1729; Thomas, b. 9/2/1731; Pleasant, b. 25/4/1733; John, b. 27/1/1735; Sarah, b. 6/1/1739; Anne, b. 7/6/1741; Nathan, b. 7/1/1743; Joseph, b. 21/10/1747; Zachariah, b. 6/10/1737.

James and Catharine Stanley, Hanover Co. Their children: William, b. 4/6/1729; James, b. 26/3/1731, Mary, b. 27/6/1733; Martha, b. 21/3/1736; Micajah, b.

6

28/4/1739; Agnes, b. 20/6/1742; Strangeman, b. 7/11/1745; Elijah, b. 7/10/1750.

Maddox & Hulday Stanley, Hanover Co. Their children: John b. 23/1/1747-8; Elizabeth b. 15/5/1749; William b. 22/7/1750; Obediah b. 27/4/1751; Mary b. 17/10/1753; Rachael b. 6/6/1757; Hulday b. 9/2/1759; Maddox b. 15/3/1760.

William & Elizabeth Stanley. Their children: Samuel b. 21/9/1759; Hannah b. 2/1/1762.

Achilles & Elizabeth Stanley. Their children: Agness b. 24/6/1768; Jesse b. 24/10/1770.

Thomas & Unity Stanley, Cedarcreek, Hanover Co. Their children: Moses b. 15/11/1781; John b. 2/11/1783; Temperance b. 22/2/1786; James b. 10/3/1787; Joseph b. 9/2/1789; Benjamin b. 10/2/1791; Judith b. 28/9/1793; Abigal b. 19/10/1796; Unity b. 19/8/1799.

Zachariah & Sarah Stanley, Louisa Co. Their children: Susanna b. 8/12/1775; Abraham b. 7/8/1777; Abigal b. 5/2/1780; Zachariah b. 15/10/1782.

Littlebury & Agness Stanley, Cedar Creek, Hanover Co. Their children: Solomon b. 26/12/1787; Martha b. 8/11/1789.

Thomas & Edith Stanley, Cedar Creek. Their children: Milly b. 7/9/1791; Edmund b. 10/2/1793; John b, 19/9/1795; Elijah b. 8/9/1796; Frances b. 1/10/1798. By Priscilla his 2nd wife: Isaac b. 24/3/1803; Thomas Binford b. 5/9/1805.

Maddy & Rebekah Stanley, Cedar Creek, Hanover Co. Their children Samuel b. 1/4/1796; Priscilla b. 15/7/1798; Lucy b. 9/4/1801; Anne b. 23/6/1803; Joel b. 18/11/1805.

Henry & Anne Terrell, Caroline Co. Their children: Henry b. 29/1/1735; Thomas b. 20/8/1736; Betty b. 7/9/1738; Anne b. 15/9/1740.

Henry & Sarah Terrell. Their children: Ursula b. 11/3/1746; Charles b. 3/8/1748; Judith b. 6/2/1750; Abigail b. 6/10/1751; George b. 28/6/1753; Tarlton b. 19/11/1754.

David & Sarah Terrell. Their children: Agga b. 17/12/1749; Benjamin b. 7/11/1750; Edward b. 12/2/1753; Sarah b. 10/1/1755; Mary b. 6/4/1757; Winifred b. 14/10/1760; David b. 11/3/1763; Henry b. 13/8/1767; Samuel b. 12/12/1769.

Pleasants & Catherine Terrell, Caroline Co. Their children: Lucy b. 17/9/1763; Jesse b. 5/10/1765; Robert b. 24/1/1768; Samuel b. 8/1/1770; Pleasants b. 26/11/1778; Mary b. 3/2/1784.

Thos & Rebecca Terrell, Caroline Co. Their children: Matthew Peatross b. 8/11/1762; Amy b. 8/11/1766; Rhoda b. 8/11/1770; Thomas b. 17/2/1772; Timothy b. 23/3/1774; Joanna b. 31/3/1776; Joseph b. 29/9/1777; Rebecca b. 22/12/1780.

Jonathan & Margaret Terrell, Caroline Co. Their children: Elizabeth b. 28/3/1778; Chiles b. 26/2/1780; Nanny b. 17/6/1782; John b. 24/5/1784; Miriam b. 2/11/1786; Matilda b. 18/3/1789.

Jesse & Mary Terrell, Caroline Co. Their children: Sarah b. 10/6/1788; Parmelia b. 27/10/1790. By Mary his 2nd wife: Rhoda b. 15/10/1796; George b. 1/1/1799; Mahion b. 17/8/1802; Samuel b. 24/8/1804; Eliza Ann b. 4/3/1807.

Matthew Peatross & Sally Terrell, Caroline Co. Their children: Mahala b. 27/4/1790; Rachael b. 2/11/1795; Thomas b. 15/2/1798; Clark b. 29/11/1799; Joanna b. 3/4/1802; Matthew b. 28/3/1804.

[blurred] & Margaret Terrell, Caroline Co. Their children: Caleb b. 17/5/1791; Thomas b. 24/2/1794.

Timothy & Miriam M. Terrell, Caroline Co. Their children: Maria b. 25/4/1799. By Mary his 2nd wife: Caty b. 11/7/1804.

Benjamin & Margaret Vaughan, Cedar Creek, Hanover Co. Their children: Matilda b. 29/1/1796 d. 24/1/1813; Samuel b. 12/8/1797; Bowling b. 30/8/1799; Joseph b. 22/8/1801; John Ladd b. 21/11/1803; Benjamin b. 30/11/1805; Anna Ladd b. 22/3/1808; Lucy Dabney b. 24/3/1810; Margaretta B. b. 2/7/1813; Mary M. b. [faded] d. 9/1813.

Nathaniel & Jemimah Winston, Caroline Co. Their children: Mary b. 28/7/1750; Samuel b. 19/9/1752; Rebecca b. 28/2/1755; Anthony b. 1/4/1757; George b. 7/12/1759.

Henry & Anne Terrell. Their children: Henry b. 29/1/1735; Thomas b. 20/8/1736; Betty b. 7/9/1738; Anne b. 15/9/1740.

Henry & Sarah Terrell. Their children: Ursula b. 11/3/1746; Charles b. 3/8/1748; Judith b. 6/2/1750; Abagail b. 6/10/1751; George b. 28/6/1753; Tarlton b. 19/11/1754.

David & [blank] Terrell. Their children: Edward b. 12/1/1753; Sarah b. 10/1/1755.

James & Elizabeth Stanley. Their child: Caleb b. 6/8/1758.

Deed for land on which Camp Creek Mtg Hse was built was given 2nd Nov 1764.

Richard & Ann Blossom. Their children: Sarah b. 14/12/1764; William b. 24/8/1766; Richard b. 18/12/1767; Obadiah b. 10/4/1770; Gregory b.17/10/1771; R[?]deon b. 17/9/1772; Ann b. 7/11/1774; Mary b. 7/9/1776; Cuzaveth b. 15/11/1779.

Pleasant & Katherine Terrell. Their children: Pleasant b. 26/11/1778; Mary b. 3/2/1784.

Micayah & Mary Davis, Their children: Susanah b. 29/4/1779; Martha & Mary b. 6/3/1780.

Moses Stanly son of Thos & Unity Stanly b. 15/11/1781.

Elizabeth Johnson of Amelia Co. d. 29/6/1783 age of 82 years.

George & Cicily Bell, Louisia Co. Their children: Robert b. 15/2/1764; George b. 13/7/1767; Nathan b. 5/4/1769; Ashley b. 2/12/1770; Anthony b. 22/7/1773; Pleasants b. 21/12/1777.

John & Lydia Johnson, Amealia Co. Their children: Judith b. 13/8/1755; Susanah b. 28/3/1757; James b. 27/8/1758; Samuel b. 19/2/1761; Joseph b. 1/10/1763; John b. 5/2/1766; Thomas b. 29/12/1769.

Jeremiah & Ann Harriss, Hanover Co. Their children: Sally b. 7/6/1767; John b. 14/8/1769; Lucy b. 15/3/1772; Cheadle b. 9/6/1774; Elizabeth b. 22/11/1779.

James & Judith Crew, Hanover Co. Their children: Unity b. 31/8/1760; Littlebury b. 18/12/1762; Jesse b. 18/1/1765; Obediah b. 31/3/1767; Sarah b. 16/7/1769; Judith b. 1/2/1772; James b 5/1/1774; Dorathy b. 27/6/1776; Benjamin b. 21/5/1779; Mary b. 20/7/1781.

John Wilson Maddox, Hanover Co. Their children: Thomas b. 2/4/1775; John b. 16/1/1777; William Griffin b. 9/3/1779; Wilson b. 9/4/1781.

William & Agatha Johnson, Amealia Co. Their children: William b. 28/7/1772; Rachal b. 30/11/1774; Charles b. 4/3/1777; Pleasant b 12/8/1780; Thomas b. 14/4/1783.

John & Tar. Peatross, Caroline Co. Their children: Mary b. 11/11/1776; Amey b. 22/1/1778; Anna b. 5/4/1780; Nelson b. 25/4/1782; Rhoda b. 27/6/1784; Elizabeth b. 9/2/1790.

John & Alce Hutchings, Goochland Co. Their children: Jonathan b. 28/2/1765; Agatha b. 21/1/1763; Susanah b. 15/1/1769; Mary b. 20/1/1771; Elizabeth b. 1/12/1772; Thomas b. 23/11/1774; Strangman b. 15/9/1776; William b. 14/8/1778; Patrick b. 3/10/1781.

Thomas & Rebecca Terrell, Caroline Co. Their children: Timothy b. 23/3/1774; Joanna b. 31/3/1776; Joseph b. 29/9/1777; Rebekah b. 22/12/1780.

Joseph & Rachael Hargrave, Caroline Co. Their child: Garlend b. 30/1/1793.

Byrom & Eleanor Ballard, Albermarle Co. Their children: Mary b. 16/6/1764; Bettey b. 1/11/1765; William b. 20/7/1767; Byrom b. 14/5/1769 d. 14/12/1769; Amos b. 15/11/1770; Byrom b. 9/6/1773 d. 9/11/1774; Mourning b. 14/5/1775; Judith b. 10/12/1779.

Jonathan & Margret Terrell, Caroline Co. Their children: Elizabeth b. 28/3/1778; Chiles b. 26/2/1780; Nanny b 17/6/1782; John b. 24/5/1784.

Thomas & Unity Stanley, Cedarcreek. Their children: James b. 10/3/1787; Joseph b. 9/2/1789; Benjamin b. 10/2/1791.

Samuel & Lucy Hargrave, Caroline Co. Their child: Sally b. 12/3/1784 d. 27/10/1786.

Pleasant & Amy Cobbs, Caroline Co. Their children: Rebecca b. 20/10/1787; Mary b. 10/3/1789; Phoebe b. 30/9/1790, Abigal b. 28/3/1795; Elizabeth b. 19/11/1793.

Mathew Peatross & Salley Terrell. Their child: Mahala b. 27/4/1790.

Nyorid[?] Johnson d. 28/8/1785.

Elizabeth Johnson w/o Jesse Johnson Senr of Amelia Co d. 29/6/1787 60 years of age.

Jane Johnson dau of Jesse & Elizabeth Johnson d. 23/6/1787 22 years of age.

Nelson Maddox son of John & Mildred Maddox d. 4/20/1793 19 years of age.

Byrum Ballard son of Byrum & Eleanor, Albermarle Co, d. 14/12/1769 aged 7 months.

Byrum Ballard son of Byrum & Eleanor, Albermarle Co, d. 9/11/1774 aged 17 months.

George Bell Senr, Campcreek, Louisa Co, d. 11/5/1787.

Mary Bunch d. 31/1/1792 Campcreek, Louisa Co.

Mary Ballard dau of Mary Bunch & Byron Ballard d. 1/9/1791.

Elizabeth Cheadle d. 16/2/1794 Caroline Co about 94 years.

Rebekah Terrell wife of Thomas Terrell d. 28/5/1794.

Nelson Peatross son of John & Sarah Peatross d. 19/4/1795.

Anne Moor d. 8/2/1792 Campcreek, Louisa Co.

Elizabeth Moorman daughter of Thos & Rachael d. 1740 (Campcreek records).

Wilson Maddox son of John W. & Mildred d. 20/4/1793.

Sarah Pleasants Parsons daughter of Samuel & Sarah Parsons d. 5/12/1784 Belleville, Goochland Co aged 3 ½ yrs & 3 days.

Elizabeth Pleasants wife of Thomas Senr d. 7/11/1788, Beaverdam, Goochland Co.

Elizabeth Pleasants daughter of Robert Pleasants Junr late of [?] (thrown out of chair) d. 1/10/1791, Beaverdam, Goochland Co.

Thomas Snowden Pleasants [son] of Thos, Beaverdam, d. 28/10/1791 Richmond 12 o'clock P.M.

Thomas Willing Pleasants son of Robert Junr late of [Ourles?] d. 11/11/1791, Chas Logans, Powhatan Co.

Nelson Peatross son of John & Sarah d. 19/4/1795 Caroline Co.

Elizabeth Snowden Pleasants daughter of Thos Snowden Pleasants d. 31/8/1796 of Genolocreek, Goochland Co. aged 4 yrs 7 mos 11 days.

Mary Pleasants widow of Thos Pleasants d. 10/11/1790 Beaverdam, Goochland Co 6 o'clock a.m aged 96 yr 7 mo.

Thomas Pleasants son of Thos Pleasants of Curles d. 4/5/1804 Beaverdam, Goochland Co aged [blank].

Margaret Pleasants daughter of Thos Pleasants d. 25/8/1806 Beaverdam, Goochland Co aged [blank].

Mary Pleasants wife of Wm H. Pleasants d. 14/3/1802 Charles Forest, Goochland Co. aged near 23 years.

Hulda Stanley wife of Maddox d. 6/9/1771 from old records.

John Stanley eldest d. 17/7/1783 Cedarcreek, Hanover Co aged about 90 years.

Temperance Stanley daughter of Thos & Unity Stanley d. 29/4/1786 Cedarcreek, Hanover Co 2 mos 7 days.

John Stanley son of Joshua & Elizabeth d. 13/3/1795 Cedarcreek, Hanover Co.

Martha Stanley wife of John Stanley eldest d. 28/5/1789 Cedarcreek, Hanover Co abt 70.

Mary Terrell wife of Jessee Terrell d. 19/11/1790 Caroline Co.

Rebeccah Terrell wife of Thomas d. 28/5/1794 (an elder) Caroline Co.

John Stanley d. 17/7/1783 aged about 90 yrs.

Martha Stanley d. 28/5/1789 aged abt 70 yrs.

Mary b. 10/2/1791.

Judith Stanley b. 28/9/1793.

Abigal Stanley b. 19/10/1796.

Unity Stanley b. 19/8/1799.

Benjamin Watkins Senr d. 9/7/1793 Genelo, Goochland Co. aged [blank] years. (Son of Benjamin)

Archilas (Accillis) Douglas (son of John Douglas) of Orange Co & Elizabeth Terrel (daughter of Micajah Terrel) of Caroline Co, married 10th da, 10th mo, 1779 in Caroline Co. Witnesses: Micajah Terrel, Pleasant Terrel, John Douglas, Elijah Johnson, Catlet Jones, Thos Terrel, Elizabeth Eastin, Sarah Terrel, Ann Barksdale, Milley Douglas, Rachel Moorman, Judith Cheadle, Martha Hargrave, Elizabeth Cheadle, Lucy Cheadle, Judith Cheadle, Salley Chiles, Ursla Cheadle, Salley Hargrove, Mary Hargrove, Rebecca Terrel, Agatha Terrel.

Thomas Stanley (son of John Stanley) and Unity Crew (daughter of James Crew) both of Hanover Co married 20th da, 12th mo, 1780 at Cedarcreek,

12

Hanover Co. Witnesses: John Stanley, James Crew, Micajah Crew, Joshua Stanley, Littlebury Stanley, Shadrack Stanley, Moses Harris, John Harris, John Shelton, Nicholas Watkins, John Stanley, Jno Anderson, Agness Stanley, Ursla Stanley, Mary Payne, Elizabeth Strong, Sara Strong, Rebecca Stanley, Huldah Stanley, Mary Strong, Margaret Stanley, Sarah Harris, Nancy Shelton, Dolley Payne, Elizabeth Harris, Susanah Stanley.

Christopher Johnson (son of Christopher Johnson) of Campbell Co and Sarah Hargrave (daughter of Samuel Hargrave deceased) of Caroline Co married 21st da of [blank] mo, 1784 in Caroline Co. Witnesses: Samuel Hargrave, Thomas Hargrave, Pleasant Terrel, Thos Terrel, John Burch, John ... el, Pleasant Cobbs, Matthew Terrel, Jesse Terrel, Rebecca Terrel, Martha Hargrave, Elizabeth McGeehee, Amey Terrel.

Thomas Pleasants Cobbs (son of Robert Cobbs) of Caroline Co and Amy Terrel (daughter of Thomas Terrel) of Caroline Co married 15th da, 6th mo, 1785 in Caroline Co. Witnesses: Rebecca Terrel, Rhoda Terrel, Aggatha Cobbs, Ursla F. Cheadle, Nancy Bates, Martha Winston, Nancy Hunnicutt, Eliza Cheadle, Milisant McGeehee, Mary Terrel, Rachel Moorman, Rebecca Winston, Nancy Maegey, Thomas Terrel, Jonathan Terrel, Pleasant Terrel, Clark T. Moorman, Matthew P. Terrel, Saml Cobbs, Lewis Cobbs, James Bates, Saml Winston, Joseph Hunnicutt, Nathan Winston.

15/4/1786. Joseph Anthony removed from Goose Creek.

20/12/1788. Charles Eastin removed from South River.

26/12/1787. I gave way to marriage with one not of the same society for which misconduct I have been sorry, desire friends to receive me again into membership. Nancy Bunch.

26/12/1787. Nanny Bunch given fourth at our preparitive meeting held at New Garden. Witnesses: Deborah Terrel, Martha Thornburgh, Eliza Stanley, Sara Rusel, Allen Unthank, Christr Hiatt Junr, Christ Hiat Senr, Wm Stanley, Thos Thornburg.

28/2/1789. Elizabeth Moorman (formerly Johnson) hath so far deviated from the known rules of Friends, as to suffer herself to be joined in marriage to a man too near of kin, by an hireling priest, we hereby disown her.

28/2/1789. Nanny Bunch who was disowned for her marrying contrary to Friends dicipline hath lately sent us a paper condemning her conduct, removed from Cedarcreek, Hanover Co, VA to Newgarden, NC.

Thomas and Sarah Hatton with several small children came from Pensylvany a few years ago, and produced to this Meeting a certificate from Friends there of their membership, but lately removed to reside within Cedarcreek, Hanover Co, we recommend the said Thomas and Sarah Hatton with their six children: Edward, Mary, Susana, Thos, Jesse and Pleasants to your notice. Signed [blank].

10/6/1786. Nathaniel & Samuel Winston in the [page torn] of a Negro contrary to our dicipline, but they failing to take the advice of their Friends, we disown them.

8/7/1786. James Crew sold one of his fellow men into bondage and refuseth to redeem him, we disown him.

9/4/1787. Robert Douglas from my heart condemn my out goings and desire to return to the fold from whence I have strayed. My wife Mary Douglas desires to come under your notice with our two children Charles & Betsey.

11/11/1786. Isaac Stanley (son of John Stanley) of Louisa Co hath been guilty of defiling a young woman that was his first cousin and lately hath married her in a manner contrary to the rules of our dicipline, we disown the said Stanley.

Littleberry Stanley (son of Thomas Stanley) and Aggatha Stanley (daughter of John Stanley) both of Hanover Co married 2nd da, 3rd mo, 1787. Witnesses: Ursley Stanley, Elizabeth Strong, Rebecca Stanley, Peggey Stanley, Judith Crew, Lucy Camron, Edith Harris, Rachel Harris, Nancy Stanley, Mary Alvis, Susanah Stanley, June Calliham, Dorothy Austin, Sarah Harris, Mildred Maddox, Susanah Harris, Elizabeth Camron, Catherine Camron, Edith Stanley, Rachel Calliham, Judith Crew, Fanney Stanley, Fanny James, Huldah Stanley, Martha Stanley, Waddy Stanley, Joshua Stanley, Thomas Stanley, James Crew, Micajah Crew, John Harris, John W. Maddox, Samuel Harris, James Stanley, John Strong, George Strong, Worth Sydnor.

14/4/1787. Zachariah Stanley hath for some time past been in the practice of drinking to excess and of being concerned in gaming, which practices (notwithstanding his having repeatedly with much seeming sincerity made professions of forsaking) he still continues, we therefore disown him.

8/15/1787. Richard Lewis of Caroline Co has absented himself from the publick worship of Friends and appears to be in a lukewarm condition, he likewise hath been in the practice of drinking spirituous liquors to excess, and playing cards for which we disown him.

13/10/1787. Jemima Winston (widow of Nathl Winston deceased) of Caroline Co for want of faithfully adhering to the reproofs of devine instruction which

14

would have preserved her from evil, and contrary to the will of her husband, by which means a number of Negros may be continued in slavery after her decease, we disown her.

8/3/1788. Margery Bunch (daughter of James Bunch) of Louisa Co hath suffered herself to be married to a man of different persuation contrary to our dicipline, we therefore disown her.

Nicholas Johnson in order for a marriage with a member of your Meeting, we do not find anything to obstruct his proceedings. Signed on behalf of South River Monthly Meeting 15th da, 3rd mo, 1788 by Acchillis Douglas clk.

Nicholas Johnson (son of Christr Johnson) of Campbel Co and Martha Hargrave (daughter of Samuel Hargrave deceased) of Caroline Co married the 16th da, 4th mo, 1788 in Caroline Co. Witnesses: Jesse Hargrave, Thomas Hargrave, Joseph Hargrave, Pleasant Terrel, Thos Terrel, Jonathan Terrel, Clark T. Moorman, Pleasant Cobbs, Matthew P. Terrel, Henry Chiles, Ben Burch, Robert Terrel, Joseph McGeehee, Saml Winston, Ann McGeehee, Margaret Terrel, Salley Chiles, Ursla F. Cheadle, Caty Terrel, Rhoda Moorman, Rachel Moorman, Sarah Pittrus, Rebecca Terrel, Salley Moorman, Salley Rogers, Polley Hewlett, Rhoda Terrel, Elizabeth Redd.

10/5/1788. Martha Winston (daughter of Natthl Winston deceased) hath suffered herself to be joined in marriage with a man of another persuation, we therefore disown her.

Matthew P. Terrel (son of Thos Terrel) of Caroline Co and Salley Moorman (daughter of Clark T. Moorman) of same co married 11th da, 5th mo, 1788 in Caroline Co. Witnesses: Thos Terrel, Clark T. Moorman, Jonathan Terrel, John Pettross, William Peatross, Pleasant Cobbs, Thos Terrel Junr, Pleasant Terrel, Achillis Moorman, James Peatross, Rachel Moorman, Rebecca Terrel, Rhoda Terrel, Rhoda Moorman, Martha Hargrave, Sarah Peatross, Amey Cobbs, Frances Moorman, Elizabeth Cheadle, Ursla F. Cheadle, Margaret Terrel, Mary Hargrave, Polley Hewlett, Jemima Nelson, Ann McGeehee, Salley Chiles, Fanney Temple, Mary Peatross.

12/7/1788. Caroline Matilda Bates for some time past wholly neglected the attendance of our religious Meetings and she showing no disposition to alter the same, but rather a desire to be discontinued from being a member, we therefore disown her.

12/7/1788. Mary Logan for some time past wholly neglected the attendance of our religious Meetings and she showing no disposition to alter the same, we therefore disown her.

11/10/1788. Rebecca Winston (daughter of Natthl Winston deceased) of Caroline Co, hath so far deviated from chastity as to have a bastard, we disown her.

11/10/1788. John Stanley (son of Maddox Stanley) of Hanover Co. acknowledged a manumition for his Negros, but refuses to have it recorded in court, and still keeps them in slavery, we declare our disunion with the said Stanley.

11/10/1788. Charles Douglas (son of Charles Douglas) of Orrange Co hath lived in the corrupt practices of the world, such as cursing, swaring, frequent places of divertion, and his general conduct being inconsistent with our profession, we therefore disown him.

20/10/1788. I have for some time past been accounted not a member of society, which has caused me sorrow of heart, I do hereby sincerely condemn that spirit which I suffered and caused me to reflect on Friends in that unbecoming manner and hope a reconciliation may take place which is my desire. Shadrack Stanley.

11/10/1788. Jesse, Samuel & Thomas Hargrave of Caroline Co acting contrary to the advice of their Friends in holding their Negroes in slavery and contrary to the intent of their father Samuel Hargrave deceased, who in his lifetime discharged several of his Negroes and placed them on his own land in a state of freedom, but they by some means have brought them into a state of bondage again, we therefore disown them.

8/11/1788. Judith Cheadle, Ursla Cheadle & Milley McGeehee of Caroline Co have deviated from the principles of justice as to keep their fellow creatures in a state of bondage, contrary to the repeated advise of Friends, we therefore disown them.

8/11/1788. Ann Machgeehee of Caroline Co signed and acknowledged in manumission for divers Negroes which she claimed a right to during her life, but now contrary to the repeated advice of Friends to allow the said Negroes any benefit therefore, we disown her.

8/11/1788. John Hunnicutt of Powhatan Co some time past signed a manumission for his Negroes and bound himself in a particular manner to support the same, but now refuses to comply and continues to hold them in a state of slavery, we therefore disown him.

4/21/17. . I freely acknowledge my past conduct to have been inconsistent with the principles of the society and hope to conduct myself in such manner in future as not to cause any reproach to fall on them. James B. Pleasants, Beaverdam.

Application being made to us by Daniel Clerk for our certificate to joined with you, it appears he is a young man of an orderly life and conversation and frequently attended our meetings and is clear of marriage engagements, therefore we recommend him to your friendly care. Signed 7th da, 2nd mo, 1789 at White Oak Swamp in Henrico Co by James Ladd clk, Isabell Ladd clk.

Catlet Jones and Ann Barksdale of Orrange Co married 2nd da, 3rd mo, 1789 in Hanover Co. Witnesses: Archillis Douglas, Christr Johnson, Clark T. Moorman, Robert Pleasants, James Hunnicutt, Benjn Johnson, John Harris, Micajah Crew, Benjn Crew, Thos Terrel, Pleasant Terrel, Nathan Bell, Thos Harris, Elijah Johnson, Thos Pleasants, Saml Parsons, Thos Hatton, Robert Watkins, Rachel Moorman, Rebecca Terrel, Rachel Harris, Edith Harris, Sarah Parsons, Chlotilda Harris, Judith Crew, Susana Watts, Deborah Pleasants, Margaret Crew, Sarah Hatton, Rhoda Moorman, Judith Harris, Salley Terrel, Mary Baughman, Mary Johnson, Ann Ladd, Priscilla Ladd, Sarah Crew, Judith Crew, Mary Pleasants.

James B. Pleasants removed to Indian Spring, MD.

Mary Bunch and her two children, Ann and James, removed to South River.

William Johnson removed to South River.

John Johnson, his wife Lidia & children Susana, John, Thomas & Lidia removed to South River.

9/5/1789. Sarah Crew (daughter of James Crew) of Hanover Co after being previously cautioned, hath married from amongst us contrary to the known rules of our dicipline. We disown her.

9/5/1789. Margaret Stanley (daughter of Thomas Stanley) of Hanover Co has joined in marriage with a man of different profession.

William Stabler requesting our certificate in order to proceed in marriage with Deborah Pleasants, a member of your Meeting, we recommend him to your care. Signed 25th da, 9th mo, 1789 James Moore clk, Fairfax.

William Stabler from Loudoun Co (son of Edward and Mary Stabler of Petersburg deceased) and Deborah Pleasants (daughter of Thomas & Elizabeth Pleasants of Goochland Co) married in Goochland Co the 4th da, 6th mo, 1789. Witnesses:
Thomas T. Pleasants, Edward Stabler, William A. Pleasants, James Pleasants Junr, Saml Parsons, James Hunnicutt, Thos W. Pleasants, Bary Pleasants, B Watkins, Joel Royster, Thos E. Pleasants, Joseph Woodson, Mary Younghusband, Sarah Parsons, Eliza Pleasants WF, Eliza Pleasants, Eliza T Pleasants, Polly T. Younghusband, Rebecca Hunnicutt, Eliza Watkins, Frances Royster, Polly Pleasants, Sarah Pleasants.

13/6/1789. Sarah Douglass (daughter of Charles Douglass) of Albermarle Co hath deviated from our rules as to suffer herself to be drawn into the customs of fashion of the world, frequenting places of diversion & nonattendance of our religious meetings, we therefore disown her.

25/8/1787. Mary Bunch (daughter of Saml Bunch) of Louisa Co hath for sometime neglected the attendance of our religious meetings and hath been guilty of frequenting places of diversion, as also giving too much way to the vain fashions & customs of the world.

Chlotilda Harris removed from White Oak Swamp, Henrico Co, by marriage and now resides within your limits, we recommend her to your Christian regard. Signed 1st da, 12th mo, 1787 James Ladd clk, Unity Ladd clk this time.

Mary Terrel removed from White Oak Swamp, Henrico Co, by marriage and now resides within your limits, we recommend her to your Christian regard. Signed 4th da, 12th mo, 1789 by James Ladd clk, Unity Ladd clk this time.

Deborah Stabler removed by marriage to Fairfax, Loudon Co.

Shadrack Stanley removed to New Garden, NC.

10/10/1789. Elizabeth Cheadle (daughter of Thomas Cheadle deceased) of Caroline Co signed a manumission for a Negro woman and declared her free, but continues to keep her in a state of slavery, we therefore disown her.

10/10/1789. Ann Harris (wife of Jeremiah Harris) hath almost wholly forsaken the attendance of our religious meetings and her general deportment also is inconsistent with our profession, we therefore disown her.

Robert Bell removed to Deep River, Gilford Co, NC.

Robert Bell returned back into the verge of your meeting. Signed the 17th da, 8th mo, 1788 by David Brooks, Deep River, Gilford Co, NC.

14/11/1789. James Harris is in the practice of overseeing slaves contrary to the established rule of our society, we therefore disown him.

George & Edmond Winston removed to White Oak Swamp, Henrico Co.

Mary Harris (wife of James Harris) and her children Judith, Benjamin, Elizabeth, Mary, Thomas, Lucy and James removed to Whiteswamp, Henrico Co.

Barksley Ballard (son of William Ballard) of Bedford Co, VA and Judith Johnson (daughter of John Johnson) of Amelia Co, VA married 27th da, 2nd mo, 1776. Witnesses: Ashley Johnson, Jesse Johnson, Garrard Johnson, William Johnson, Ben Johnson, Mary Johnson, Elizabeth Johnson, Judith Johnson, Agatha Johnson, Jane Johnson, Susana Johnson, John Johnson Senr, Lydia Johnson, Senr.

Samuel Hargrave (son of Samuel Hargrave deceased) of Caroline Co and Lucy Terrell (daughter of Pleasant Terrell) of said co married 10th da, 1st mo, 1779. Witnesses: Pleasant Terrell, David Terrell, Micajah Terrell, Thos Terrell, Thos Chiles, Jesse Hargrave, Anthony Winston, Geo Winston, Robt Farish, Stephen Farish, Mary Hargrave, Elizabeth Hargrave, Mary Harris, Salley Chiles, Elizabeth Terrell, Rachel Burruss, Ann Mackgee, Rachel Moorman, Molly Chiles, Rebecca Winston, Judith Cheadle, Lucy Cheadle, Deborah Terrell.

Ashley Johnson of Campbell Co and Milley Johnson of Amelia Co married 13th da, 3rd mo, 1782. Witnesses: William Johnson, Ashley Johnson Senr, Jesse Johnson, Garrard Johnson, John Johnson, Joseph Johnson, Samuel Johnson, Thomas Johnson, Elizabeth Johnson, Elizabeth Johnson Junr, Mary Johnson, Lidia Johnson, Jane Johnson, Sara Johnson, Drusilia Johnson.

Elisha Johnson (son of Robert Johnson) of Surry Co, NC and Jane Johnson (daughter of Ashley Johnson) of Amelia Co, VA married 16th da, 3rd mo, 1785. Witnesses: Agatha Johnson, Judith Johnson, Elizabeth Johnson, Jane Johnson, Susanah Johnson, Drusilla Johnson, Anne Johnson, Lydia Johnson, Elizabeth Piller, Agatha Johnson, Jesse Johnson Junr, Ben Johnson, Thos Johnson, Saml Johnson, Wm Johnson Junr, Wm Johnson of ... , Andrew Moorman, Ashley Johnson, Garrard Johnson, John Johnson, Wm Johnson, Garrard Johnson Senr, Ashley Johnson Senr, Jesse Johnson Senr, Milley Piller, Judith Johnson, Lucy Winston, Christian Winston, Sarah Johnson.

James Candler (son of John Candler) of Campbell Co and Agness Johnson (daughter of James Johnson) of Louisa Co married 16th da, 1st mo, 1786. Witnesses: James Johnson, Catlet Jones, George Bell Senr, Elijah Johnson, ...

Johnson, Peter Crawford, George Bell Junr, Nehemiah Bloomer, Martha Johnson, Patty Johnson, Mary Johnson, Massey Johnson, Cisley Bell, Betsey Johnson, Lucy Johnson, Ashley Johnson.

13/3/1790. Milley Stanley (wife of John Stanley) of Hanover Co signed a manumission with her husband for several slaves but since has showed a disposition not to suffer it to take effect, we disown her.

Joseph Hargrave (son of Samuel Hargrave deceased) of Caroline Co & Rachel Terrell (daughter of Pleasant Terrell) of said co married the 14th da, 3rd mo, 1790. Witnesses: Jesse Hargrave, Saml Hargrave, Thos Hargrave, Saml Terrell, John Hargrave, Robt Terrell, Obediah Crew, Christr Terrell, Wm Burrus, Henry Burrus, Pleasant Cobbs, Matw P. Terrell, Jonathan Terrell, Jno Peatross, Clark T. Morman, Thos Terrell, Saml Chiles, Millicent Hargrave, Nancy Terrell, Rachel Moorman, Rebecca Terrell, Margt Terrell, Salley Terrell, Rhoda Terrell, Rhoda Moorman, Judith Harris, Elizabeth Cheadle, Ursla F. Cheadle, Lu.. Temple, Catharine Ellis, Susana Hargrave, Molly Terrell, Sarah Terrell, Lealey Cobbs, Polly Hewlet, Amey Cobbs, Lucy Hargrave, Millicent Hewlet.

8/5/1790. Nathan Winston of Caroline Co hath suffered himself to be drawn into the vain customs of the world, such as frequenting places of diversion, cursing, swareing and offering to fight, we therefore disown him.

Gerard Johnson removed to South River, Campbell Co with his wife Judith, their children: Benjamin, Samuel, John,, Gerard, Wat... , David, Elizabeth, Jane & Judith.

11/4/1784. Benjamin Johnson of Surry Co, NC, through unwatchfulness have given way so far to the spirit of the world as to suffer myself to be joined in marriage contrary to the known principle of friends, which practice I do condemn, and am heartily sorry for, and shall be glad if friends can find freedom to pass my misconduct.

Mary Johnson through unwatchfulness have given way so far to the spirit of the world as to suffer myself to be joined in marriage contrary to the known principle of friends, which practice I do condemn and am heartily sorry for and shall be glad if friends can find freedom to pass by my misconduct.

These may certify that Benjamin Johnson and Mary his wife have been pretty deligent in attending meetings and have behaved orderly. Signed the 28th da, 3rd mo, 1784 Deep Creek, Surry Co, NC by John Hutchings, Daniel Huff, Simon Hadly, John Johnson, Nicholas Hutchins, Bridget Hadly, Elizabeth Huff, Sarah Hutchins, Lidia Johnson.

8/1/1785. Jacob Cheadle of Caroline Co hath married one of two near kin by an hireling priest contrary to good order used among friends, we disown him.

11/12/1784. Jeremiah Harris hath sold a slave which we believe to be an iniquitious practice & contrary to our dicipline, we disown him.

10/7/1790. Ann Bates (daughter of James Bates late of York Co deceased) hath deviated so far from the principles we profess as to join in marriage with a man of a different profession, we therefore disown her.

11/9/1790. John Hargrave (son of Samuel Hargrave deceased) of Caroline Co is in the practice of keeping his fellowmen in the state of slavery which being contrary to our principles we disown him.

John Johnson (son of Jesse) of Amelia Co and Nancy Hunnicutt of Powhatan Co (daughter of John Hunnicutt deceased) married at Genito the 12th da, 12th mo, 1790. Witnesses: Joseph Hunnicutt, Jesse Johnson, Ashly Johnson Junr, Ben Watkins, Joseph Watkins, Watkins Johnson, Thos Watkins, Thos Stanley, Saml Parsons, John S. Pleasants, Thos S. Pleasants, Cary Pleasants, Ruben Pleasants, Danl Clark, Robert H. Ross, James Pleasants Junr, John Hunnicutt, Elizabeth Watkins, Mary Watkins, Salley Watkins, Polley Pleasants, Mary Watkins, Elizabeth T. Pleasants, Mary Brooks, Mary Watkins, Nancy Judi.

Thomas Snowden Pleasants of Goochland Co (son of Thomas & Elizabeth Pleasants of said co) and Elizabeth Tucker Pleasants of same co (daughter of Jacob & Sarah Pleasants of Henrico Co) married at Genito , Goochland Co the 16th da, 12 mo, 1790. Witnesses: Lane Parsons, John S. Pleasants, Thos W. Pleasants, Philip Pleasants, Thos E. Pleasants, Cary Pleasants, Thos Harris, Obediah Crew, B Watkins, John Harris, Achillis Barksdale, Sarah Parsons, Elizah Pleasants Winsor, Polly Pleasants, Mary Younghusband, Eliza Pleasants, Mary Brooks, Agness Royster.

8/11/1788. Samuel Chiles (son of John Chiles) of Caroline Co hath married a woman of another persuasion by a hireling minister contrary to the rules of our society, we declare our disunion with him.

8/1/1791. Benjamin Stanley hath joined himself in marriage with a woman not of our religious society, we disown him.

Certificate that Benjamin Vaughan removed from Whiteoak Swamp, Henrico Co, we recommend him to your Christian care. Signed 5th da, 2nd mo, 1791 by Thomas Ladd clk.

9/4/1791. Edith Stanley (daughter of John Stanley) hath suffered herself to be joined in marriage contrary to the known rules of friends, we therefore disown her.

9/4/1791. Judith Crew (daughter of James Crew) hath suffered herself to be joined in marriage contrary to the known rules of friends, we therefore disown her.

9/4/1791. Sarah Harris (daughter of Jeremiah Harris) hath suffered herself to be joined in marriage contrary to the known rules of friends, we therefore disown her.

9/4/1791. Lucy Chiles (daughter of John Chiles) of Caroline Co has late married contrary to the good order used among us, we disown her.

Gary Pleasants removed to Whiteoak Swamp, Henrico Co.

11/7/1791. Joseph Anthony of South River requested a certificate in order for marriage with Rhoda Moorman of Cedar Creek.

14/5/1791. Solomon Stanley (son of William Stanley) of Hanover Co hath suffered himself to be joined in marriage contrary to the rules of friends, we do therefore disown him.

Isaac Stanley and Elizabeth Stanley were guilty of indecent familiarity with each other before they were married, our marriage also was contrary to the good order used among friends, which practices we have seen the evil of and do condemn them as they have been cause of sorrow to us, we hope friends will reinstate us.

4/12/1791. William Johnson some time past left my parents in a very disorderly manner greatly to the dishonour of them, I am heartily sorry for the same.

11/6/1791. Robert Bell (son of George Bell) of Louisa Co hath suffered himself to be joined in marriage contrary to the known rules of Friends, we therefore disown him.

2/7/1791. Benjamin Bates Junr removed to Cedar Creek from Whiteoak Swamp, Henrico Co, we recommend him to your Christian care.

Joseph Anthony of Campbell Co & Rhoda Moorman of Caroline Co married the 15th da, 5th mo, 1791. Witnesses: Clark T. Moorman, Matthew Terrell, Thos Terrell, John Payne, Catlet Jones, Jonathan Terrell, Ursla F. Cheadle, Salley Terrell, Ann Stevens, Pleasant Cobbs, Jno Peatross, Anthony New, Isaac

Winston, Joanna Terrell, Lucy Winston, Salley Chiles, Judith Cheadle, Rachel Moorman, Salley Terrell, Rebecca Terrell, Rhoda Terrell.

9/7/1791. William Johnson (son of Wm Johnson), at the time his father obtained our certificate for himself & family to join the Friends at South River, Campbell Co, was absconded from his fathers house by which he was not included in the said certificate, but since returning and condemning such conduct we do now recommend him as a member & to your Christian care.

Rhoda Anthony who by marriage removed to South River, Campbell Co.

Benjamin Russel and his two daughters Sophia & Rebecca removed to Cedar Creek from Burleigh, Prince George Co.

Jane Johnson (wife of Elisha Johnson) removed by marriage (some time ago).

19/8/1791. I forsook the things that brought trouble on me, particularly that of drunkenness & adultery, for which I stand disowned, requesting you may again be reconciled to me. Nicholas Crew, Campbell Co..

28/8/1791. We think Nicholas Crew is disposed to make satisfaction for this misconduct and we are able to say that he is a man of good report in his neighbourhood of late. Signed Micajah Davis, David Terrell, Richd Bloxsom, Wm Davis.

Daniel Clark removed to Center, Gilford Co, NC.

Thomas Snowden Pleasants and his wife Elizabeth Tucker removed to White Oak Swamp, Henrico Co.

10/12/1791. George Bell (son of George Bell deceased) of Louisa Co has given way to the vanities of the world so far as to be guilty of fighting & frequenting places of diversion, we therefore disown him.

12/5/1791. I now embrace this opportunity of condemning my conduct in marrying contrary to the known rules of friends and hope friends will pass by my offence. Elizabeth Moorman.

Betty Moorman is a constant attender of our meeting and appears orderly in her deportment. Signed Agatha Johnson, Ann Bloxsom, Dosha Moorman, Nancy Moorman, Richard Bloxsom Senr, Joseph Johnson, James Johnson Saml Johnson, Gerrard Johnson, Micajah Moorman.

Melicent Johnson (formerly Hargrave) removed to South River.

Elizabeth Moorman removed to South River.

12/5/1792. To the Militia Officers of Goochland Co. We certify that Isaac Stanley is a member of our religious society.

9/6/1792. Sophia Harris (daughter of Moses Harris) hath joined in marriage contrary to the known rules of friends, we therefore disown her.

John Winston removed Henrico Co.

Thomas Exum Pleasants removed to Henrico Co.

13/10/1792. Judith Douglas (daughter of Charles Douglas) of Orrange Co hath married contrary to our dicipline to a man not professing with us, we therefore disown her.

25/8/1792. I once being a member of your society & marrying contrary to the rules of friends I was disowned. I can truly say which conduct has been sincerely condemned by me, and would be glad to be once more a member among you. Patty Jones.

13/10/1792. Thos Harris Junr informed this Meeting that he had a desire to attend the yearly Meeting in NC.

13/10/1792. Rachel Moorman informed this Meeting that she had a desire to attend the yearly Meeting in NC.

13/10/1792. Thos Pleasants informed this Meeting that he had a desire to attend the yearly Meeting in NC.

Ashley Johson [sic] Senr, his wife Mary, their children Ashley, Thomas, Watkins, Drusila, Anna & Edith removed to South River, Campbell Co.

Benjamin Johnson & wife removed to South River, Campbell Co.

Benjamin Bates Junr removed to Henrico Co.

David Terrell of Campbell Co and Patty Johnson (daughter of Ashly and Martha Johnson) of Louisa Co married 25th da, 2nd mo, 1793. Witnesses: Henry Terrell, Samuel Parsons, Micajah Crew, Clark T. Moreman, Wm Johnson, Benjamin Bates Junr, Thomas Harris, John Harris, Jonathan Terrell, Matthew Terrell, Thomas Ladd, Wm Stabler, Nathan Bell, Joshua Stanley, Thos Hatton, Tho Doswell, Catlit Jones, Waddy Stanley, Saml Terrell, Leml Crew, Ro: H. Crew, Gerrard Johnson, John Crew Junr, Judith Crew, Rachel Moreman, Ann Jones, Rachel Harris, Edith Harris, Margaret Crew, Sarah Bell, Mary Ladd, Tace Crew, Mary Hatton, Mary Brookes, Rachel Ladd, Sarah Harris, Susannah Harris, Nancy Hunnicutt, Betsy Watkins, Salley Watkins, Salley Ladd.

4th mo, 1793. I heartily confess my conduct for some time past has been inconsistent with the principles of the society, I sincerely hope to conduct myself in future so as to give no uneaseness to Friends & greater peace in my own mind. Jesse Crew.

William Jackson removed from Chester Co, PA.

11/5/1793. John Harris (son of Jeremiah) hath been in the practice of overseeing slaves contrary to the rules of our religious society and manifests a disposition to continue it. Therefore we disown him.

Elijah Johnson of Louis Co (son of Ashley & Martha Johnson) and Betsey Watkins (daughter of Benjamin & Prissilla Watkins) of Goochland Co married 13th da, 4th mo, 1793. Witnesses: Polley Watkins, Sarah Harris, Betsey Johnson, Ann Jones, Janey Ristole, Rachel Moorman, Margaret Crew, Unity Stanley, Mary Pleasants, Rachel Harris, Sarah Parsons, Sarah Hatton, Sarah Pleasants, Judith Crew, Mary Hatton, Tace Crew, Edith Harris, Thos Stanley, Catlet Jones, Wm Jackson, Saml Terrell, Saml Parsons, Thos Harris, Thos Hatton, John Harris, Joshua Stanley, Benjamin Russel, Clark T. Moorman, Micajah Crew, Thos Harris, Pleasant Cobbs.

24/8/1793. Thomas Johnson (son of Jesse deceased) has married contrary to the known rules of our discipline to a woman not of our society. Therefore we disown him.

Shadrack Vaughan removed from Whiteoak Swamp, Henrico Co.

Benjamin Bates from York Co (son of Benjamin & Hannah Bates of same place) and Tace Crew (daughter of Micajah & Mary Crew) of Hanover Co married 16th da, 12 mo, 1793. Witnesses: Deborah Darby & Rebecca Young from old England, David Cumings from PA, Margaret Crew, Chlotilda Harris, Mary Pleasants, Sarah Pleasants, Mary P. Younghusband, Unity Stanley, Edward Stabler, Thos Hatton, Fleming Bates, Lemuel Crew, Wm H. Pleasants, Wm Jackson, Thos Ladd, Micajah Crew, Clark T. Moorman, Thos Stanley, Joshua Stanley, Thos Harris Junr.

11/1/1794. Peter Fitzgerald late of Hanover Co has deviated from good order as to be guilty of drinking spirituous liquors to excess, using ill words & neglecting the attendance of our religious meetings, therefore we disown him.

Edward Stabler of the Town of Alexandria (son of Edward and Mary Stabler deceased of the Town of Petersburg and Mary Pleasants (daughter of Thomas and Elizabeth Pleasants the latter deceased) of Goochland Co married 27th da, 2nd mo, 1794. Witnesses: Thos Pleasants, James B. Pleasants, William H.

Pleasants, JW Pleasants, Philip Pleasants, Gerrard Hopkins, Saml Parsons, Micajah Crew, Benjamin Russel, James Vaughan, R Turner, Ruben Pleasants, Robert Pleasants, John Pleasants, Jno P. Watson, Saml P. Parsons, Thos Hunnicutt, Sarah Pleasants, Deborah Pleasants, Mary Younghusband, Elizabeth T. Pleasants, Jane Pleasants, Sarah Parsons, Mary P. Younghusband, Rebecca Hunnicutt, Elizabeth Stanley, Polley Watkins, Milley M. Hunnicutt.

22/2/1794. Sarah Winstone (daughter of Nathl Winstone deceased) hath suffered herself to be joined in marriage with a man not of our profession contrary to the known rules of friends, we therefore disown her.

22/2/1794. Mariam Pleasants of Powhattan Co some time past signed manumissions for the slaves she had in possession but since refuses to suffer them to take effect and continues to hold them in a state of bondage, therefore we disown her.

18/1/1794. John Johnson (son of James) removed from South River, we recommend him to your Christian care. Signed Samuel Davis clerk this time, South River.

4/1/1794. James Vaughan removed from Henrico Co, we recommend him to your Christian care. Signed Thomas Ladd, clk, Henrico Co.

8/3/1794. Jesse Terrell requested a certificate to join in marriage with a member of Whiteoak Swamp, Henrico Co.

8/3/1794. Pleasant Winstone (son of Nathl Winstone) of Caroline Co hath of late married contrary to the rules and good order used among us, therefore we disown him.

8/3/1794. Rhoda Terrell (daughter of Thomas Terrell) of Caroline Co hath joined in marriage to a man not of our society, therefore we disown her.

12/4/1794. Benjamin Vaughan proposed marriage with a member of White Oak Swamp, Henrico Co and requested certificate.

5/4/1794. Benjamin Bates Junr removed from White Oak Swamp.

12/7/1794. To Friends of Richsquare Monthly Meeting in NC. Our friend Richard Jourdan in the course of his religious visit to several of our meetings, produced minute of concurrence dated 11th mo last. Also Jeremiah Outland companion to the above said friend attended at the same time and produced your minute of concurrence dated 12th month last year.

23/8/1794. Mary Stabler removed to Fairfax, Loudoun Co

23/8/1794. Waddy Stanley intends to join in marriage with a member of White Oak Swamp, Henrico Co and requests certificate.

10/5/1794. William Crew of Albemarl Co hath been in the practice of using ill words, fighting & has absented himself from the attendance of our religious meetings, we therefore disown him.

2/8/1794. Margaret Vaughan removed by marriage from Henrico Co.

Robert Crew (son of Benjamin Crew deceased) of Charles City Co and Nancy Terrell (daughter of Pleasant & Caty Terrell) of Caroline Co married 14th da, 9th mo, 1794. Witnesses: Rachel Hargrave, Margaret Crew, Ann Jones, Amy Cobbs, Margaret Terrell, Sally Chiles, Salley Terrell, Lucy Hargrave, Jonathan Terrell, Pleasant Cobbs, James D. Ladd, Jesse Hargrave, John Peatros, John Johnson, Pleasant Terrell, Saml Terrell, Robert Terrell, Matthew Terrell, Joseph Hargrave, Catlet Jones, Saml Hargrave.

13/12/1794. Lucy Harris (daughter of Jeremiah Harris deceased) lately joined in marriage contrary to our discipline to a man not of our society, we therefore disown her.

28/2/1795. Hutchins Barnett (son of Arthanasious Barnett) late hath so far deviated from our known principles against war as to be in the capacity of a soldier, we do therefore disown him.

7/2/1795. Rebecca Stanley removed by marriage from Whiteoak Swamp.

7/2/1795. Mary Bailey Terrell removed by marriage from Whiteoak Swamp.

7/3/1795. Samuel Couch Junr removed from Whiteoak Swamp, Henrico Co.

9/5/1795. Obedience Harding removed to Deepcreek, Surry Co, NC.

9/5/1795. Shadrack Vaughan removed to Whiteoak Swamp, Henrico, Co.

13/6/1795. Pattey Terrell (wife of David) removed to South River, Campbell Co.

22/8/1795. William Henry Pleasants having intentions of marrying a member of Whiteoak Swamp, Henrico Co requests a certificate.

22/8/1795. Pattey Jones removed to South River.

22/8/1795. Thomas Watkins (son of Benjamin) has joined himself in marriage to a woman not in religious profession with us, we therefore disown him.

22/8/1795. Cary Pleasants neglected the attendance of our religious Meeting and lived in conformity to the vain customs and fashions of the world, we therefore disown him.

14/11/1795. William Johnson (son of Jesse Johnson deceased) hath joined in marriage with a first cousin by consanguinity, and by an hireling priest, therefore we disown him.

14/11/1795. Mary Watkins (daughter of Benjamin Watkins deceased) hath joined herself in marriage with her first cousin by consanguinity & by an hireling priest, we therefore disown her.

9/1/1796. Cheadle Harris (son of Jeremiah Harris deceased) of Hanover Co hath neglected the attendance of our religious Meeting and given into the customs of the world, we therefore disown him.

Mary Pleasants (daughter of James Ladd) removed by marriage to Whiteoak Swamp.

12/34/1796. Richard Harris who for sometime hath resided in or about Richmond removed to Henrico Co.

5/17/1796. Sarah Pleasants (wife of Jno S. Pleasants) with her two children Sarah & Mary removed to White Oak Swamp, Henrico Co having for some time past resided there.

9/4/1796. James Vaughan removed to Whiteoak Swamp, Henrico Co.

14/5/1796. Thomas Maddox (son of Jno Wilson Maddox) removed to Goos Creek, Bedford Co.

14/5/1796. Ann Chiles (daughter of John & Mary Chiles) of Caroline Co hath late joined herself in marriage contrary to the known rules of friends, we therefore disown her.

14/5/1796. Thomas Barnett (son of Arthanasious Barnett) removed to Deep Creek, NC.

14/5/1796. Jane Barnett (wife of Arthanasious) and children Milicent, John, Jesse, Arthanasious, Elizabeth, Nancy & Mary removed to Deep Creek, NC.

5/3/1796. Littleberry Crew removed from Wrightsbourough, GA.

8/10/1796. Cicily Johnson (daughter of James Johnson deceased) of Louisa Co hath married a man not of our religious profession, we therefore disown her.

John Johnson (son of James Johnson) of Bedford Co and Dorothy Crew (daughter of James Crew deceased) of Hanover Co married 16ᵗʰ da, 11ᵗʰ mo, 1796. Witnesses: Judith Crew, Elizabeth Johnson, Unity Stanley, Chlotilda Harris, Rachael Moorman, Judith Hart, Mary Crew, Ann Jones, Margaret Crew, Tace Bates, Margaret Vaughan, Unity Crew, Susannah Hatton, Susanna Davis, Micajah Crew, Thos Harris, Littleberry Crew, Jesse Crew, Obadiah Crew, Catlett Jones, Joshua Stanley, Thomas Stanley, Waddy Stanley, Edmund James, Maleolin Hart, Benj Bates Junr.

22/9/1796. James Wilson removed from Deep Creek, MD.

8/4/1797. Plummer Harris removed to Whiteoak Swamp.

1/4/1797. Fleming Bates removed from Whiteoak Swamp.

25/2/1797. Alban Gelsun removed from Fairfax.

10/6/1797. William Jackson removed to Cornwall, NY.

8/7/1797. Joseph Hargrave for a considerable time past been in the practice of gaming and neglecting the attendance of our religious meetings, and also too free use of spirituous liquors and fighting, therefore we disown him.

8/7/1787. Ashley Bell (son of George Bell deceased) of Louisa Co hath lately been married contrary to the known rules of the society to a woman not of our religious profession, we therefore disown him.

Littleberry Crew (son of James and Judith Crew) of Hanover Co and Huldah Stanley (daughter of John and Milly Stanley) of same co married 11ᵗʰ day, 7ᵗʰ mo, 1797. Witnesses: Jno Stanley, Jesse Crew, Obadiah Crew, Jonathan Stanley, Joshua Stanley, Thomas Stanley, Waddy Stanley, Benj Bates Junr, Thomas Hatton, Catlitt Jones, Leml Crew, Fleming Bates, Micajah Crew, Edm James, Jno Thompson, Tho Mallory, Judith Crew, Huldah Stanley, Unity Stanley, Edith Stanley, Rebecca Stanley, Mary Crew, Agness Stanley, Chlotilda Harris, Rachael Moorman, Margaret Vaughan, Priscilla Mallory.

9/9/1797. Douglass Barkesdale hath declined the attendance of our religious meetings and is in the practice of holding his fellow men in slavery and also has joined himself in marriage to a first cousin, we therefore disown him.

7/1/1797. John Winston returned to Cedar Creek from Whiteoak Swamp.

12/11/1797. William E. Harris (son of Moses Harris) of Hanover hath lately joined in marriage with a woman not of our religious profession, we therefore disown him.

14/4/1798. Samuel Couch Junr removed to Bedford Co.

Timothy Terrell (son of Thomas Terrell) of Caroline Co and Miriam Murdock Hunnicutt (daughter of James Hunnicutt deceased) late of Goochland Co married in Genelo, Goochland Co the 10th da, 6th mo, 1798. Witnesses: John Hunnicutt, Joseph Terrell, James Hunnicutt, James Hunnicutt, William H. Pleasants, Obadiah Crew, Samuel Couch, ... [faded] ..., Ann Hunnicutt, Elizabeth Winston, Mary Peatross, Mary P. Younghusband, Elizabeth Peatross, Mary Pleasants, Elizabeth Pleasants, Henrietta M. Pleasants, Mary Hatton, Sarah Parsons, Mary Brookes, Elizabeth Stanley, Susannah Hatton, Amy Peatross, Margaret P. Parsons.

23/8/1798. Catlett Jones to pay visit to Friends of Fairfax and Redstone Quarters and to attend the next annual meeting in Baltimore. Signed: John Johnson, Obadiah Crew, Dadely Stanley, Elijah Johnson, Jonathan Terrell, Joshua Stanley, Thos Harris, Benj Bates Junr, Matthew Terrell, Joseph Terrell, Fleming Bates, James Wilson, Pleasants Terrell, Micajah Crew, Clark Moorman, Saml Parsons, Thos Hatton, Tho Stanley, Saml Couch, Pleasant Cobbs, Thos Harris, Jesse Crew, William H. Pleasants.

2/6/1798. Shadrack Vaughan removed from Whiteoak Swamp.

10/11/1798. Robert Douglas of Orange Co for a considerable time neglected the attendance of our religious meetings and removed his habitation remote from any settlements of them & out of reach of any of our meetings. And has lately manifested a disposition to violate our discipline by removing several Black people out of this state in quality of slaves, we therefore disown him.

9/6/1798. Edith Stanley condemns her outgoings and sincerely desires that friends may be reconciled to her.

12/1/1799. Thomas Coppage of Orange Co continuing in the practice of holding slaves, we therefore disown him.

Joshua Stanley (son of John Stanley) of Hanover Co and Rachael Harris (daughter of John Harris deceased) of said co married 12th da, 12th mo, 179-. Witnesses: John Stanley, Thomas Harris, Jonathan Stanley, Joshua Stanley, Thomas Harris, Littlebury Crew, Catlitt Jones, Clark Moorman, Thomas Stanley, Thos Stanley Junr, Waddy Stanley, Thomas Hatton, Jesse Crew, Fleming Bates, Lemuel Crew, Obadiah Crew, John Johnson, Rachael Harris, Edith Harris, Sarah Harris, Rebecka Stanley, Unity Stanley, Rachael Moorman, Margaret Vaughan, Judith Crew, Chlotilda Harris, Mary Hatton, Susanna Hatton, Unity Crew.

Jonathan Stanley (son of John Stanley) of Hanover Co and Mary Crew (daughter of James Crew deceased) of said co married the 10th da, 12th mo, 1798. Witnesses: John Stanley, Littleberry Crew, Jesse Crew, Joshua Stanley Senr, Joshua Stanley Junr, John Johnson, Thomas Stanley Senr, Obadiah Crew, Thomas Stanley Junr, Waddy Stanley, Catlitt Jones, Clark Moorman, Micajah Crew, Thos Harris, Thos Maddox, Lemuel Crew, Moses Stanley, Fleming Bates, Judith Crew, Dorothy Johnson, Judith Hart, Unity Stanley, Rachel Moorman, Margaret Vaughan, Sarah Harris, Rachel Stanley, Unity Crew, Margaret Crew, Jane Hart, Ann Jones.

5/1/1799. Thomas Stanley removed from Wrights Borough, GA.

Obadiah Crew of Goochland Co (son of James Crew deceased) and Mary Peatross (daughter of John and Sarah Peatross) of Caroline Co married in Caroline Co the 10th da, 3rd mo, 1799. Witnesses: John Peatross, Thomas Terrell, John Johnson, Jesse Crew, Timothy Terrell, Thomas Peatross, William Peatross, Malcolm Hart, Richard Peatross, Anthony New, Pleasant Terrell, Pleasant Cobbs, Matthew Terrell, Dorothy Johnson, Joanna Terrell, Sally Terrell, Caty Terrell, Rhoda Anthony, Amey Cobbs, Anna Peatross,
Nancy New, Elizabeth Peatross, Rebecca Terrell.

8/6/1799. Samuel Parsons and his wife Sarah Parsons and their infant children Samuel & Margaret, also Elizabeth Tucker Pleasants, removed to Whiteoak Swamp.

8/6/1799. Fleming Bates removed to Whiteoak Swamp.

11/5/1799. Thomas Maddox removed from South River.

3/6/1799. (Redstone Quarterly Meeting) Father Jones in the course of a religious visit in the 9th mo last, we think it right of us to inform you that his company of Gospel labors were acceptable and satisfactory. Signed: Jos Townsend clk.

10/12/1799. John Maddox removed to Pipe Creek.

29/9/1799. Letter to Cedar Creek Meeting. Charles Wardell has been some years removed from Burlington, NJ and settled at Fredericksburg and he has accomplished his marriage with one not in membership with us, we ask that you deal with him on these or any other diviations and inform us of your disposition. A letter by a safe hand directed to us to the care of Henry Drink or William Lavery or any other friend in Philadelphia will be likely to reach us. Signed William Allinson, John Griscom at Burlington, NJ.

12/3/1739. David Terrell appointed overseer for [page torn]. Thos Stanley & James Stanley overseer for Cedar Creek.

12/3/1739. The case of Jno Sanders respecting his not being fully paid for building the meeting house at Cedar Creek.

12/3/1739. Appoint Jos Cheadle, David Terrell, Thos & James Stanley or either two of them to attend the yearly meeting at Nansamond.

9/12/1739. John Elmore & Elizabeth Harris publish their intention of marriage. John Elmore to furnish a certificate from meeting he belongs to. Cathron Stanley & Elizabeth Stanley appointed to inquirer into the clearness of Eliz Harris.

4/8/--. David Terrell & Thos Stanley to attend the marriage of John Elmore & Eliza Harris.

John Elmore & Elizabeth Harris married the 19th da, 1st mo, 1739/40. Witnesses: Mary Harris, Stanley Harris, James Stanley, HG Stanley, Mary Elmore, John Stanley, John Crew Junr, John Cheadle, David Terrell, Milason Cheadle, Elizabeth Crew, George Hubbard, Thos Cheadle, Thos Lame, Hugh Red, Judeth Red, Mary Harris Junr, Eliz Stanley, Maddox Stanley, Daniell Lo... .

7/2/1740. Thos Pleasant advised sundry necessary things repeating the decipline of the Church.

7/2/1740. John & Charles Johnson brothers to be dealt with about their neglect in friends not knowing whether they own & keep slaves.

7/3/1740. Friends appointed to ask John & Charles Johnson which meeting they belong to.

7/4/1740. Wm Lain desires a certificate signifying his unity with friends. Thos Stanley & James Stanley appointed to inquire into the said Wm Lain & his wife. Appoint Stanley Harris & Henry Terrell to advise with Joseph Butler.

2/7/1740. Armiges Toather & Melicent Cheadle publish their intention of marriage. Armiges father is deceased and to bring a certificate from monthly meeting he belongs to.
Mary Stone & Anna Terrell are appointed to inquire into the clearness of Melicant Cheadle.

2/7/1740. An accounting given of the disorderly walking of David Crew, whereupon meeting appoints John Hubbard & Henry Terrell to inquire into same.

11/6/1740. Hugh Red (Read) of Caroline Co & Judeth his wife admitted several shamefull practices and they have been advised & tenderly delt with in love but they prosist, we testify against them. William Ladd, Armiges Toather, John Cheadle, John Benford, Stanley Harris, Robt Ellison, Andrew Crew, Willm Crew, Henry Terrell, David Terrell, Nicolas Stone.

7/4/1741. David & Henry Terrell, Jno Cheadles, Jno Hubbard of Caroline Co, Thos & James Stanley & Daniell Harris of Hanover Co or either two of them are appointed to attend the Quarterly meeting of friends at Whiteoak Swamp, Henrico Co.

These friends have bestoed there boundeys: John Cheadle 8 pounds, David Terrell 10 pounds, Nicolus Stone 5 pounds, Stanley Harris 4 pounds, Strangman Hutchason 4 pounds, John Johnson 5 pounds, Henry Terrell 6 pounds, Benjamin Wadkins 7 ½ pounds.

Remley Harris, Jno Sanders of Hanover Co, Henry Terrell & John Cheadle of Caroline Co or either two of them are appointed to attend the meeting at Whiteoak Swamp in Henrico Co.

12/7/1741. Joseph Butler continues to disorderly walking.

12/7/1741. David Terrell & Jno Cheadle who hath been appointed overseers of the meeting in Caroline Co desires that Jno Hubbard & Nicolas Stone may be appointed in their roome.

12/9/1741. Joseph Butler of Caroline Co guilty of severall disorders, therefore we disown him.

27/9/1741. Wm Laine request our certificate signifying his unity with friends.

27/9/1741. James Stanley desires that Jno Sanders should be appointed overseer in his roome.

27/11/1741. James Stanley desires Jno Sanders be appointed overseer in the room of Thos Stanley.

18/12/1741/2. Jno Sanders not producing a certificate, not yet appointed to overseer in Thos Stanley'e roome.

1st mo 1741/2. Jno Hubbard, Henry & David Terrell of Caroline Co & Jno Sanders & Stanley & Daniell Harris of Hanover Co or either two of them are appointed to attend quarterly meeting of Friends at Whiteoak Swamp in Henrico Co.

4th mo 1742. Accounts rendered against Jno Standley for his disorderly walking.

4th mo 1742. Thos Stanley & Stanley Harris & Daniell Harris of Hanover Co, Jno Cheadle, Henry Terrell & Jno Hubbard of Caroline or either two of them to attend the Quarterly meeting at Whiteoak Swamp.

10/8/1742. For friends suffering [list of goods] from : Jno Sanders, Mary Harris widdow, Daniell Harriss, Humphry Jones, Daniell Coleman, Nicolas Stone, Richd Bullord, Henry Terrell, David Terrell.

11/7/1742. Jno Hubbard, & David Terrell from Hanover Co, Stanley Harris, Jno Sanders & Thomas Stanley appointed to attend Quarterly meeting at Whiteoake Swamp, Henrico Co.

13/9/1742. Manoak Chiles & Anne Cheadle publish their intention of marriage. David Terrell & Richd ... [page torn] are appointed to inquire into the clearness of Manoak Chiles. Mary Stone & Agatha Terrell are appointed to inquire into the clearness of Anne Cheadle.

11/10/1742. Read certificates of Edmond Peckover.

5/5/1742. William Thomas, he in his visit to friends, produced certificate.

5/5/1742. Manoak Chiles & Anne Cheadle marriage being contrary to the custom amongst friends, proceeding too early in second marriage. John Hubbard & Richd Ballard are appointed to attend the marriage.

Manoak Chiles (son of Henry Chiles deceased) of Hanover Co and Anne Cheadle (daughter of Jno Cheadle) of Caroline Co married 12th da, 10th mo, MDCCXIII. Witnesses: David Garland, Geo Hubbard, Richard Brime, Squire Johnson, James Turner, James Southworth, Wm Jones, Robt Mackelborough, Jno H, Edmond Peckover, Eliza Pleasants, Fleming Bates, Chas Woodson, Jno Pleasants, Wm Winston, Tarlton Woodson Junr, Mary Pleasants, Kesenhappuck Brime, Robt Pleasants, Manoak Miles, Anne Chiles, Jno Cheadle, Walter Chiles, David Terrell, Agatha Terrell, Rachel Railey, Hannah Burch, Elizh Railey.

19/1/1742/3. Richd Butler, David Terrell & Jno Hubbard ... [page torn] ... Harris, Stanley Harris & Jos Sanders of Hanover Co appointed as representatives to attend meeting at Whiteoak Swamp.

11/4/1743. Jno Cheadle, Jno Hubbard, David & Henry Terrell of Hanover Co, Strangeman Hutchings, Stanley Harris appointed to attend Quarterly meeting in Whiteoak Swam, Henrico Co.

9/5/1743. Account of friends suffering brought in for malitia fines from friends in Caroline Co [list of goods]: Jno Cheadle, Nicolas Stone, Jason Meader, Jno Hubbard, ... [blurred] ... , Henry Terrell.

5/8/1743. Stanley Harris & Jno Hubbard appointed to inquire into the state of friends of both meetings.

19/9/1743. Jno Stanley and Marthy Hutchings publish their intension of marriage. John Sanders & Stanley Harris appointed to inquire in to the clearness of Jno Stanley. Elizh Stanley & Jane Sanders appointed to inquire into the clearness of Marthy Hutchings.

19/9/1743. Joseph Crew (son of Andrew Crew) of Caroline Co & Angness Stone (daughter of Nicolas Stone) of Caroline Co publish their intention of marriage. Joseph Crew is required to produce a certificate from the meeting he belongs to. Agatha Terrell & Mary Ballard are appointed to inquire into the clearness of Agness Stone.

10/--/1743. David Terrell & Richd Ballard are appointed to attend the marriage of Joseph Crew and Angness Stone.

10/--1743. Jno Cheadle, David & Henry Terrell of Caroline Co, Jno Sanders, Stanley Harris & Strangeman Hutchings of Hanover Co to attend Quarterly meeting at Whiteoak Swamp.

Joseph Crew (son of Andrew Crew) of Charles City Co and Agness Stone (daughter of Nicolas Stone) of Caroline Co married 11th da, 10th mo, 1743. Witnesses: Jason Meader, Anne Chiles, Stanley Cheadle, Abagail Railey, ... Terrell, ... , Geo Hubbard, Andrew Crew Junr, Matthew Elloson, Daniel Terrell, Micah Johnstone, Richd Ballard, Jonas Meader, Manoak Chiles, Andrew Crew, Nicolas Stone, Henry Terrell, Jno Cheadle.

John Stanley & Marthy Hutchings of Hanover Co married 11th da, 10th mo, 1743. Witnesses: Wm Stanley, Strangeman Hutchings, Thos Stanley, Ashley Johnson, Daniell Laine, Wm Laine, Joseph Harris, Thos Glass, James Stanley,

Benj Wadkins, Jane Hutchings, Mary Harris, John Sanders, Charles Johnson, Mary Harris Junr, Elizabeth Stanley, Madox Stanley.

[date blurred]. George Hubbard requests our certificate to the meeting in Henrico Co in relation of marriage. David Terrell & Joshua Cheadle are appointed to inquire into his clearness. 11/19/1743 found clear.

10/1/1743. Henry Terrell, Jno Hubbard of Caroline Co, Stanley Harris, Jno Sanders of Hanover Co are appointed to attend the Quarterly meeting of friends at Whiteoak Swamp, Henrico Co.

10/1/1743. Henry Terrell requested our certificate in relation of marriage. Nicolas Stone & Richd Ballard are appointed to inquire into the clearness of him. 14/2/1744 found clear.

9/4/1744. [blurred] by the friends, each 5 pounds: John Hubbard, Jno Cheadle, Nicolas Stone, David Terrell, Manoak Chiles, Rich Ballard, Henry Terrell.

9/4/1744. Acct of Friends sufferings brought in this year for malitia fines [list of goods]: Jno Cheadle, Nicolas Stone, David Terrell, Henry Terrell, by Jno Taylor high sheriff. Henry Terrell for church rates so called by Henry Guttrey.

10/3/1744. David Terrell is appointed overseer of this meeting in the roome of John Hubbard.

10/3/1744. Charles Morman & Thos his son appointed overseers of the meeting lately settled in Louisa Co.

10/3/1744. Peter Hubbard & Angness Chiles publish their intention of marriage. Jno Cheadle & Henry Terrell are appointed to inquire into the clearness of Peter Hubbard. Sarah Terrell & Mary Ballard are appointed to inquire into the clearness of Agness Chiles.

8/10/1744. David Garland and Mary Cheadle publish their intention of marriage. Manoak Chiles & Richd Ballard appointed to inquire into the clearness of David Garland. Sarah Ballard and ... Terrell appointed to inquire into the clearness of Mary Cheadle.

Peter Hubbard of Caroline Co (son of John Hubbard of Amelia Co) and Angess Chiles (daughter of Manoak Chiles) of Caroline Co married 9th da, 10th mo, 1744. Witnesses: Mary Stone, Christian Stone, Sarah Ballard, Sarah Terrell, Joel Meader, David Garland, Lettice Cheadle, Judeth Hubbard, Mary Cheadle, Henry Terrell, Richard Ballard, David Terrell, Thos Cheadle, Manoak Chiles, Geo Hubbard.

12/11/1744. Joseph Harris hath been treated with in love by the overseers yet refuses to hear them. Therefore David & Henry Terrell appointed to treat yet further with him to gaine upon him to forsake his disorderly [blurred].

12/11/1744. David & Henry Terrell are appointed to attend the marriage of David Garland & Mary Cheadle.

12/11/1744. John Cheadle is appointed in the roome of Jno Hubbard to inquire into the nese... of friends.

David Garland (son of Edward Garland of Hanover Co deceased) and Mary Cheadle (daughter of John Cheadle) of Caroline Co married 13th da, 11th mo, 1744. Witnesses: ... Brame, ... [blurred] ..., David Terrell, Richd Ballard, George Hubbard, Thos Moreman, Henry Terrell, ... Chiles, Jno Cheadle, Thos Cheadle, Manoak Chiles.

6/4/1745. Friends have concluded that a paper be written against Joseph Harris denying & disowning him. David & Henry Terrell stand by Harris.

6/4/1745. Jno & Charles Johnson from Hanover or either of them appointed to attend the Quarterly meeting at White Oak Swamp, Henrico Co.

13/5/1745. Joseph Harris (son of John Harris deceased) of Hanover Co is disowned. Signed by: Henry Terrell, Jno Creadle, David Terrell, John Sanders, James Stanley, Richd Ballard, Stanley Harris, Manoak Chiles.

10/6/1745. Distress made on Jno Cheadle for church taker called by Henry Guttery.

14/7/1745. Henry Terrell, David Terrell & Jno Cheadle of Caroline Co and Jno Sanders & Stanley Harris of Hanover Co or either two of them appointed to attend the Quarterly meeting at Whiteoak Swamp, Henrico Co.

14/10/1745. Madox Stanley desires our certificate to Henrico signifying his unity with friends & clearness in respect of marriage. Jno Sanders & Stanley Harris appointed to inquire into his clearness.

8/12/1745. George Hubbard desiring the advise of friends about suing for some land he hath a right to by his father and the heir at law refuses to acknowledge the same. Henry & David Terrell & Jno Cheadle appointed to inquire into the truth of the matter.

8/1/1745. It is ordered that a paper be written against Wm Fulcher (Fuliker) denying & disowning him.

8/1/1745. Henry & David Terrell, Richd Ballard of Caroline Co, Stanley & Daniell Harris & Jno Sanders of Hanover or either two of them appointed to attend the Quarterly meeting at White Oak, Henrico Co.

12/2/1746. About 17 shillings of collection money is ordered for the use of James Buchannan a friend at Greene Spring, Louisa Co.

10/3/1746. Wm Fulcher (son of Joseph Fulcher) hath committed several gross crimes which is a scandal to his profession and therefore disown him. Signed by: Henry Terrell, David Terrell, Stanley Harris, Jno Sanders, Thos Moreman, Richd Ballard, James Stanley, George Hubbard.

8/9/1746. Meeting at Fork Creek, Louisa Co, Francis Clarke & Wm Haley appointed overseers.

8/9/1746. Francis Clarke Junr & Christion Stone publish their intension of marriage. ... Haley are appointed to inquire into the clearness of Francis Clarke. ... & Ann Chiles are appointed to inquire into the clearness of Christion Stone.

[date blurred]. Stanley Harris & Wm Haley appointed to attend the marriage of Francis Clarke Junr & Christion Stone.

Jno Sanders & Stanley Harris from Cedar Creek, David Terrell and Nicholas Stone from Caroline Co or either two of them appointed to attend the Quarterly meeting at Whiteoak Swamp, Henrico Co.

Francis Clark (son of Francis Clark) of Louisa Co and Christion Stone (daughter of Nicholas Stone) of Caroline Co married the 11th da, 10th mo, 1746. Witnesses: Nichs Stone, Jonas Meador, Stanley Harris, Joel Meador, Mary Stone, Wm Haley, David Terrell, Benja Clarke, David Terrell Junr, Geo Hubbard, Manoak Chiles, Richd Ballard, Sarah Ballard, Elizh Stone, Agatha Terrell, Thos Cheadle, Judith Hubbard.

10/9/1746. Ashly Johnson & Agatha Stanley publish their intention of marriage. Jno Sanders & Stanley Harris appointed to inquire into the clearness of Ashley Johnson. Catron & Jane Sanders appointed to inquire into the clearness of Agatha Stanley.

14/10/1746/7. Jno Sanders & Wm Lane appointed to attend the marriage of Ashley Johnson & Agatha Stanley.

Ashley Johnson (son of Jno Johnson) of ... Co and Agatha Stanley (daughter of Jno Stanley) of same co married 5th da, 10th mo, 1746/7. Witnesses: Gidron

Johnson, Jesse Johnson, Benj Johnson, Wm Thornton, Wm Stanley, Benj ... Junr, Eliz Johnson, Jno Johnson, Jno Stanley, Jno Lane, Jno Crew Junr, Squire Johnson, Jno Coleman, Henry Terrell, Jesse Sanders, ... Johnson, Mary M... .

11/2/1747. Certificate of friend Thos Greath... from meeting at Westmoreland.

19/8/1747. Sarah Glistine & Eliz Jordan from Nansemond Co to the comfort of friends at Green Spring Creek meeting.

13/4/1747. Henry Terrell & Richd Ballard appointed to treat with Joel Meador about the cattle laid to his charge.

13/4/1747. Jno Sanders, Nicholas Stone, James Stanley, Strangeman Hutchings and Stanley Harris or either two of them appointed to attend the Quarterly meeting at White Oak Swamp, Henrico Co.

.../1747. Jane Sanders, Mary Stone & Sarah Ballard or either two of them will treat with Mary Harris Junr considering the disorder laid to her.

8/6/1747. Joel Meador not appearing, order to be written denying and disowning him.

12/7/1747. Joel Meador (son of Janoh Meador) of Caroline Co having committed several crimes which is a ... against his profession, is disowned. Signed by: Stanley Harris, Richd Ballard, Henry Terrell, David Terrell.

12/7/1747. David Terrell & George Hubbard of Caroline Co, Stanley Harris & John Sanders of Hanover Co appointed to attend the Quarterly meeting at White Oak Swamp, Henrico Co.

10/8/1747. William Fulcher reconciled with the society.

10/8/1747. Thomas Cheadle desires a certificate to the friends in Henrico Co in relation to marriage. David Terrell & Nicholas Stone appointed to inquire into the clearness of Thomas Cheadle.

12/10/1747. Stanley Harris, Jno Sanders, Jno Cheadle, Henry Terrell or either two of them appointed to attend the Quarterly meeting at White Oak Swamp, Henrico Co.

12/1/1747/8. Thomas Stockdon hath some time heretofore desired to be taken under the care of friends with his family. He and his family walks orderly, they are therefore excepted as members.

12/1/1747/8. Jno Cheadle, Nicholas Stone, Henry & David Terrell, Stanley Harris, Jno Sandars or either two of them are appointed to attend the meeting at Whiteoak Swamp, Henrico Co.

13/8/1748. David Terrell & Nicholas Stone desire to be discharged from their overseers place in this meeting whereupon Henry Terrell and Thomas Stockdon are appointed.

11/4/1748. David Terrell, Thomas Stockdon, Nicholas Stone, Jno Sanders, Strangman Huchans, Stanley Harris or either two of them appointed to attend Quarterly meeting at Whiteoak Swamp, Henrico Co.

9/5/1748. All that desire to be members: John Cheadle & his family, David Terrell & his family, Henry Terrell & his family, Thos Cheadle & his family, Willm Elless & his family, Joseph Crew & his family, Nicolas Stone & his family, Richd Bullard & his family, Peter Hubbard & his family, Menoak Chiles & his family, David Garland & his family, Sarah Bullord (wife of Wm Bullord) request to come under the care of the meeting.

13/6/1748. An acct of members of this meeting that desire to come under the care of friends are: John Sandors & his family, James Stanley & his family, Strangman Hutchings & his family, Benj Watkins & his family, Stanley Harris.

10/7/1748. George Hubbard desires himself & family to be taken under the care of friends, motion excepted.

10/7/1748. David Terrell & Jos Crew of Caroline ... [page torn] ... Jno Sanders of Hanover or either two of them appointed to attend the Quarterly meeting at Whiteoak Swamp, Henrico Co.

10/10/1748. Henry Terrell, Jos Crew & George Hubbard from Caroline Co, Stanley Harris & Strangman Hutchings of Hanover appointed to attend the Quarterly meeting at White Oak Swamp.

14/11/1748. Jno Sanders is appointed to receive the collection of friend for the use of friends & Jno Cheadle is continued for this meeting to do the like.

11/12/1748/9. David Terrell Junr request our certificate to Green Springs, Louisa Co in relation to marriage. Henry Terrell & Jos Crew appointed to inquire to his clearness.

11/1/1748/9. Jno Cheadle, David & Henry Terrell of Caroline Co, Jno Sandors, James Stanley, Benj Harriss & Stanley Harris of Hanover appointed to attend Quarterly meeting at Whiteoak, Henrico County.

10/4/1749. Jno Cheadle desires our certificate in relation to marriage to friend at Pagin Creek, Isleshill Co. David Terrell & Nicholus Stone appointed to inquire into his clearness.

10/4/1749. Jno Cheadle, David Terrell, Stanley Harris, Jno Sandors appointed to attend the Quarterly meeting at Whiteoak Swamp, Henrico Co.

8/5/1749. Jno Cheadle owned that he had declined his intention and no certificate was issued.

8/5/1749. Sara Ballord (wife of Wm Ballord) is excepted as a member.

12/6/1749. John Stanley desires to be taken under the care of the friends, motion is excepted.

12/6/1749. Taken from Strangman Hutchings ... rails & rug & blanket. From Richd Ballord saddle & plow.

9/7/1749. Elizabeth (daughter of Menoak Chiles) having not walked so orderly as becomes those of our profession, deneigh her as being a member of our society.

9/7/1749. Jno Cheadle & Jno Crew of Caroline, Stanley Harris & Strangman Hutchings of Hanover appointed to attend the Quarterly meeting at Whiteoak Swamp, Henrico Co.

9/7/1749. David Terrell Junr desire himself & his wife to come under the care of friends. Excepted as members 11/9/1749.

9/10/1749. James Stanley, John Sanders, Jno Cheadle, David Terrell appointed to attend the Quarterly meeting at Whiteoak Swamp, Henrico Co.

10/12/1749. Jno Moore Junr of Louisa Co & Elizabeth Sanders (daughter of Jno Sanders) of Hanover Co publish their intension of marriage. Jno Moore is desired to bring a certificate of clearness from the meeting to which he belongs. Cathron Stanley & Martha Stanley are appointed to inquire into the clearness of Elizabeth Sanders.

10/1/1749/50. Jno Moore Junr produced a certificate signifying his clearness. Stanley Harris & Thos Stanley appointed to attend the marriage of Jno Moore Junr & Elizabeth Sanders.

10/1/1749/50. Henry & David Terrell, Thos Cheadle of Caroline Co, Stanley Ho... [blurred] ... of Hanover Co to attend the Quarterly meeting at Whiteoak Swamp, Henrico Co.

10/1/1749/50. Elizabeth (daughter of Menoak Chiles) married out from among friends for which cause we disown her. Signed by: James Stanley, Joseph Crew, John Sandors, Henry Terrell, Nicholas Stone, Jno Cheadle, Thos Stockdon.

John Moore Junr of Louisa Co & Elizabeth Sanders (daughter to Jno Sanders) of Hanover Co married 11th da, 1st mo, 1749/50. Witnesses: Jno Moore, Jno Sanders, Stanley Harris, Thos Stanley, Wm Stanley, James ... , Jno Harris, Jno Higgason, Jno Coleman, Jno Stanley, Jno Stanley Junr, Daniell Harris, Wm Lane, James Stanley, Jno Sanders Junr, Cathren Stanley, Rebackeh Harris, Sarah Harris, Anne Moore, Hulda Stanley.

9/4/1750. Benj Wadkins, Stanley Harris of Hanover, David Terrell & Nicholas Stone appointed to attend the Quarterly meeting at Whiteoak Swamp, Henrico Co.

14/5/1750. Joseph Crew & Henry Terrell, appointed to treat with Peter Hubbard concerning some disorders which he hath acted, ordered a paper to be written deneighing & disowning him.

11/6/1750. David Terrell desires ... between him and Thomas Wild merchant of Caroline Co.

11/6/1750. Joshua Ladd produced a certificate from friends at Haddenfield in the Jarseys.

8/7/1750. Friends have ordered a paper to be written & brought disowning Thos Ballard (son of Richard Ballard).

8/7/1750. Jno Cheadle & David Terrell, Stanley Harris & Benjamin Harris appointed to attend the Quarterly meeting at Whiteoak Swamp, Henrico Co.

8/7/1750. Acct of sufferings brought this year from: Jno Cheadle 2 pounds 10 shillings, Nicolas Stone 1 pound 15 shillings, Henry Terrell 3 pounds 9 shillings, David Terrell 1 pound 5 shillings.

11/6/1750. Peter Hubbard of Caroline Co hath been guilty of several disorders, therefore we disown him. Signed by: David Terrell, Stanley Harris, Benj Harris, James Stanley, Nathl Winston, Jno Sanders, Strangman Huchens, Nicolus Stone, George Bell.

18/8/1750. Testimony against Thos Ballard publickly read.

11/11/1750. Samuel Hargrave produced a certfycates from the Pagan Creek, Isleswhite Co signifying his clearness in relation to marriage. Likewise Samuel Hargrave to be taken under the care of this meeting.

9/12/1750. Taken by distress, to the value of, from: Nicholas Stone 15 pounds, Benjamin Harris 11 pounds 6 shillings, Thos Cheadle 3 pounds 10 shillings, Henry Terrell 4 pounds, John Cheadle 6 pounds.

9/1/1750. Saml Hargrave excepted as member of our meeting.

9/1/1750. Nicholas Stone, Henry Terrell, Stanley ... [blurred] ... Sanders to attend Quarterly meeting at Whiteoak Swamp, Henrico Co.

8/4/1751. Stanley Harris, Strangeman Hutchings, Joseph Crew & Henry Terrell appointed to attend Quarterly meeting at Whiteoak Swamp, Henrico Co.

8/4/1751. Friends reject Ashley Johnson in relation to marriage.

8/4/1751. It is appointed that Benja Harris ask John Johnson what monthly meeting ... .

10/6/1751. Samuel Hargrave & Martha Cheadle publish their intention of marriage. Nicholas Stone & David Terrell appointed to inquire into the clearness of the man & Mary Stone & Sarah Ballard into the clearness of the young woman.

10/6/1751. Jesse Johnson & Elizabeth Wadkins publish their intention of marriage. Strangeman Hutchings & Jno Stanley to inquire into the clearness of the man and Cathren Stanley & Eliza Cobbs Hutchings to the clearness of the woman.

10/6/1751. Willm Moors certificate from NC of 8/5/1751 approved.

--/--/1751. John Sanders, Stanley Harris, Benj Harris, David Terrell & Thos Cheadle appointed to attend Quarterly meeting at Whiteoak Swamp, Henrico Co.

Samll Hargrave of Caroline Co & Martha Cheadle (daughter of Jno Cheadle) of same co married 15th da, 7th mo, 1751. Witnesses: Ann Chiles, Mary Garland, Micajah Terrell, Benj Harris, Jno Sanders, Henry Terrell Junr, Andrew Crew, Jno Cheadle, Thos Cheadle, Manoak Chiles, Willm Fulcher, Joseph Crew, Henry Terrell.

Jesse Johnson (son of John Johnson) of Amelia Co & Elizabeth Watkins (daughter of Benj Watkins) of Goochland Co married 12th da, 8th mo, 1751.

Witnesses: Mary Johnson, [blurred], Jno Johnson, Willm Stanley, James Stanley, Ashley Johnson, Charles Johnson ... [blurred] ... .

14/10/1751. Stanley Harris, Jno Sanders, Thos Cheadle & Thos Stockton appointed to attend Quarterly meeting at Whiteoak Swamp, Henrico Co.

2/2/1752. Christopher Clark of Louisa Co & Elizabeth Stone of Caroline Co publish their intension of marriage. Ann Chiles & Elizabeth Cheadle are appointed to inquire into clearness of Elizabeth Stone. Christopher Clark is requested to produce a certificate.

14/3/1752. Thos Stockton & Nathall Winston appointed to attend the marriage of Christopher Clark & Elizabeth Stone.

14/3/1752. Henry & David Terrell, Jno Sanders & Stanley Harris appointed to attend Quarterly meeting at Whiteoak Swamp, Henrico Co.

Christopher Clark (son of Francis Clark) of Louisa Co & Elizabeth Stone (daughter of Nicholas Stone) of Caroline Co married 15th da, 3rd mo, 1752. Witnesses: Ursula Clark, Jno Cheadle, Thos Stockton, David Terrell, Daniell Matthews, Stanley Harris, Ann Chiles, Sarah Ballard, Elizabeth Cheadle, Agatha Terrell, Jemima Winston, Nicolas Stone, Cristion Clark, Joseph Crew, Francis Clark, Jno Stone.

7/4/1752. Benja Harris appointed overseer of this meeting in James Stanley's stead who being unable to act.

9/5/1752. Thos Stockton desires some other friend be appointed overseer in his stead.

11/7/1752. It is ordered that Henry Terrell receive the tobacco at the hands of Thos Turner of King George Co which was left for the use of friends by our deceased friend Elizabeth Duff and give that Turner bond to ... .

8/8/1752. [blurred] ... he is acquitted & David Terrell is appointed in his place.

7/9/1752. Joseph Crew, David Terrell, Benj Harris & Stanley Harris appointed to attend the Quarterly meeting at Whiteoak Swamp, Henrico Co.

7/9/1752. Gidion Ellyson & Margory Stanley publish their intensions of marriage. Jno Sanders & Stanley Harris appointed to inquire into the clearness of Gidion. Cathron & Martha Stanley to inquire into the clearness of Margory.

14/10/1752. John Stanley and Stanley Harris appointed to attend the marriage of Gidion Elleson & Margory Stanley.

44

Gidion Ellyson (son of William Ellyson) of New Kent Co and Margrey Stanley (daughter of Thos Stanley) of Hanover Co married [page torn]. Witnesses: Ashley Johnson, Benja Watkins, Jane Sanders, Susanah Ellyson, Hezekiah Sanders, Rebeckah Harris, Ann Stanley, Joseph Harris, Shadrack Stanley, Archelaus Elmore, Jno Stanley Junr, Jno Sanders Junr, Jno Crew, Willm Ellyson, Thos Stanley, Jno Sanders, Benj Ellyson.

11/11/1752. David Terrell request our certificate to friends at Hawfield & Cain Creek.

9/12/1752. Read certificate of Thos Branson from Cain Creek, NC.

9/12/1752. Read certifycate of Abigail Pike from Cain Creek, NC.

9/12/1752. Read certificate of Martha Thornton from Cain Creek, Orrange Co, NC.

9/12/1752. ... Ballard (daughter of Richd Ballard) hath married out from friends.

9/12/1752. Thos Cheadle, ... Stone, Benj Harris & Stanley Harris appointed to attend the Quarterly meeting at Henrico Co.

10/2/1753. Whereas Rachell Wright hath been severall times in these parts in the service of truth & hath requested our certificate to the parts she belongs. There is one provided. Also one for Mary Jackson & one for William Hunt who was with Rachell Wright her last visit to this meeting.

10/3/1753. Attended by the ministry of our esteemed friend Michal Lightfoot whose certificate from the monthly meeting of friends held at Philadelphia 23/2/1753 was read. As was the certificate of our friend Samuell Emlin from the said meeting (who was companion to the said Michall Lightfoot).

10/3/1753. David Terrell, Joseph Crew, Benj Harris & Stanley Harris appointed to attend the Quarterly meeting at Whiteoak Swamp, Henrico Co.

14/4/1753. Jno Stanley being summoned to the Generall Court by Ashley Johnson, desires the advice of meeting in the case.

12/5/1753. Attended by our friend Michall Lightfoot in his returneth.

12/5/1753. Joseph Crew is appointed overseer of this meeting in David [blurred].

12/5/1753. David Terrell & Thos Stockton to carry copy of the testif... [blurred] ... against Susanah Stone (daughter of Richd Ballard) ... .

9/6/1753. Strangeman Hutchins, Benj Harris & Stanley Harris appointed to attend Quarterly meeting at Whiteoak Swamp, Henrico Co.

8/9/1753. John Sanders & Benj Harris appointed to treat with Ann (daughter of Jno Stanley) in relation to her marrying out.

8/9/1753. Jno Cheadle, Henry Terrell, Benj Harris & Strangeman Hutchings appointed to attend Quarterly meeting at Whiteoak Swamp, Henrico Co.

13/10/1753. Ordered that a certificate be provided for Willm Stanley and Ann Chiles companions for Jane Haggitt in her visit.

13/10/1753. Jno Cheadle, David Terrell & Thos Stockton appointed to treat with Richard Ballord.

13/10/1753. Susanah Stone (daughter of Richard Ballord) of Caroline Co married out from amongst friends & testify against and deney her as being a member. Signed by: Strangman Hutchings, Willm Stanley, Henry Terrell, Benja Harris, Thos Cheadle, David Terrell.

8/12/1753. Anne (daughter of Jno Stanley) contrary to friends advice married out from friends. A paper of testifycation to be drawn.

8/12/1753. Prudence Stockton (the seposed daughter of Thos Stockton) of Caroline Co married out from friends. A paper of testifycation to be drawn.

8/12/1753. Charles Moorman Junr, Philys Hoggitt, Benj Harris, Jno Sanders, Nicolas Stone & Thos Stockton appointed to attend Quarterly meeting at Whiteoak Swamp, Henrico Co.

8/12/1753. Jno Cheadle desires liberty to appoint his son Thos Cheadle his attorney in a case against Richard Abell at Opeckin who he saith stand indebted to him. Request is granted.

12/1/1754. Micajah Terrell & Sarah Lynch both of Albermarle Co publish their intensions of marriage. Nicolas Stone & Thos Cheadle are appointed to make the inquirey into the clearness of Micajah Terrell. Anne Moore & Mary Moreman to inquire into the clearness of Sarah Lynch.

12/1/1754. Wm Stanley requests a certificate in clearness in relation to marriage to friends at Caine Creek, NC.

12/1/1754. Geo Robenson certificate from [blurred] was read & approved.

12/1/1754. Daniell Mathews certificate from Fairfax was read & approved.

12/1/1754. Thos Moorman appointed to ask the mountain friends whether they are truly desirous to keep up their meeting at the mountains.

9/2/1754. Prudence Stockton (the seposed daughter of Thos Stockton) of Caroline Co and Ann Strong (daughter of Jno Stanley) hath married out from friends, we therefore disown them. Signed by: Thos Cheadle, Jno Sandors, Henry & David Terrell, Wm Haley, Michall Stone, Benj Harris, Strangeman Hutchings, Francis Clark.

Micajah Terrell of Albermarle Co and Sarah Lunch of same co married 10th da, 2nd mo, 1754. Witnesses: Wm Halley, Ashley Johnson, Chas Moorman, Daniell Mathews, Wm Matthews, Thos Cheadle, Agatha Terrell, Sarah Lynch, Jane Haggitt, Anne Moore, David Terrell, Chas Lynch, Chas Moorman Junr, Thos Moorman.

13/4/1754. Attended by worthy friends Mary Peasley & Catherine Patton which certificate was read.

13/4/1754. Certificates for our worthy friends Rachell Wright & Mary Jackson from meeting at Caine Creek, NC, who was accompanied by Jerimiah Paggit.

13/4/1754. Anthony Hoggitt & Mary Stanley publish their intentions of marriage. Wm Halley & Francis Clarke Junr appointed to inquire into the clearness of said Anthony Haggitt and Jane Sanders & Mary Harris to inquire into the clearness of Mary Stanley.

Strangman Hutchings & Jno Barnett Junr report on clearness of Benjamin Wadkins in relation to marriage, they find nothing to obstruct his having a certificate.

11/5/1754. Jane Hoggitt's certificate from NC was read.

11/5/1754. Benja Harris, Daniel Harriss, Jane Saunders, Sarah Harris appointed to attend marriage of above couple.

11/5/1754. Henry Terrell & Benja Harriss are appointed to treat with Thos Clark in a matter of disorder.

11/5/1754. Ordered that a certificate be prepared for Wm Diggs against the return of Rachall Wright.

11/5/1754. Ordered that a preparative meeting be held each weekday before the mo meeting. David & Henery Terrell & Jno Saunders are appointed to lay this motion before the Quarterly meeting.

8/6/1754. Thos Cheadle appointed clerk in the roome of Henry Terrell. David Terrell Junr appointed clerk in the absence of Thos Cheadle & Wm Standley to act as clerk in the absence of the said Cheadle.

8/6/1754. William Digs not appearing clear obstrucks his having a certificate.

8/6/1754. Benja Harriss, Thos & Charles Mooreman appointed to treate with Henery Terrell Junr (son of David Terrell) considering his disorderly walking.

8/6/1754. John Johnson & Ledy Watkins published their entention of marriage., Charles Johnson & Garrat Ellison appointed to enquire into clearness of Jno Johnson. Eliza Huchings & Mary Harriss appointed to enquire into clearness of Ledy Watkins.

8/6/1754. Nicklas Stone, Henery Terrell & John Cheadle appointed to treat with Thos Standley & Madox Standley in matter of disorder.

Antoney Hoggatt of Goochland Co and Mary Stanley of Hanover Co married 12th da, 5th mo, 1754. Witnesses: Jane Hoggatt, Rebeccah Harris, Jane Sanders, E:De Harris, James Standly Junr, William Standly, Pleasant Standly, Cornelius Harris, Strangeman Hutchin, Joseph Hoggatt, Daniel Harriss, John Standley, John Harris.

13/7/1754. Daniel Harriss & family, Thomas Standley Junr, Pleasant Standley, John Harriss (son of Daniel Harriss) under the care of Friends.

13/7/1754. John Daviss, Charles Mooreman appointed to treat with Charles Doughless in a matter of disorder.

13/7/1754. Mathew Johnson and Rachall Mooreman appointed to treate with the said Dougless' wife in a matter of defferance.

13/7/1754. Saml Hargrave & Thos Cheadle appointed to treate with Nathaniel Winston for not complying with his lawfull contract with David Terrell Junr.

13/7/1754. Christopher Clark (son of Thos Clark) petion for a certificate to Friends at P.D., NC. Wm Haley & John Davis appointed to enquire into said Clark's clearness.

13/7/1754. Jno Standley petion for a certificate to Friends at Whiteoak Swamp, Henrico Co in relation to marriage. John Saunders & Benj Harris appointed to enquire into the said Standley's clearness.

13/7/1754. The epistles of our Worthy friends Mary Peasley & Catheran Payton were read.

13/7/1754. Benja Watkins & Strangeman Huchings appointed to attend the marriage of John Johnson & Ledy Wadkins.

13/7/1754. John Saunders, Thomas Mooreman & John Cheadle appointed to attend Quarterly meeting.

10/8/1754. William Haley, Francis Clark, Phillip Hoggett, George Robesson, Charles Mooreman & Jno Daviss appointed to meet at this meeting house 24th this instant to settle the differences betwixt Nathl Winston & David Terrell Junr.

14/9/1754. John Standley & Edey Huchings publish their entention of marriage. John Saunders and Benja Harriss appointed to enquire into the said Standley's clearness.

14/9/1754. Micajah Mooreman & Sushannah Chiles publish their entention of marriage. Wm Haley & Jno Daviss appointed to enquire into the said Mooreman's clearness.

14/9/1754. Antoney Hoggitt petion for a certificate to friends at New Garden, NC. Wm Haley and Francis Clark appointed to enquire in the said Hoggett's clearness.

14/9/1754. Jno Harriss petion for liberty to sue for a just debt, petion granted.

12/10/1754. John Saunders and Benja Harriss appointed to attend the marriage of John Standley & Edey Huchings.

12/10/1754. Henery Jerrell & Nichs Stone appointed to attend the above marriage.

12/10/1754. Francis Clark petioned for himself and family for a certificate to Friends in NC. Phillip Hoggett & Richd Stone appointed to enquire into their clearness.

12/10/1754. William Haley requesting the like & same friends are appointed into enquire into the life and conversation.

12/10/1754. James Cunch desire to be under the care of this meeting. Charles Mooreman & Ashley Johnson appointed to make enquirey into the said Cunches conversation.

12/10/1754. John Pleasants Junr and Strangeman Huchings appointed to enquire of Thos Pleasants, John Pleasants (son of John), Talton & Jacob Woodson & Joseph Woodson whether they were willing to go under the denomination of Quakers.

12/10/1754. Bowlen & Adward Clark to be overseer of the weekday meetings.

12/10/1754. Jno Cheadle, Charles Mooreman, Jno Sanders appointed to attend the Quarterly meeting.

9/11/1754. George Bell Junr produced a certificate from meeting at Whiteoak, Henrico Co, read & approved.

9/11/1754. Jane Hoggett produced a certificate from yearly meeting held in Pequammin Co, NC at which place she had been on the service of the truth 13/10/1754.

9/11/1754. Benja Harriss and John Cheadle appointed to treat Wm Terrell Junr (son of David Terrell) for his disorderly behavour.

9/11/1754. Benja Clark appointed overseer of Fork Creek meeting instead of Francis Clark Junr.

9/11/1754. A certificate for Francis Clark & Christopher Clark and families and for Esom Haley (son of Wm Haley) was granted to the meeting at Cane Creek, NC.

9/11/1754. Henry Phillip Hart and John Roberts petioned for a certificate relative to marriage. Jno Clark appointed to enquire into the life and conversation of the said Hart.

9/11/1754. Jane Hoggitts petition for a certificate to Friends in New Garden, NC.

12th mo/1754. Zacariah Mooreman & Caty Terrell published their entention of marriage. John Davis & Thos Cheadle appointed to enquire into the said Mooreman's clearness.

Charles Lynch & Anna Terrell published their entention of marriage. Edward Clark and Bowlen Clark appointed to enquire into the said Lynches clearness.

14/1/1755. Those appointed to attend the marriage of John Standle give a clear account.

14/1/1755. David Terrell & Thos Cheadle appointed to attend the marriage to the two above.

14/1/1755. Sarah Lynch petion for liberty to sue a man for a just debt, request granted.

14/1/1755. Charles Lynch requested liberty to sue for a just debt which was granted.

8/2/1755. James Bunch is taken under the care of friends.

8/3/1755. Benja Harris, David Terrell, Robert Pleasants & John Crew appointed to enquire and treat with Jno & Thos Pleasants, Jacob & Talton Wodson, & Jos Woodson living in Goochland Co.

8/3/1755. Friends appointed to treat with Henry Terrell (son of David Terrell) report that he appears to be sorry he has been a scandal to friends.

8/3/1755. Charles Mooreman and Henery Terrell appointed to treate with Thos Standley concerning his son Thos. Thos Standley Junr married out from amongst us. A paper of denial is ordered.

8/3/1755. David Terrell, Benja Harris & Charles Mooreman appointed to attend Quarterly meeting.

12/4/1755. Thos Pleasants, Jacob & Talton Wodson Junr of Goochland Co shall produce a certificate from the meeting they did belong to.

12/4/1755. Jos Woodson & Wm Matox desire to be under this meeting. Benja Watkins & Strangeman Huchings appointed to make further enquirey.

12/4/1755. No account of Henery Hart and John Roberts. Rilley Mooreman & George Bell appointed to make further enquirey.

12/4/1755. Robert Cobbs & Wm Candler of Bedford Co desire to be taken under this meeting. Edward and Bowlen Clark appointed to enquire into their clearness.

10/5/1755. Certificate granted to Henery Hart & John Robert with respect to an orderly removal.

10/5/1755. Wm Candler & ... Clark request a certificate to Friends at Cane Creek, NC, request granted.

10/5/1755. John Johnson (son of John Johnson) of Amelia Co and Lydia Watkins (daughter of Benjamin Watkins deceased) of Goochland Co married the 13th da, 7th mo, 1754. Witnesses: Benj Harriss, Benj Watkins, Nicho Stone, Strangeman Huchings, Jno Newby.

Micajah Morman (son of Thos Moreman) of Louisa Co & Susanna Chiles (daughter of Manoak Chiles) of Caroline Co married 13th da, 10th mo, 1754. Witnesses: Rachel Morman, Ann Chiles, Martha Hargrave, Mourning Clark,

Milla Terrell, Anna Terrell, Thos Morman, Manoak Chiles, Henry Terrell, John Cheadle, John Pleasant, Pleasant Terrell.

Zachariah Morman (son of Thos Morman) of Louisa Co & Betty Terrell (daughter of Henry Terrell) of Caroline Co married 12th da, 5th mo, 1755. Witnesses: Sarah Terrell, Rachel Morman, Sarah Lynch, Agatha Terrell, Mary & Milla Terrell, Micajah Terrell, John Stone, Henry Terrell, Thos Morman, Henry Terrell Junr, Thos Terrell.

Charles Lynch (son of Charles Lynch deceased) of Bedford Co & Anne Terrell (daughter of Henry Terrell) of Caroline Co married 12th da, 1st mo, 1755. Witnesses: Sarah Terrell, Sarah Lynch, Mary & Milla Terrell, Judith Cheadle, Henry & Thos Terrell, Martha ... , Thos Cheadle, ... Terrell, Henry Terrell, John Moreman, David Terrell, Nicolas Stone.

John Stanly (son of John Stanly) of Hanover Co & Ede Huchens (daughter of Strangeman Hutchens) of Goochland Co married 16th da, 10th mo, 1754. Witnesses: Judeth Watkins, Jane Watkins, Mary Hutchens, Mary Strong, James Benford, Benj Watkins, Strangeman Hutchins, Jno Harris, Wm Standley, ... , ...

12/4/1755. Thos Standley (son of Thos Standley) having proceeded in marriage contrary to the principles of our profession, we therefore disown him. Signed by: George Bell, Benj Harris, John Standley, Nichs Stone, Jos Crew, Thos Cheadle, Strangeman Hutchins, Henry Terrell, David Terrell.

14/6/1755. Certificate ordered for Jos Hoggat to Friends in New Garden, NC.

14/6/1755. Nathll Winston not complying with his just contracts with David Terrell Junr. Reports that he is willing to comply as soon as possible by selling lands or any other thing.

14/6/1755. Joseph Crews requests to be released from being overseer of the meeting. Saml Hargrave is appointed overseer in his room.

12/7/1755. Philip Hoggitt's requesting a certificate is reserved till next meeting in expectation of his returning back from Caroline Co in order to clear up a charge laid against him.

12/7/1755. Thos Pleasants & John Pleasants Junr produced a certificate from the meeting at Whitcoak Swamp, Henrico Co 5/7/1755.

12/7/1755. Wm Johnson & Susanah Johnson publish their intentions of marriage. Thos & Charles Morman to inquire into his clearness.

12/7/1755. John Sanders, Thos Moreman & John Cheadle appointed to attend the Quarterly meeting.

9/8/1755. Thos & Charles Moreman appointed to attend the marriage of Wm Johnson & Susanah Johnson.

9/8/1755. Wm Haley leaving our parts, hath petitioned for a certificate to Friends at Cane Creek, NC. Thos & Charles Moreman appointed to enquire into his life & conversation.

9/8/1755. Edward Clark requests a certificate in order to travel to NC. Robt Clark & Wm Cheadle appointed to enquire into his life & conversation.

12/9/1755. Robt Cobbs & Mary Terrell publish their intentions of marriage. Edward & Bonler Clark appointed to enquire into his clearness.

12/9/1755. Nicols Stone petitions a certificate to NC. Henry Terrell & John Cheadle appointed to enquire into his life & conversation.

11/10/1755. Thos Cheadle & Manoak Chiles appointed to attend the marriage of Robt Cobbs & Mary Terrell.

11/10/1755. Nicolas Stone & John Sandors appointed to attend Quarterly meeting.

8/11/1755. William Ballard hath acquainted us of his intentions to remove himself & family to NC, requests a certificate.

8/11/1755. John Clark desires to be taken under the care of Friends. Thos & Charles Morman appointed to enquire to his life & conversation.

13/12/1755. David Candler desires to be taken under the care of Friends. Edward & Bowler Clark & Charles Lynch appointed to enquire into his life & conversation.

13/12/1755. Isaac & John Clark desire to be taken under the care of Friends. Thos & Charles Moreman appointed to inquire into their lifes & conversations.

13/12/1755. Joseph Crew & Henry Terrell Senr appointed to treat with Thos Stocton on account of his not tending meetings.

13/12/1755. Joshua Dickson produced a certificate from the meeting of Rays in Old England in County of Durham.

13/12/1755. Accounts Friends sufferings brought in: David Terrell 6 pounds, Francis Clark 15 shillings, Wm Haley 14 shillings, Antony Hoggitt 6 pounds, Henery Terrell 6 pounds, Nichls Stone 3 pounds, Thos Cheadle 5 pounds.

Robert Cobbs of Bedford Co & Mary Terrell (daughter of David) of Caroline Co married 11th da, 10th mo, 175-. Witnesses: Thos Cheadle, Henry & Thos Terrell, Wm Candle, Henry Terrell, ... , David Terrill, Agatha Terrell.

Ashley Johnson of Amelia Co & Mary Watkins (daughter of Benjamin Watkins) of Goochland Co married 9th da, 4th mo, 1751. Witnesses: Elizabeth Watkins, Rachel Harris, Mary Woodson, Elee Standley, Madox Standley, Jos Harris, Thos Woodson, Archileus Standley, John Johnson Senr, Benjamin Watkins Junr.

10/1/1756. John Stone & Lucy Clark published their entention of marriage. Henery Terrell & Saml Hargrave appointed to enquire into his clearness.

14/2/1756. George Taylor acknowledges and condemns his outgoing.

14/2/1756. John Cheadle & Henery Terrell appointed to treate with Thos Stockton.

14/2/1756. Benj & Thos Clark appointed to attend the marriage of John Stone.

14/2/1756. Sarah Ballard petioned for a certificate for herself & children respecting her united with Friends at Cane Creek, NC, granted.

13/3/1756. Friends appointed to enquire into the life & conversation of Isaac & John Clark report things do not appear so clear as could, continues for further consideration.

13/3/1756. David Terrell petitioned for liberty to sue Wm Harriss of Bedford Co for a just debt, liberty granted.

10/4/1756. Nicholas Stone is appointed with Henery Terrell to treate with Thos Stockton on account of him absenting himself from meetings & other things which he stands charged.

10/4/1756. Benja Harris and John Saunders appointed to treate with Henry Terrell (son of David Terrell) not attending meetings & sundry other disorderly practices.

10/4/1756. Charles & Ashley Johnson appointed overseers of the first day meeting in Amelia Co.

10/4/1756. Garrat Ellison & Archelious Ellmord have married out by the hurling priest contrary to our Christian disipline. Order to be prepared against them.

10/4/1756. Charles Mooreman, Jno Sanders & John Cheadle appointed to attend the Quarterly meeting.

John Stone (son of Nichs Stone) of Caroline Co & Lucy Clark (daughter of Jos Clark) of Louisa Co married 14th da, 2nd mo, 1756. Witnesses: Ursula Clark, Rachel Morman, Agness Jonson, Mary Morman, Anne Terrell, Elizabeth Morman, John Davis, Charles Moreman, John Standley, Charles Morman Junr, Wm Candler, David Terrell Junr, Thos Moreman, Benj Harris, Wm Stanley.

9/5/1756. Benja Johnson & Lucy Moreman publish their intention of marriage. Benja Clark & John Stone appointed to enquire into his clearness.

12/6/1756. Joseph Newby's certificate from meeting at Perquemen, NC was read.

12/6/1756. Papers of denial against Gerard Elmore (son of Archilius Elmore) are continued.

12/6/1756. William Candler applied for a certificate for Friends at New Gardian, NC, ordered to be prepared.

12/6/1756. Thos & Charles Morman appointed to attend the marriage of Benj Johnson & wife.

12/6/1756. Joseph Mackgeehee petitions to be taken under the care of Friends. [blurred] & Nicolas Stone appointed to enquire into his life & conversation.

12/6/1756. Joseph Mackgeehee & Mary Chiles publish their intentions of marriage. Charles Morman Junr & Benj Clark appointed to enquire into.

10/7/1756. Benj Harris, David Terrell & Henry Terrell appointed to attend Quarterly meeting.

10/7/1756. John Saunders requests a certificate to friends in NC. David Terrell & John Cheadle to make enquirey into his life & conversation.

10/7/1756. Strangeman Huchens & John Jonson requests the same and same persons to make enquirey.

14/8/1756. Joseph Mackgeehee is agreeable therefore he is taken under Friends care.

14/8/1756. Thos & Charles Moreman appointed to attend the marriage of Joseph Mackgeehee & Mary Chiles.

14/8/1756. John Stone Junr petitioned for a certificate to travel to NC. Charles Moreman & John Davis to enquire into his life & conversation.

14/8/1756. Thos & Charles Moreland request a certificate to travel to NC. Jno Davis & Ashly Johnson appointed to enquire into their life & conversation.

14/9/1756. David Terrell & Natha Winston appointed to ... Thos Stockton instead of Henry Terrell & Nichs Stone.

14/9/1756. John Saunders (son of Jno Saunders) hath married out from amongst Friends, a paper of denial is ordered.

9/10/1756. Jesse Johnson appointed overseer in the stead of Charles Johnson at Amelia meeting.

9/10/1756. David Terrell & Benja Harriss appointed to attend Quarterly meeting.

13/11/1756. Joseph Mackgeehee has acquainted us of his intention to remove to NC & requested a certificate, which was granted.

John Saunders (son of Jno Saunders) of Hanover Co hath lately married out contrary to the order of Friends, therefore we disown him. Signed by: John Davis, David Terrell Junr, Ashley Johnson, John Haley, David Terrell, Thos Moreman, Charles Moreman.

Garrat Elleson (son of Robert Elleson) of Newkent Co hath married out by priest contrary to the advice of Friends, therefore we disown him. Signed by: Strangeman Huchens, Benja Harriss, David Terrell, Saml Hargrave, John Sanders, Nichs Stone, Thos Cheadle, Jno Cheadle, Henery Terrell.

Archillus Ellmore of Amelia Co hath lately married out by a hireling minister contrary to Friends advice, therefore we disown him. Signed by: Henery Terrell Senr, Strangeman Hugings, David Terrell, Benj Harriss, John Cheadle, Nichs Stone, Saml Hargrave.

11/12/1756. Friends sufferings brought in: Saml Hargrave 5 shillings, Nichs Stone 2 pounds 10 shillings, John Cheadle 1 pound 15 shillings, ... , Isaac Cheadle 2 pounds 12 shillings, Strangeman Hugings 7 pounds.

8/1/1757. Christopher Clark requests to be taken under the care of Friends. Jno Davis & Charles Moreman Junr to enquire into his life & conversation.

8/1/1757. Jno Saunders requests to be released from being overseer. Wm Standley appointed overseer in the room of Jno Saunders.

Joseph Mackgehe of Louisa Co & Mary Chiles of Caroline Co married 12th da, 8th mo, 1756. Witnesses: Mary Woodson, Mary Bunch, Ann More, Jean Saunders, Sarah Lunch, Sarah Harris, Thos Moreman, Benja Mackgehe, George Bell, Chas Morman Junr, David Terrell Junr, Henry Terrell Junr, Jno Saunders, Ashley Johnson.

12/2/1757. Report of Jno Davis & Chas Morman Junr, Christopher Clark was taken under the care of Friends.

12/2/1757. Christopher Clark & Milla Terrell publish their intentions of marriage. Jno David & Chas Moreman appointed to enquire into his clearness.

12/3/1757. Henry Terrell & Nicolas Stone appointed to attend the marriage of Clark & wife.

12/3/1757. John Standley (son of Thos Standley) & Ann Ballard publish their intentions of marriage. Benj Harris & John Sanders appointed to enquire into his clearness.

12/3/1757. Charles Lynch requests for Friends consent to sue Jno ... Pain for a just sum & liberty is granted.

9/4/1757. Nicho Stone & Thos Cheadle appointed to attend the marriage of John Standle.

9/4/1757. David Terrell, John Sanders & Benja Harriss appointed to attend the Quarterly meeting.

14/5/1757. Henery Terrell to collect the tobacco lodged in the hand of Thos Turner by the Widow Duff for the use of Friends.

14/5/1757. A certificate of our worthy friend John Woolman of NJ colony was read.

Christopher Clark (son of Micajah Clark) of Albermarle Co & Milla Terrell (daughter of David Terrell) married the 13th da, 3rd mo, 1757. Witnesses: Aggatha Terrell, Sarah Terrell, Sarah Harris, Eliza Cheadle, Mourning Clark, Jno Cheadle, Nicolas Stone, Micajah Terrell, Pleasant Terrell, Zacharias Morman, David Terrell, Henry Terrell, Manoak Chiles.

John Standley (son of Thos Standley) of Hanover Co & Ann Ballard of Caroline Co (daughter of William Ballard of NC) married the 10th da, 4th mo, 1757.

Witnesses: John Harris, John Crew, John Standley, Susannah Sanders, Moore Bell, Cornelis Harriss, David Terrell, Strangeman Hugins, Thos Standley, Wm Standley.

11/6/1757. George Mathews certificate from the meeting at Cane Creek was read.

11/6/1757. From the womens yearly meeting at York in Great Briton an epistle from Mary Waite dated 10/2/1679 was read.

11/6/1757. Henery Terrell (son of David Terrell) acknowledged he was sorry for the miss steps which he hath made and the scandal he had brought upon friends. Desires to continue under the care of friends.

9/7/1757. Thos Pleasant requested a certificate to friends in West River, MD in relation to marriage. Strangeman Huchens & David Terrell appointed to make enquiry thereof.

9/7/1757. Joseph Crew Senr complains that Thos Standley neglects payment on a just contract. Benja Harris & David Terrell appointed to treat with the said Standley for his non pay.

13/8/1757. Hezikiah Saunders desires a certificate in relation to marriage to meeting at Whiteoak Swamp, Henrico Co. Benja Harris & William Standley are to enquire into his clearness.

11/9/1757. Elizabeth Price complains that John Moore Junr stands justly indebted to her and neglects payment from time to time. Thos & Charles Moreman appointed to go to Thos Moore & request of him payment of the money or give security.

11/9/1757. Friends suffering brought in: Samuell Hargrave 10 shillings, Nicolas Stone 1 pound 7 shillings 9 pence, Thos Cheadle 6 pounds, Jno Jonsons 2 pounds 10 shillings, Ceslah Elmond 13 shillings, John Johnson 7 pounds 10 shillings.

8/10/1757. Joseph Crews reports that he received satisfaction of Thos Standley by a promise of payment.

8/10/1757. Pleasant Standley request a certificate to friends at Whiteoak Swamp in relation to marriage. Jno Saunders & Chas Moreman appointed to enquire into his clearness.

8/10/1757. Thos Nicleson certificate read. Henry Terrell & Thos Pleasant appointed to draw up a certificate for him.

8/10/1757. John Husband & Alce Standley publish their intentions of marriage. John Barnet & Benja Watkins to enquire into his clearness.

8/10/1757. John Saunders, Benj Harris, Henry Terrell, Jno Cheadle appointed to attend the Quarterly meeting.

12/11/1757. John Smith & Thos Lain (Thos Lain from NC) produced a certificate, read & approved. Charles Mooreman & William Standley appointed to draw up a certificate for the said Smith & Lain & send to their respective meetings.

12/11/1757. Richd Stone, John Cheadle, Benja Harriss, John Saunders & Thos & Charles Mooreman to treate with David Terrell & Christopher Clark for their disorderly walking.

12/11/1757. Ashley & James Johnson appointed to reconcile a matter of difference between David Terrell Junr & Agnis Going (Gowing).

12/11/1757. Charles Mooreman appointed clerk in room of David Terrell Junr.

11/12/1757. Jno Saunders & Benja Harris appointed to attend the marriage of John Hutchens & Mary Standley.

11/12/1757. Manock Chiles Junr doth proceed disorderly. Henry Terrell & Samuel Hargrave appointed to treate with him.

14/1/1758. Nichelaus Standly requests to be taken under the care of Friends. Benj Harris & John Saunders to make enquiry into his life & conversation.

14/1/1758. Benja Harris, Thos Morman, Henry Terrell & ... Hargrave appointed to attend Quarterly meeting.

11/2/1758. Thos Mooreman, John Davis, Henery Terrell, Samuel Hargrave, Benja Harris & John Saunders to meet before next Quarterly meeting in order to settle the same.

14/3/1758. Nicolas Stone & Nath Winston appointed assistants with the other friends in treating with Thos Stockton.

14/3/1758. Manoak Chiles Junr still continues walking on sundry matters inconsistent with the principles of truth. A paper of denial to be drawn.

14/3/1758. John Cheadle, Thos Cheadle Wm Standley, John Harriss, Charles Mooreman & George Bell, with the other friends before appointed, to meet the day preceeding the Quarterly meeting.

59

14/3/1758. Joseph Chouning petioned to be taken under the care of Friends. Thos & Charles Mooreman appointed to enquire into his life and conversation.

8/4/1758. Jos Chouning for some time heretofore did attend some meetings at Camp Creek but is now removed towards Caroline. Henery Terrell & Saml Hargrave to make necessary enquiry.

8/4/1758. Archales Standle request a certificate in relation to marriage. John Sanders & Benja Harriss to make enquiry.

8/4/1758. Saml Hargrave appointed clerk in the roome of Thos Cheadle.

8/4/1758. Appointed Benja Harris & Standley Harris to make enquiry into a report brought against Hezakiah Sanders not being clear of some disorders.

8/4/1758. Benja Harriss, Thos Mooreman, Henery Terrell & Saml Hargrave to attend Quarterly meeting.

8/4/1758. Manoak Chiles Junr hath for sometime given way to the vain customs & practices of the world such as going to publick places, fighting & sundry other disorders, therefore we disown him. Signed by: John Sanders, Thos Mooreman, Henery Terrell, Thos Cheadle, Samuel Hargrave, Benja Harris, John Harris.

John Hutchens (son of Strangeman Hutchens) of Goochland Co and Alce Standley (daughter of John Standley) married the 11th da, 12th mo, 1757. Witnesses: Rebeca Harris, Ede Harris, Eliz Huchens, Mary Hutchens, Martha Standly, Jno Standley, Jno Saunders, Benj Harris, Jno Harris, Willm Standley, Jno Standley Junr, Moses Harris.

13/5/1758. John Haley desires to be released from being overseer of Fork Creek meeting.

10/6/1758. Law sute between David Terrell Junr & Agness Going is now ended to his shame.

10/6/1758. Strangeman Hugings and William Standley appointed to treate with Hezakiah Sanders in stead of Benj & Standly Harris.

10/6/1758. John Moore Junr petitioned for a certificate to Old England. Thos Mooreman and John Davis appointed to enquire into his life & conversation.

10/6/1758. John Davis & James Johnson appointed to enquire into a report against Benja Johnson (son of Agness Johnson) of Louisa Co of some disorders.

60

10/6/1758. Thos Clark appointed overseer of Fork Creek meeting in the roome of Jno Haley.

10/6/1758. Benj Harriss request liberty to attach a man's estate which was his tenant, who he suspected was endeavoring to go off and defraud him of his rents, request was granted.

7/7/1758. Thos Mooreman & Benja Johnson appointed to treate with David Terrell Junr concerning his disorderly walking.

7/7/1758. Henery Terrell, Benj Harriss, Thos Mooreman, William Standley, Samuel Hargrave & John Sanders appointed to attend Quarterly meeting.

7/7/1758. Complaint brought against Wm Fulcher not tending meetings & other disorderly proceedings. Henery Terrell & Saml Hargrave to write to the said Fulcher.

12/8/1758. David Terrell Junr hath given satisfaction as is thought reasonable for his disorderly proceeding.

12/8/1758. John Moore Junr hath declined his entention of going to Old England.

12/8/1758. Henery Terrell & Thos Mooreman to draw up a paper of denial against Benjamin Johnson.

9/9/1758. John Cheadle, Benja Harriss, Nich Stone & David Terrell to meet the 16th instant at John Standley's with Hezakiah Sanders to reconcile a difference which hath happened between them, concerning some building.

9/9/1758. It appears William Fulsher is guilty of sundry things inconsistent with the principles of truth. Saml Hargrave to draw up a paper of denial against him.

9/9/1758. William Diggs some years ago apply himself for a certificate to NC. But some things appeared to hinder this meeting to allow him but since hath removed that complaint and continues a member of our society.

9/9/1758. William Standley requests certificate to meeting at Fairfax, Loudon Co, John Sanders & Benja Harriss to enquire into his clearness in relation to marriage.

9/9/1758. Complaint against Henery Terrell Junr (son of David Terrell) being guilty of some disorders. Jno Cheadle, Thos Cheadle & Saml Hargrave to treat with him.

9/9/1758. Received of the estate of Eliza Duff ... [blurred] ... Edward Dixon 10 pounds 18 shillings ... .

9/9/1758. Jno Cheadle 9 pounds 5 shillings of the balance to Henery Terrell to defray former charges.

9/9/1758. Benja Johnson (son of Benja Johnson deceased) of Louisa Co hath given way to the delusions of Saton, we therefore disown him. Signed by: Thos Mooreman, Henery Terrell, John Davis, Thos Ballard, Ashley Johnson, James Johnson, Achillas Mooreman, David Terrell Junr.

13/10/1758. A paper of denial to be drawn up against Henery Terrell Junr.

13/10/1758. James Johnson & Mildred Mooreman publish their entention of marriage. Ashley & Jesse Johnson to enquire into his clearness.

13/10/1758. Robert Johnson & Cisley Elmore publish their entention of marriage. John Davis & Charles Mooreman appointed to enquire into his clearness.

13/10/1758. William Diggs & Judith Haley publish their entention of marriage. Saml ... & David Terrell appointed to enquire into his clearness.

13/10/1758. A complaint against George Taylor being guilty of some things. John Davis & Ashley Johnson appointed to treate with him.

13/10/1758. William Standley petioned to be released of being overseer. John Sanders is appointed overseer in his stead.

13/10/1758. Saml Hargrave appointed to search the monthly meeting records to know whether Gidion Johnson hath ever been taken under the care of this meeting.

13/10/1758. John Sanders, Jno Cheadle, Benja Harriss, David Terrell & William Standley appointed to attend the Quarterly meeting.

13/10/1758. William Fulsher of Orange Co hath given way to the delutions of saton such as gaming, going to places of divertion & absenting himself from meetings, we therefore disown him. Signed by: Saml Hargrave, Henery Terrell, John Cheadle, John Davis, David Terrell, Benja Harriss.

11/11/1758. John Davis & Charles Mooreman appointed to attend the marriage of James Johnson.

11/11/1758. Ashley & Jesse Johnson appointed to attend the marriage of Robert Johnson.

11/11/1758. John & Thos Clark appointed to attend the marriage of William Diggs.

11/11/1758. Charles Johnson petitioned for assistance towards the maintaining of his family.

11/11/1758. Joseph Chouning petitioned for a certificate to the meeting at Whiteoak Swamp. John Cheadle & David Terrell to enquire into his clearness in relation to marriage.

11/11/1758. Henry Terrell (son of David Terrell) of Caroline Co hath given way to vain practices of the world such as gaming, going to places of publick divertion & other disorderly practices. Therefore we disown him. Signed by: Thos Mooreman, John Davis, John Saunders, Ashley Johnson, Saml Hargrave, Benja Harriss.

9/12/1758. Hezekiah Sanders condemns the faults which he's stood accused of upon which he continues a member of our society.

9/12/1758. James Crew & Judith Harriss published their intention of marriage. The said Crew is desired to produce a certificate.

James Johnson (son of John Johnson) of Amelia Co and Mildred Mooreman of Louisa Co (daughter of Thos Mooreman) married the 12th da, 11th mo, 1758. Witnesses: John Davis, Saml Hargrave, Benja Johnson, James Johnson, George Bell, David Terrell Junr, George Robinson, ... Mooreman, Francis Ballard, Mary Johnson, Thos Mooreman, Rachal Mooreman, Cisley Johnson.

12/1/1759. Ordered the sum of 5 pounds be raised for the support of Charles Johnson and his family, the money to be put into the hands of Ashley Johnson.

12/1/1759. James Crew produced a few lines from James Ladd and John Crew.

12/1/1759. John Sanders & Standley Harriss appointed to attend the marriage of James Crew & Judith Harriss.

12/1/1759. William Standley, John Sanders, Benja Harriss & Thos Mooreman to attend Quarterly meeting.

10/3/1759. Agreeable to an order of the Quarterly meeting, John Cheadle, Henery Terrell, Nichlos Stone, Charles & Thomas Mooreman, John Davis, Benja Harriss & John Sanders appointed members to constitute meetings of ministers & elders.

Robert Johnson (son of Ashley Johnson) of Louisa Co & Cisley Elmore (daughter of Thos Elmoore) of Amelia Co married the 19th da, 11th mo, 1758. Witnesses: ... [blurred] ... , Jno Johnson, Chas Johnson, Jesse Jonson, Garrard Elleson, Ashley Johnson.

5/4/1759. Eliza (wife of William Standley) lately removed to Fairfax. Certificate dated 3/12/1758.

5/4/1759. James Johnson of Amelia Co desired the advice of friends in a matter of difference between him & Gidion Johnson. Jno Pleasants of Cumberland & Thos Pleasants are appointed to endeavour to settle the same.

5/4/1759. John Saunders, Henery Terrell, ... , & William Standley appointed to attend the Quarterly meeting.

5/4/1759. Thos Parsons appointed to visit George Taylor on acct of his disorderly conduct, not being present we have no account of the same. Thos & Charles Mooreman appointed to assist the other friends.

15/4/1759. Strangeman Hugins, William Standley, Saml Hargrave, Catherine Standley, Elizabeth Standley, Ann Chiles, Eliza Cheadle, Sarah Harris, Sarah Terrell & Rachal Mooreman added to the friends appointed to sit in meetings of ministers and elders.

13/5/1759. The case of George Robenson's marrying out, its ordered that Benja Johnson & Zachariah Mooreman draw up a denial paper.

13/5/1759. Nicks Stone, John Cheadle, Henery Terrell, Saml Hargrave, Jno Standley Junr, Benja Harriss, John Sandors to meet and reconcile a difference between Standle Harriss & Daniel Harriss family.

13/5/1759. Nathll Winston, Saml Hargrave, John Sanders & Benja Harriss appointed to treate with Thos Terrell concerning a report tending much to the dishonour of truth.

William Diggs of Louisa Co (son of Marshall Diggs deceased) and Judith Haley (daughter of Jno Haley) of same co married the 12th da, 11th mo, 1758. Witnesses: Benja Johnson, George Robinson, John Sanders, Thomas Mooreman, George Bell, James Johnson, David Terrell Junr, John Davis, Zachariah Mooreman, Lucy Stone.

9/6/1759. Charles Mooreman & John Davis ordered to draw up denial paper against George Taylor.

9/6/1759. George Robenson of Louisa Co hath forfeited his privileges of membership by marrying out to a woman of an other persuation by a hurling minister, we therefore disown him. Signed by: Charles Mooreman, Thos Mooreman, John Davis, William Standley.

9/6/1759. Money expended by William Standley traveling to Operkon as a guide to John ...nand, Saml Emlen ... .

9/6/1759. Money expended by John Harriss going to MD as guide to Mary Kerby & Grace Croasdall. By John Cheadle.

13/7/1759. James Crew (son of Andrew) of Charles City Co and Judith Harriss (daughter of Benja Harriss) of Hanover Co married the 14th da, 1st mo, 1759. Witnesses: John Pleasants Junr, Thos Pleasants, Thos Moreman, Jos ... , Robert Pleasants, Benja Harriss, Jno Sanders, William Standly, Edward Stablers, Andrew Crew, Benja Crew.

11/8/1759. Concerning James & Gidion Johnson, it appears Gidion Johnson is not in unity with friends therefore James Johnson can proceed against him.

11/8/1759. Standly Harriss found guilty of sundry disorders. Saml Hargrave to draw up denial paper against him.

11/8/1759. Thos Terrell refuse to resolve any questions that shall be asked him on account. Samuel Hargrave appointed to draw up denial paper.

11/8/1759. Jamima Chouning produced a certificate from meeting at Whiteoak, Henrico Co.

11/8/1759. John Pleasants Junr of Cumberland Co married contrary to the advise of friends to woman of another society. Wm Standley & Jno Sanders appointed to draw up denial paper.

4/8/1759. John Sanders and Benja Harriss appointed to present Standly Harris with his denial.

4/8/1759. Nicks Stone & Thos Stocton appointed to present Thos Terrell with his denial.

4/8/1759. Cornelious Harriss of Hanover Co (son of Daniel Harriss) hath married out from among us. Henery Terrell appointed to draw up denial paper.

4/8/1759. Henery Terrell requests release from being overseer. Richd Stone appointed in his stead.

4/8/1759. Money ordered to reimburse Stephen Hambler, F... Bayley & Saml Pleasant for sundry expenses. Raised by this meeting: Benja Harris 12 pounds, Garret Johnson 2 shillings 6 pence, Moses Harris 2 shillings 6 pence, Saml Hargrave 2 shillings 6 pence, Jno Cheadle 10 shillings 6 pence, Henery Terrell 2 shillings 6 pence, Natha Winston 2 shillings 6 pence, John Sanders 2 shillings 6 pence, John Harriss 2 shillings 6 pence, Zacariah Stanly 2 shillings 6 pence, Wm Stanly 2 shillings 6 pence.

8/9//1759. John Pleasants Junr of Cumberland Co contrary to the known rules of our disipline married a woman of an other society by a hireling minister, therefore we disown him. Signed by: Thos Stocton, Natha Winston, Henery Terrell, Nicks Stone, Samuel Hargrave, John Standly, John Cheadle, Thomas Cheadle.

8/9/1759. Stanley Harriss of Hanover Co forfeited his previlidge of membership amongst us by endeavoring to defile his brothers daughter and sundry other things, therefore we disown him. Signed by: Samuel Hargrave, Henery Terrell, Thos Cheadle, John Standley, Nicks Stone, John Cheadle, Thos Stocton.

4/9/1759. Thos Terrell of Caroline Co forfeited his prevelidge of membership amongst us by a familiarity with a lude woman to the disgrace of himself and our profession. Signed by: Samuel Hargrave, Thos Cheadle, Thos Stockton, Jno Sanders, John Cheadle, Nicks Stone.

12/10/1759. John Harriss requests a certificate to friends at West River, MD. Samuel Hargrave & Wm Standly appointed to enquire into his life & conversation in relation to marriage.

12/10/1759. Nicks Stone, Henery Terrell, John Harriss & Saml Hargrave appointed to attend the Quarterly meeting.

12/10/1759. Cornelious Harriss of Hanover Co forfeited his privilege of membership amongst us by joining in marriage to a woman of different persuation. Signed by: Samuel Hargrave, clerk.

11/11/1759. Produced from Whiteoak Swamp, Henrico Co meeting, a certificate of Sarah Stanley and Eliza Stanly wifes of Archilon and Pleasant Standly, read & approved.

11/11/1759. A compliant against Christopher Clark being guilty of sundry disorders. James Johnson and Chas Mooreman appointed to treate with him.

11/1/1760. Jno Davis is added to assist in treating with Christopher Clark.

11/1/1760. Jno Moore Junr married out from among us. Saml Hargrave to draw up denial against him.

11/1/1760. Henery Terrell, Benja Harriss, John Sanders & Thos Mooreman to attend Quarterly meeting.

9/2/1760. Garrard Ellison petitioned to be taken under the care of Friends. Ashly & Jesse Johnson to enquire into his life and conversation. 4/4/1760. His wife also desires to be taken under the care of Friends.

4/4/1760. Charles Mooreman & James Johnson ordered to prepare a paper of denial against Christopher Clark.

4/4/1760. Orders of the Quarterly meeting relating to the sufferings of Friends not being complied, ordered that they be collected and John Sanders to forward them.

4/4/1760. A paper was presented signed by John Sanders & Benj Harriss setting fourth a complaint against Wm Standly & Zacariah Stanly for sundry reproachfull and infamous expressesions against Strangeman Huchins & his ministry. Jno Harriss, Thos Mooreman, Thos Pleasants, Robert Pleasants & Edward Stabler to examine into the said complaint and treate with them.

4/4/1760. Benja Harriss, Jno Sanders, Thomas Pleasants appointed to attend the Quarterly meeting.

10/5/1760. Suffering brought in by Thos Mooreman & John Barnart 5 pounds 3 shillings.

10/5/1760. Jno Sanders, Benja Harriss & Samuel Hargrave to treate with Wm & Zacariah Stanley.

14/6/1760. John Cheadle & Nicks Stone appointed to treate with Wm & Zacariah Stanley.

14/6/1760. Rachal Harris requests a certificate to West River, MD.

14/6/1760. A complaint against Shadrack Standly for scandalizing Sarah Sanders in a very reproach full manner in sundry matters. Jno Cheadle, Nicks Stone and Benja Harriss to treate with the said Standly.

14/6/1760. Our Worthy friend Jos Newby from NC visited this meeting.

11/7/1760. James Johnson & Charles Mooreman appointed to draw up a paper of denial against Christopher Clark.

11/7/1760. Benja Harris and Saml Hargrave appointed to draw of paper of denial against Shadrick Standly.

11/7/1760. John Harriss petioned to sue R... Harriss for a track of land which he apprehends he hath a right to but cannot be determined without a determination at the law, meeting grants him liberty.

11/7/1760. A complaint against Micajah Terrell and Henery Terrell (son of Henery Terrell) of their being guilty of sundry things, gameing, dancing, being at marriages contrary to the rules of our disappline. Saml Hargrave appointed to treate with them.

11/7/1760. Jno Sanders, Benja Harriss, Nathll Winston & Samuel Hargrave appointed to attend Quarterly meeting.

9/8/1760. Christopher Clark sent a paper of condemnation to pretty good satisfaction.

9/8/1760. William & Zacariah Standly sent a paper of condemnation which was read and was satisfactory.

9/8/1760. Saml Hargrave appointed to draw up a paper of denial against Henery & Micajah Terrell.

9/8/1760. Cair Mcgehee requests to be taken under the care of Friends. John Cheadle & Sam Hargrave appointed to enquire into his life & conversation.

9/8/1760. Shadrick Standly of Hanover Co hath by advancing sundry discretions and enfamous expressions against Sarah Sanders, boasting to several persons that he had used to greate ... with her in order to demeane her cauactor. Therefore we disown him.

13/9/1760. Henery & Micajah Terrell appears to good satisfaction, there to continue under the care of Friends.

13/9/1760. Shadrick Standly applied himself to this meeting to be again received into unity and a member of this meeting.

13/9/1760. A complaint against Newbery Stockton (son of Thos Stockton) being guilty of sundry disorders & is removed from the reach of this meeting. Thos Cheadle to write to him & let him know he must make this meeting or paper of denial to be drawn up.

13/9/1760. Agreeable to an order of the yearly meeting, hath disposed of a list of books sent to us by Robt Pleasants & others appointed for that service.

10/10/1760. Jno Sanders, Jno Davis & Jno Cheadle appointed to attend Quarterly meeting.

13/12/1760. Nicks Stone & Thomas Cheadle to draw up paper of denial on Newbery Stockton.

13/12/1760. Our friend Thomas Farmer produced his certificate from Pequammans, NC.

13/12/1760. Garratt Johnson & Judith Watkins published their entention of marriage. Charles & Ashley Johnson to enquire into the clearness of Garratt Johnson.

13/2/1761. Friends appointed to draw up paper of denial against Newbery Stockton not appearing, Saml Hargrave appointed to draw up one.

13/2/1761. Strangeman Huchings & Benja Watkins appointed to attend the marriage of Garratt Johnson & Judith Watkins.

13/2/1761. William Ferrell a publick friend from Fredricksburg Township, SC produced a certificate. Samuell Hargrave & Benja Harris appointed to draw up a certificate for him to his meeting.

13/2/1761. Also a certificate for Thomas Farmer from NC.

13/2/1761. Garratt Ellison requests a certificate to Whiteoak Swamp, Henrico Co. Also one for his wife. Jesse & Ashley Johnson appointed to enquire into the life & conversation of them.

14/3/1761. The matter concerning Cair McGehee is discontinue for his proceeding in marriage contrary to the rules of friends.

14/3/1761. Newbery Stockton (son of Thos Stockton) forfeited his preveledge of membership amongst us by absenting himself from meetings & suffering himself to be drawn away into the vain and libertines fashion of the world frequenting places of diversion, we therefore disown him. Signed by: Saml Hargrave, John Cheadle, Jno Sanders, Thos Stockton, Nicks Stone.

13/6/1761. Micajah Standly request a certificate to meeting at Fairfax. Benja Harriss & John Sanders to enquire into his life & conversation.

13/6/1761. A complaint against John Standly Junr (son of John Standly) that he is guilty of sundry disorders such as drinking to access. Jno Davis and Thos Mooreman appointed to treate with him.

13/6/1761. A complaint against Collass Johnson & Thos Douglass hath married contrary to the advice of friends by a hireling priest. Wm Standly to draw up paper of denial.

10/7/1761. Zachariah Mooreman is ordered to read the papers of denial against Thomas Douglass & Collass Johnson at publick meeting to which they did belong.

10/7/1761. Jno Sanders, Benja Harris, Jno Cheadle, Thos Cheadle & Wm Stanly appointed to attend the Quarterly meeting.

10/7/1761. Thomas Douglas & Colless Johnson of Louisa Co joined themselves in marriage to women of an other persuasion in matters of religion by a hireling priest. We therefore disown them. Signed by: Thos Cheadle, Wm Stanly, Saml Hargrave, Jno Sanders, Benja Harriss, John Cheadle.

8/8/1761. John Harriss & Zachariah Stanly appointed to draw up paper of denial against John Stanly Junr.

8/8/1761. Shardrick Standly requests to be again received into full unity with friends, request granted.

8/8/1761. Moses Harriss request a certificate in relation to marriage to meeting in West River, MD. Strangeman Hugings & Benja Harris appointed to enquire into his clearness.

8/8/1761. Samuel Robert Broocks acquainted some friend of his desire of being joining in membership with us. 12/9/1761 John Sanders & Wm Standly to enquire into his life and conversation.

8/8/1761. Samuel Hargrave is appointed to read Ann Chiles paper of denial at meeting to which she did belong.

12/9/1761. Obediah Harriss requests a certificate in relation to marriage to meeting in Henrico Co. William Stanly & John Harriss appointed to enquire into the same.

12/9/1761. Richard Lewis of Caroline Co requests to be taken under the care of friends. Jno Cheadle & Thos Stockton appointed to enquire into his life and conversation.

12/9/1761. John Stanly Junr of Hanover Co having taken undue liberties in the excessiveness of strong drink to the extreame of drunkenness, also behaving himself in a abusfull manner to others in profaine language with quarelling and fighting, we therefore disown him. Signed by: John Cheadle, John Sanders,

Benja Harriss, John Harriss, Thomas Cheadle, Thomas Stockton, Natha Winston.

14/11/1761. This meeting attended by our friend George Matthews from Cane Creek, NC who produced a certificate.

14/11/1761. Our friend Wm Hunt from New Garden, NC produced a certificate. 8/1/1762 Wm Stanley appointed to draw up certificate for him.

8/1/1762. This meeting attended by our worthy friend John Stephenson from England who produced a certificate from Stockton, County of Durham monthly meeting held at Yarmo.

8/1/1762. Complaint against Henery Terrell Junr being guilty of sundry disorders tending to the dishonour of truth. Samuel Hargrave to treat with him.

8/1/1762. John Sanders, William Stanly, Nicks Stone & Samuel Hargrave appointed to attend Quarterly meeting.

13/2/1762. The clerk failing to appear, Wm Stanly appointed in his stead for this time.

13/2/1762. William Stanly is appointed to draw a certificate for George Matthews & Wm Hunt.

13/3/1762. Samuel Hargrave appointed to draw up a paper of denial against Henery Terrel Junr.

13/3/1762. William Stanly appointed overseer in roome of Benja Harriss who is lately removed by death.

13/3/1762. John Sanders & John Harriss appointed to secure the land on which Ceder Creek meeting house stands.

9/4/1762. John Davis & David Terrell to secure the land on which Camp Creek meeting house stands.

9/4/1762. Saml Robert Broocks and Mary Hutchings published their entention of marriage. John Harriss & Wm Stanly appointed to enquire into his clearness.

9/4/1762. Moses Harriss removed within the verg of Sourthriver meeting & requests a certificate. John Harriss & Wm Stanly appointed to enquire into his life & conversation.

9/4/1762. John Sanders, John Harriss & Wm Stanly appointed to attend the Quarterly meeting.

8/8/1762. Report that Christopher Clark acts contrary to the rules of our disappline. 9/7/1768. Thos Stockton, Jno Davis & Thos Mooreman appointed to treat with him.

8/5/1762. Henery Terrell (son of Henery Terrell) is guilty of sundry disorderly practices, such as appearing at places of diversion, dancing & absenting himself from meetings. Therefore we disown him. Signed by: John Davis, John Sanders, David Terrell, S R Broocks, John Harriss.

12/6/1762. Micajah Terrell hath removed within the verge of the meeting in Bedford Co. Jno Cheadle & Saml Hargrave to make enquirey into his life & conversation to draw up a certificate.

9/7/1768. Jno Stanly (son of Thos Stanly) requests a certificate to meeting at New Garden. NC. Jno Sanders & Wm Stanly appointed to enquire into his conversation and affairs.

9/7/1768. John Cheadle, Nicks Stone, Samuel Hargrave, John Sanders & William Stanly appointed to attend Quarterly meeting.

14/8/1762. Wm Stanly & John Sandors appointed to draw up paper of denial against Christopher Clark.

14/8/1762. Samuel R. Broocks request a certificate in order to joyne the meeting held in Henrico Co. Jno Harris & Jno Sanders appointed to enquire into his conversation & affairs.

8/10/1762. John Sanders Junr request to be taken under the care of this meeting. John Douglass & Thomas Mooreman appointed to enquire into his life & conversation.

8/10/1762. Charles Johnson petion for something towards the releafe of himself & family. Meeting ordered 1 pound 10 shillings to him for that purpose.

8/10/1762. John Sanders 2 shillings 6 pence, John Douglass 5 shillings, Wm Stanly 2 shillings 6 pence, Saml Hargrave 2 shillings 6 pence, John Harris 2 shillings 6 pence.

8/10/1762. William Stanly & Shadrack Stanly appointed to attend the Quarterly meeting.

13/11/1762. Money raised for the support of Chas Johnson: John Cheadle 5 shillings, of the meeting money 7 pounds 6 shillings, Thomas Stockton 2 pounds 6 shillings.

13/11/1762. John Barnet lately suffered on an account of pr... demands so much that is feared his family may suffer. Jno Sanders & Jno Harris appointed to enquire into the same.

13/11/1762. Pleasant Terrell hath lately married out from amongst friends by a hireling priest. Wm Stanly & John Harriss appointed to draw up a testification against him.

11/12/1762. The matter respecting meeting house ... fully complied with, Cha Mooreman and John Davis to secure that at Camp Creek. Strangeman Huchings to secure that at Geneto.

11/12/1762. Pleasant Terrell (son of David Terrell) of Caroline Co hath joined himself in marriage with a woman of an other presuation in matter of religion by a hireling priest. Therefore we disown him. Signed by: Samuel Hargrave, John Davis, Strangeman Huchings, John Sanders, John Harriss, William Stanly, Cha Mooreman, William Ballard.

7/1/1763. Money raised for John Barnat of Camp Creek: Ceder Creek: Jno Sanders 2 shillings 6 pence, John Harriss 2 shillings 6 pence, William Stanly 2 shillings 6 pence; Caroline: Saml Hargrave 2 shillings 6 pence, Nicks Stone 2 shillings 6 pence; Jeneto: Strangeman Huchings 5 shillings, Thos Pleasants 5 shillings.

7/1/1762. Byrom Ballard (son of William Ballard) requests a certificate to meeting in Bedford Co. Thomas Mooreman & Charles Mooreman appointed to make enquiry into his life & conversation.

7/1/1762. Thomas Mooreman, John Davis & John Sanders appointed to attend Quarterly meeting.

12/2/1763. Thos Clark not being present Wm Stanly chosen this time.

12/2/1763. John Sanders Junr hath sent a few lines condemning his past conduct desiring to be received into unity with friends, received as a member again.

8/4/1763. A complaint brought in by Joshua Stone in behalf of his wife Susanah Stone against Talton Woodson at being guilty of reporting things tending to her ... . Thomas Pleasants appointed to treat with the said Woodson.

8/4/1763. A complaint against Geo Bell's being guilty of sundry things. John Davis appointed to treate with him.

8/4/1763. John Sanders, John Harriss & Shadrick Stanly appointed to attend Quarterly meeting.

11/6/1763. Wm Stanly and John Harriss appointed to deliver a coppy of minutes to Talton Woodson, he is to attend next meeting.

8/7/1763. Nicks Stone appointed to visit George Bell & let him know he must give satisfaction, or denial will go fourth.

8/7/1763. John Cheadle, Nicks Stone & Samuel Hargrave appointed to attend Quarterly meeting.

13/8/1763. Minutes delivered to Talton Woodson, his answer was he did say Sushannah Stone was guilty of forgery but it was no other than what she herself did acknowledge, that is to say, wrote a letter to Charles Woodson to enform him of an affair of [blurred] Pleasants which he the said Pleasants desird her to do and she set his hand instead of her own by his consent which [blurred] .... Report being satisfactory & sufficient to cleare the said Sushannah Stone.

13/8/1763. John Harriss & William Stanly appointed to draw a denial on Geo Bell.

13/8/1763. This meeting thinks is reasonable to treate with Ashly Johnson concerning his daughter marrying from amongst friends. John Davis & John Sanders appointed for that service. Also to treat with Ashly Johnson Junr for accompanying [Geo] Bell to the priest and let him know he might be accountable to this meeting for such disorder.

10/9/1763. William Ballard and Ann Stanly publish their intention of marriage. He is desired to produce a certificate from meeting he belongs to.

10/9/1763. A complaint against Pleasant Stanly being guilty of drinking spirituous liquers to excess and fighting. John Cheadle, John Sanders & Strangeman Hugings to treate with him.

10/9/1763. George Bell of Louisa Co hath taken undue liberties in appearing at places appointed for military exercise also frequenting places for divertion and hath married a woman by a hireling priest and nearer of him than is allowed. We therefore disown him. Signed by; John Sanders, John Cheadle, Strangeman Hugings, John Harriss, Shadrick Stanly, William Standly.

8/10/1763. John Sanders appointed to deliver a coppy of the minutes to Ashly Johnson Junr, he is to appear at next meeting.

8/10/1763. William Ballard produced a certificate from meeting at New Garden, NC signifying his clearness of marriage ingagements, and has consent of parents. John Harriss & John Sanders appointed to attend the marriage of William Ballard & Ann Stanly.

12/11/1763. Edward Booeken one of his Majesties Justices of the Peace for Amelia Co sent a few lines setting fourth that Agness Roynolds made oath before him that Ashly Johnson (son of Ashly Johnson) had committed adultery with her and got her with child. Thomas Mooreman & John Davis to treat with the said Johnson.

12/11/1763. William Johnson and Aggatha Mooreman publish their entention of marriage. Ashly & Jesse Johnson (sons of John Johnson) appointed to enquire into his clearness.

12/11/1763. Thomas Ballard hath married to a woman of a different way of thinking in matters of religion by a hireling priest. John Sanders & William Stanly appointed to draw a denial.

12/11/1763. Charles Mooreman (son of Acculas Mooreman) guilty of appearing at places appointed for military exercises and wearing surpurflous apparel. Thomas Mooreman & John Davis to treat with him.

12/11/1763. Benjamin Johnson & Zachariah Mooreman request a certificate to meeting at South River, Bedford Co for them & families. John Davis & Charles Mooreman appointed to enquire into their lives & conversation.

12/11/1763. Zachariah Stanly request a certificate to joyne the meeting of New Garden [blurred]. John Sanders and John Harriss appointed to enquire into his life, conversation & affairs.

12/11/1763. Strangeman Stanly request the same to same meeting. Same friends appointed for same service.

William Ballard (son of William Ballard) of Roan Co, NC and Ann Stanly (daughter of Thos Stanly) of Hanover Co married 11th da, 11th mo, 1763. Witnesses: John Harriss, William Stanly, Nathan Stanly, Sarah Stanly, Ursula Stanly, Milly Stanley, Sarah Ladd, Jane Sanders, Cathrine Stanly, Madox Stanly, Pleasant Stanly, Shadrick Stanly, John Stanley, Strangeman Stanly, John Sanders, James Ladd, Stanlus Enough.

10/12/1763. John Davis & Thos Mooreman appointed to draw a denial against Ashley Johnson Junr.

10/12/1763. Charles Mooreman & James Johnson appointed to attend the marriage of William Johnson and Aggatha Mooreman.

14/1/1764. Wm Stanly appointed to assist in the matter of securing lands on which Camp Creek & Jenato meetinghouses stand.

14/1/1764. A subscription for John Barnat read: John Cheadle 10 shillings, Samuel Hargrave 2 shillings 6 pence, Nicks Stone 8 shillings, William Stanly [blurred].

14/2/1764. James Johnson (son of John Johnson) request a certificate to friends at New Garden, NC meeting . Ashly and Jesse Johnson appointed to enquire into his life, conversation and affairs.

14/2/1764. Talton Johnson requests the same to the same place. John Davis & John Sanders appointed to enquire into his life & conversation.

14/2/1764. Strangeman Huchings, Nicks Stone, John Sanders & John Harriss appointed to attend the Quarterly meeting.

14/4/1764. John Harriss & Wm Stanly appointed to treate with Pleasant Stanly.

14/4/1764. Micajah Stanly produced a certificate from Fairfax meeting, he desires to be joined membership with this meeting, received as a member of this meeting.

14/4/1764. James Crew produced a certificate from the meeting at Whiteoak Swamp, Henrico Co for self and wife, desires to be joynd in membership with his meeting, received as members thereof.

14/4/1764. John Sanders requests a certificate for himself and his wife Jane Sanders to the meeting at New Garden, NC. John Harriss and Wm Stanly appointed to enquire into his life and conversation and also his son Joel Sanders.

14/4/1764. Nicks Huchings request a certificate to meeting in Henrico Co in relation to marriage. John Harriss & Shadrick Stanly appointed to enquire into his clearness.

14/4/1764. Nathan Stanly requests a certificate for the meeting at New Garden, NC. John Harriss and Shadrick Stanly appointed to enquire into his life & conversation.

14/4/1764. A bal of 6/9 due to John Barnet of sum ordered to be raised for him.

12/6/1764. Account of sufferings brought in: Strangeman Hugings 4 pounds 10 shillings, Nicks Stone 3 pounds 18 shillings.

76

12/6/1764. John Harriss appointed overseer in the stead of John Sanders.

11/2/1764. Ashley Johnson Junr (son of Ashley Johnson) of Louisa Co having given way to his own lusts so far as to beget a bastard child by his cuzan Agness Runalds, we disown him. Signed by John Harriss, William Stanly, John Sanders, Nicks Stone.

11/8/1764. Ashley Johnson appeared and gave such satisfaction in respect to his daughters marriage, was thought reasonable.

11/8/1764. Pleasant Stanly sent paper condemning his past conduct giving some assurance of a more circumspect life hereafter which was pretty good satisfaction.

11/8/1764. Friend appointed to treat with Charles Mooreman reports that he hath complied with no satisfaction, and also that the said Charles Mooreman hath married to a woman of another presuation in matter of religion by a hireling priest. John Harriss and William Stanly appointed to draw a denial against him.

11/8/1764. John Harriss & William Stanly appointed to draw up certificate for James Johnson (son of John Johnson) of Amelia Co to joyne the meeting of New Garden, NC.

11/8/1764. William Stanly requests a certificate to the meeting at New Garden, NC for himself, wife and children. John Harriss & James Crew appointed to make enquiry into his life, conversation & affairs.

11/8/1764. Micajah Stanly requests a certificate to the meeting held at Fairfax. Samuel Hargrave appointed to make enquiry into his life, conversation & affairs.

11/8/1764. Zachariah Stanly request a certificate to the friends of New Garden, NC meeting. William Stanly & James Crew appointed to enquire into his life, conversation & affairs.

11/8/1764. William Lane and his family, within the limits of the meeting at New Garden, NC, for some time have neglected to attend meetings, still have a right of membership. Obediah Harriss and William Stanly appointed to enquire into the lives & conversation of said family.

11/8/1764. Strangeman Hugings motioned his entention of traveling into some parts of NC and requests a certificate. John Harriss & Samuel Hargrave appointed to enquire into his life & conversation.

11/8/1764. David Broocks produced a certificate from meeting at Hopewell, VA which was read & approved. Received as a member.

11/8/1764. Strangeman Hugings, William Stanly, John Davis and Samuel Hargrave appointed to attend Quarterly meeting.

8/9/1764. John Payn & Mary his wife request to be taken under the care of friends. John Harriss & James Crew appointed to enquire into their lives & conversation.

8/9/1764. Joseph Ray requests the same. John Harriss and Shadrick Stanly appointed to enquired into their lives and conversation.

8/9/1764. John Pleasants (son of John Pleasants) of Cumberland Co sent a paper of condemnation for his past misconduct signed by his own hand before his death, which was read & much approved.

13/10/1764. The clerk being absent by reason of sickness, William Stanly appointed to act for this time.

13/10/1764. James Crew appointed overseer in the roome of Wm Stanly.

13/10/1764. Shadrick Stanly request certificate in relation of marriage to meeting held at Whiteoak Swamp. John Harriss & James Crew to enquire into his clearness.

13/10/1764. John Ladd and Unity Harriss publish their intention of marriage. He is to produce a certificate from the meeting at Whiteoak Swamp, Henrico Co.

13/10/1764. Charles Mooreman (son of Accallus Mooreman) of Louisa Co hath fallen into many disorderly things and late hath suffered himself to be joined in marriage to a woman of an other persuation in matters of religion and by a hireling priest. Therefore we disown him. Signed by: Samuel Hargrave, Nicks Stone, John Cheadle, William Stanly, John Harriss, Shadrick Stanly, Nathaniel Winston, James Crew.

10/11/1764. John Harris & James Crew to attend the marriage of John Ladd and Unity Harriss.

10/11/1764. James Pleasant of Cumberland Co requests a certificate to the meeting at Whiteoak Swamp in relation to marriage. John Harriss and Strangeman Hugings appointed to make enquiry into his clearness.

9/2/1765. The clerk failing to attend by reason of sickness, John Harriss to act for this time.

9/2/1765. Thomas Mooreman requests a certificate for himself and wife Rachall in order to joyne the meeting at South River, Bedford Co. John Davis & Samuel Buch appointed to enquire into their lifes and conversation.

9/2/1765. Charles Mooreman appointed overseer of Camp Creek meeting in stead of Thomas Mooreman.

9/2/1765. Nicks Stone, Strangeman Hugings, James Crew, John Harriss & Shadrick Stanly appointed to attend Quarterly meeting.

John Ladd of Charles City Co and Unity Harriss (daughter of Benja Harris) of Hanover Co married 11th da, 11th mo, 1764. Witnesses: James Harriss, Nicks Harriss, Strangeman Hugings, James Crew, Benja Johnson, Shadrick Stanly, James Ladd, William Ladd, Obediah Harris, John Payn, Benjamin Crew, John Harriss, Judith Crew, Rebecca Harriss, Ede Harriss, Mary Harriss, Rachall Harriss, Milly Stanly, Mary Payn, Ursula Stanly.

13/4/1765. A complaint against Robt Cobbs being a disorderly person. Samuel Hargrave and John Cheadle appointed to treate with him.

14/5/1765. John & Mary Payne received as members.

14/5/1765. John Stanly (son of Maddox Stanly) and Milley Stanly (daughter of John Stanly) publish their intention of marriage. John Harris and James Crew appointed to make inquiry into his clearness.

14/5/1765. John Harris, James Crew & Samuel Hargrove appointed to attend Quarterly meeting.

14/5/1765. Judeth Mooreman (daughter of Charles Mooreman) and Rebeckar Bunch (daughter of Samuel Bunch) hath married out from amongst friends. John Harris and Samuel Hargrove to know if the said Charles Mooreman and Samuel Bunch consents to their daughter marrying.

14/5/1765. It appears a manifest neglect in the members attending meetings in Amelia Co, and not sending any acct to the monthly meeting. John Harris and James Crews to go to meeting or send in writing the judgement of this meeting.

3/6/1765. John Cheadles and Samuel Hargrove to treat with Robert Cobbs.

3/6/1765. John Harris and James Crews appointed to attend the marriage of John Stanly and Milley Stanly.

3/6/1765. Strangeman Hutchens and Thomas Pleasants appointed overseers of Jenato meeting.

3/6/1765. This meeting attended by our worthy friends Sarah Rigbie from meeting at Dear Creek, MD and her companion Anne Rigbie who produced certificate. John Harris and Samuel Hargrove to draw a certificate for them.

3/6/1765. John Harris, Strangeman Hutchens, Thomas Pleasants, John Payne, James Crew and Samuel Hardgrove to examine the minutes of this meeting not recorded.

10/8/1765. John Cheadle reports Robert Cobbs desirous to be continued in the society. John Davis and John Sanders to treate with Robert Cobbs once more.

10/8/1765. Angess Stanley produced a certificate from meeting at Whiteoak Swamp, Henrico Co, now removed to this meeting, and received as a member.

10/8/1765. Strangeman Hutchens, John Harris, John Davis, James Crew, John Cheadle, John Payne and Samuel Hargrove appointed to attend Quarterly meeting.

10/8/1765. Robert Johnson hath removed to New Garden, NC. Ashly Johnson and John Harris to make inquirey into his life and conversation.

John Stanly (son of Maddox Stanly) of Hanover Co and Milley Stanly (daughter of John Stanly) of same co married 12th da, 6th mo, 1765. Witnesses: John Stanly, Maddox Stanly, Pleasant Stanly, John Harris, Stanly Harriss, James Crew, Thomas Coller, Archaldous Stanly, Joshua Stanly, Thomas Harris, Daniel Harris, Ursula Stanly, Rachal Harris, Edeth Harris, Mary Payne, Agness Stanly, Elizabeth Stanly, Judeth Crew, Mary Strong.

14/9/1765. Christopher Payne and his wife requested a certificate to the meeting in New Garden, NC. John Harris and Samuel Hargrave to inquire into his life, conversation and affairs.

12/10/1765. Benjamin Clark (son of Francis Clark) of Louisa Co and Elizabeth Price published their intention of marriage. Shadrack Standly and David Broockes to enquire into his clearness.

12/10/1765. Jeremiah Harris (son of Benjamin Harris deceased) and Ann Chiles (daughter of Manoak Chiles deceased) published their intentions of marriage. Shadrack Stanly and Archaldes Stanly appointed to enquire into his clearness.

9/11/1765. The clerk being absent, John Harris appointed to act as clerk this time.

9/11/1765. Armsley Crew and Joseph Clark appointed to attend the marriage of Benjamin Clark and Elizabeth Price.

9/11/1765. Nathaniel Winston and John Harris appointed to attend the marriage of Jeremiah Harris and Ann Chiles.

Benjamin Clark (son of Francis Clark) of Louisa Co and Elizabeth Price of said county married 10th da, 11th mo, 1765. Witnesses: Nathaniel Winston, Sarah Harris, Cair Mcgehee, John Chiles, Joseph Chewning, Martha Hargrove, Lucy Stone, Milley Clark, Elizabeth Cheadle, Judeath Cheadle, Jemima Winston, Molley Winston, Molley Cheadle, Mary Mcgehee, Jemima Chewning, John Harris.

Joseph Harris (son of Benjamin Harris deceased) of Hanover Co and Ann Chiles (daughter of Manoak Chiles deceased) of Caroline Co married 10th da, 11th mo, 1765. Witnesses: Sarah Harris, Cair Mcgehee, John Chiles, Joseph Chewning, ... Crew, Martha Hargrove, Luce Stone, Elizabeth Cheadles, Jamima Winston, Judeth Cheadles, Jemima Chewing, John Harris, Ann Mcgehee.

11/12/1765. Thomas Elmore made application for a certificate to joine himself to the meeting at New Garden, NC. Ashley Johnson and Jesse Johnson appointed to inquire into his life, conversation & affairs.

11/12/1765. John & William Johnson made application for a certificate for themselves and families in order to join the meeting at New Garden, NC. James Crew and John Harris appointed to inquire into their lives, conversation & affairs.

11/1/1766. This meeting attended by our worthy friend James Rigbie who produced a certificate from Dear Creek, MD meeting and his companion Isaac Harford from PA produced a certificate from New Garden, NC meeting. Thos Clark appointed to draw certificate for the above friends.

11/1/1766. Obadiah Harris requests a certificate to joine himself and family to the meeting of New Garden, NC. John Harris and Maddox Stanly appointed to make enquirey into his life, conversation and affairs.

11/1/1766. A complaint brought against Benjamin Clark and Elizabeth his wife being guilty of sundry things, such as fornication. John Harris and Samuel Hargrove appointed to draw a testification against them.

8/2/1766. Hezekiah Sanders made application for a certificate for himself, wife and children in order to joyne themselves to friends of New Garden, NC.

Shadrack Stanley and John Harris appointed to enquire into his life and conversation.

8/2/1766. Shadrack Stanly, Archeldas Stanly & John Harris appointed to attend the Quarterly meeting.

8/2/1766. Benjamin Clark and Elizabeth Clark his now wife are guilty of fornication and other things, we therefore disown them. Signed by: Rachal Harris, Edeth Harris, Ann Magehee, Mary Harris, Sarah Harris, Hulda Stanly, Agness Stanly, Ann ... , ... Stanly, ... Stanly, John Stanly, Pleasant Stanly, Thomas Harris, Jeremiah Harris, Joseph Ray, John Harris, Shadrack Stanly, Maddox Stanly, Daniel Harris, James Crew, James Harris.

12/4/1766. Charles Moorman (son of Charles Moorman) hath married from amongst friends to a woman of another profession. John Harris to draw a testification against him.

10/5/1766. John Harris & James Crew appointed to attend the Quarterly meeting.

10/5/1766. John Harris, Rachal Harris and Martha Hargrove ... the Quarterly meeting.

10/5/1766. Sufferings: Nichlous Stone 9 pounds 4 pence, John Cheadels 6 pounds, Strangeman Huchens 17 pounds 10 shillings.

10/5/1766. Charles Moorman (son of Charles Moorman) of Louisa Co hath suffered himself to be joined in marriage by a hireling priest to a woman of a deferante profesion in matters of faith. Therefore we disown him. Signed by: Strangman Huchens, Armslee Crew, John Chiles, James Crew, Nathaniel Winston, Jerimiah Harris, Samuel Hargrove, John Cheadles, Nichlous Stone.

9/8/1766. Ashley Johnson informs this meeting that Charles Johnson stands in need of some assistance toward the maintainance of himself and family. Money subscribed: Samuel Hargrove 2 pounds 6 shillings, James Crew 2 pounds 6 shillings, Strangeman Hutchens 2 pounds 6 shillings, John Harris 2 pounds 6 shillings, Shadrack Stanley 2 pounds 6 shillings, Ashley Johnson 2 pounds 6 shillings, John Davis 2 pounds 6 shillings, John Cheadles 2 pounds 6 shillings.

9/8/1766. Ashley Johnson requested a certificate to the meeting at New Garden. John Harris & Shadrack Stanly appointed to enquire into his life & conversation.

82

9/8/1766. Strangeman Hutchens, John ... [blurred] ..., James Crew and Samuel Hargrove appointed to attend Quarterly meeting.

15/9/1766. John Hart merchant of London made application for the members to use their endeavours to have a matter of difference settled between himself and Thomas Pleasants relating to a ballance of money which the said Hunt supposes Thomas Pleasants stands indebted to him. John Harris appointed, and requests George Elless and Joshua Stone to meet and settle the said account.

15/9/1766. Edward Stabler made application in behalf of Wilson and Nixon in company to appoint proper persons to settle an account between the said Wilson and Nixon and Thomas Pleasants. Samuel Hargrove and John Harris appointed, and also requests George Elless and Joshua Stone to meet to settle the said account.

14/10/1766. Joseph Chewning ... his wife Jamima, hath not conducted with that prudence which she ought to have done. Strangeman Hughens, Saml Hargrove & Nichlous Stone appointed to join the women friends in treating with her.

14/10/1766. The money raised for Charles Johnson: Edward Statler 5/, Daniel Harris Junr 2/6, James Harris 2/6, Archalus Stanley 2/6, Thos Pleasants 5/. Shadrack Stanley appointed to ... the collection for Charles Johnson.

2/7/1766. Benjamin Clark writes condemnation letter for his disorderly ways.

8/11/1766. Samuel Hargrove, James Crew & John Harris appointed to draw a denial against Joseph Chewning.

8/11/1766. John Harris, and James Crew appointed to attend the Quarterly meeting at Whiteoak Swamp.

13/12/1766. The clerk being absent, Thos Pleasants appointed for this time in his stead.

13/12/1766. James Crew & Thos Pleasants, John Harris & Strangman Hutchens appointed to collect the sentiments of friends concerning the slave trade.

10/1/1767. James Harris and James Crew appointed to collect and examine loose papers of the women's meeting.

14/2/1767. The clerk failing to attend, John Harris to act for this time.

14/2/1767. Moses Harris produced a certificate from South Pine meeting in order to joyne himself in membership.

14/2/1767. Our well esteemed friend Robert Willis attended this meeting and produced a certificate from meeting in East Jersey. James Crew and John Harris appointed to draw a certificate for him to produce to next Quarterly meeting.

14/2/1767. James Crews, John Harris, Shadrack Stanley, Archaldous Stanley & Moses Harris appointed to attend the Quarterly meeting.

11/3/1767. A complaint against Joseph Ray being guilty of many disorders . John Harris and Moses Harris to treate with him.

11/3/1767. John Barnett requested that his three children Athnatious, Anna and Martha Barnett be received as members. John Harris appointed to enquire into their lives & conversation. 9/5/1767 received as members.

11/3/1767. An epistle of our friend Nathon Dicks deceased late of NC meeting was read to good satisfaction.

11/4/1767. John Harris appointed to joyne the women friends in treating with Sarah Terrell (wife of David) on account of her daughter marrying out.

9/5/1767. Samual Hargrave appointed to produce a denial against Robert Cobbs.

9/5/1767. John Harris appointed to draw a denial against Joseph Ray.

9/5/1767. Concerning the slave trade ... George Foxes advice to friends ... in the printed epistle from 1758 the most likely to take affect.

9/5/1767. Nichlous Stone requests a certificate to North and South Carolina. Samuel Hargrove to draw one.

9/5/1767. Complaint against Pleasants Stanly being guilty of drinking to access and cursing. James Crew and Moses Harris appointed to enquire into the truth of the same.

9/5/1767. John Harris, James Crew and Moses Harris appointed to attend the Quarterly meeting.

--/6/1767. James Harris requested a certificate to joyne him in membership with friends of New Garden, NC meeting. Shadrack Stanly and John Harris appointed to enquire into his life and conversation.

--/6/1767, There hath been a neglect in the clerk attending meetings, Nicklous Stone and John Harris appointed to speak to him. Meeting desires to know his reasons.

11/7/1767. Strangeman Hutchens desires to be released from treating with Jemime Chewning. Moses Harris appointed his stead.

11/7/1767. James Crew and Moses Harris examined into the truth of a report against Pleasant Stanly & that there is some truth in the report. Samuel Hargrove and Nathaniel Winston to treate with the said Pleasant Stanly.

11/7/1767. Samual Hargrove give reasons for not attending several monthly meetings which was satisfactory ones.

--/6/1767. Robert Cobbs of Caroline Co grew lukewarm and endefrent about religion, for sook coming to our meetings, and was too much in the practise of vaine fashions of the world such as using prulal [sic] language, we therefore disown him. Signed by: Shadrack Standly, Armsbe Crew, Archaldous Stanly, Moses Harris, James Crew, Nathanual Winston, Samual Hargrove, John Cheadles, John Harris.

8/8/1767. Moses Harris hath treated with Jameme Chewnins and she hath sent in writing in which she condemns the things lade to her, much to the satisfaction of friends.

8/8/1767. John Barnett and Elizabeth Huthens publish their ententions of marriage. Thomas Pleasants and Moses Harris appointed to make the necessary enquirey.

8/8/1767. Samual Hargrove Thomas Pleasants, James Crew and John Harris appointed to attend the Quarterly meeting.

8/8/1767. John Harris, Thomas Pleasants, John Davis, Charles Moorman, Samual Hargrave and Ashley Johnson appointed to collect the names of male members of respective meetings to which they belong in order to form certificates to send to Leftenant Coln in the county where they belong accorden to act of assembly.

10/10/1767. Athanathous Barnett and Jane Hutchens published their intentions of marriage. Thomas Pleasants and Moses Harris appointed to enquire into his clearness.

10/10/1767. John Sanders Junr requested a certificate to joyne New Garden, NC meeting. John Davis appointed to enquire into his life and conversation.

10/10/1767. Richard Blocksom requested to be taken under the care of friends. John Davis, Charles Moorman & David Terrell appointed to enquire into his life and conversation.

11/14/1767. John Davise, John Harris, Thomas Pleasants and Samual Hargrove to collect the sums which they will forward for good undertaking. They will lodge the money in the hands of John Harris.

11/14/1767. John Harris and Daniel Harris to attend the marriage of Arlanashoush Barnett and Jane Hutchens.

11/14/1767. David Brookes requested a certificate to the meeting at New Garden, NC. John Harris and John Davis appointed to enquire into his life and conversation.

11/14/1767. John Harris and Daniel Harris to attend the Quarterly meeting.

12/9/1767. Moses Harris appointed to draw a denial against Pleasant Stanly.

12/9/1767. John & Moses Harris appointed to attend the marriage of John Barnett and Elizabeth Hutchens.

12/9/1767. John Harris & Moses Harris appointed to draw a bill of dementions for the addition & repairing to the meeting house.

12/12/1767. Moses Harris requested a certificate in relation to marriage to the meeting at the Western Branch, Isle of White Co. Strangeman Hutchens and John Barnett appointed to make necessary enquirey.

13/2/1768. Edward Stabler wrote that the hole matter between Wilson and Nixon and Thomas Pleasants be dismissed as there was no probility of determining the matter.

12/2/1768. Thomas Pleasants should give his reasons for refusing to have the matter determined. Strangmon Hutchens appointed to tender him a copy of this minit.

12/2/1768. Money collected by John Davis from friends about Camp Creek which he delivered to John Harris is 3 pounds 6 shillings.

12/2/1768. Strangmon Hutchens, John Davis, John Harris, Nichlous Stone, James Crew and Samual Hargrave appointed to attend Quarterly meeting.

13/12/1766. Joseph Chewming hath walked disorderly, more especiley has been subject to the vile sin of taking strong drink to excess, we do publickly disown him. Signed by: Thomas Harris, Nathanial Winston, Jeremiah Harris, Deanel Harris Junr, James Crew, Shadrack Stanley, John Stanley, John Harris.

12/3/1768. Thos Pleasants roat not to their satisfaction. John Harris and Samual Hargrave to treat with him.

12/3/1768. Nichlous Stone, John Davis and John Harris to treat with several members belonging to Fork Creek meeting that do not live to cursumspect as the truth and our discipline, and friends cannot be free in giving them certificates to the commanding millita offesor.

12/3/1768. Produced certificates from New Garden, NC for Wm Johnson and his wife Aggatha Johnson. Also certificates for John Johnson and his wife Elizabeth, John Johnson and their grandson John Johnson.

12/3/1768. Thomas Dugless (son of John Dugless) requests to be received as a member of this meeting. John Davis and David Terrell appointed to enquire into his life and conversation.

9/4/1768. Strangmon Hutchens desiring to be released from being overseer of Jeneto meeting. John Barnett appointed in his stead.

9/4/1768. Pleasant Terrell requested to be taken under the care of Friends. Samual Hargrove and Nathanual Winston appointed to make enquirey into his life and conversation.

14/5/1768. William Ratliff and his wife Elizabeth requested to be reseved as membours. Samual Hargrove and Nathanual Winston to make the necessary enquirey into their lives and conversations.

14/5/1768. Henery Terrell (son of Henery Terrell) requested to be reseved as a member of this meeting. Samual Hargrove and Nathanual Winston appointed to enquire into his life and conversation.

14/5/1768. Moses Harris and John Harris appointed to attend the Quarterly meeting.

11/6/1768. The matter conserning Thomas Dugliss is not fully comployed with, William Ballard, John Davis & David Terrell appointed to make the necessary inquiry into his life and conversation.

11/6/1768. Pleasant Terrill sent a letter condemning the practice of his marring from amongst friends. He is reseved as a membour.

11/6/1768. John Harris, Moses Harris and Samual Hargrove appointed to collect 3 pounds 10 shillings to reimburse certin number of friends, according to extract from the Quarterly meeting.

11/6/1768. John Harris, Moses Harris, James Crew, Shadrack Stanly and Samual Hargrove appointed to draw a plan for a house & meeting place to accommodate the Quarterly meeting.

9/7/1768. The matter of William Ratliff & wife is refered. John Harris, Nathanual Winston and Saml Hargrove appointed to make forther inquirey. 3/8/1768 received as members.

9/7/1768. John Harris, Shadrack Stanly, James Crew, Saml Hargrove or any three of them to lett meeting house out to the lowest bidder. To be built and completed by the 7th da, 7th mo, 1769. John Harris appointed to reseve the money subscribed & apply to the use mentioned.

9/7/1768. Meeting house at Ceder Creek where it now stand is veary inconvenant on acct of the badness of the ways which leades to it. James Crew, John Harris, John Davis, Charles Moormon, Thomas Pleasants, Pleasant Terrell & Samual Hargrove appointed to pioynt out a moor proper place to build the meeting house.

9/7/1768. William Ballard requests a certificate to the meeting at South River in relation to marriage. David Terrell and John Davis appointed to enquire into his clearness.

9/7/1768. Henry Terrell reseved as a member due to letter which he roat condemning his past conduct.

9/7/1768. Archable Pleasants, Charles Woodson Junr and Ann his wife produced certificates from the meeting held in Henrico Co. Reseved as membours.

9/7/1768. A complaint against John Barnett and his wife Elizabeth that she was delivered of a child in about seven months after their marriage. John Harris, Shadrack Stanly and James Crew to make inquirey into the truth. 3/8/1768 Appears they are clear.

3/8/1768. Several disorders found subsisting amongst friends at the Fork Creek meeting. Thomas Clark appointed overseer of the Fork Creek meeting some years past and it appears that he hath been defishent in the performance of his duty and therefore discontinued from that service. John Davis and Nichlous Stone still continue to treat with them. John Harris and Shadrack Stanly appointed to their assistance.

3/8/1768. The commity appointed to lett the building a meeting house, let the building the same to John Harris for 38 pounds.

3/8/1768. George Bell and Cisly his wife roat desiring to be reseved as members, also condemning the practice of their marring from amongst friends. John Davis and Charles Moorman to inquire into his life and conversation.

3/8/1768. John Davis, Charles Moorman, John Harris & Samual Hargrove appointed to attend Quarterly meeting.

10/9/1768. Nichlous Stone request for himself and his grandson Joseph Crew a certificate to joyne themselves to the meeting in Cain Creek, Orange Co, NC. Richard Lewis and Samual Hargrove appointed to make inquirey into their lives and conversation.

10/9/1768. William Diggs and his wife Judeth and six children Sarah, Rebacer, Agness, William, Pleasant and Marshall Diggs, hath removed from within the limits of this meeting without a certificate. Nichlious Stone to make inquiry into their life and conversation.

8/10/1768. Friends in Amelia Co have failed to attend or send any acct of the state of that preparative meeting. Moses Harris, John Haley and John Harris appointed to visit them on that occation.

12/11/1768. Complaint against Francis Clark (son of John Clark) of Fork Creek meeting who hath married to a woman of an other proswastion in matter of religion by a hireling priest. John Harris appointed to draw a testification against him.

12/11/1768. John Harris, James Crew and Thomas Harris appointed to attend the Quarterly meeting.

12/11/1768. Report of the Amelia meeting, it appears that Charles Johnson and his wife Sarah, two poor friends, stand in need of some releaf. Ashley and Jesse Johnson and John Harris appointed to make inquirey into the matter.

10/12/1768. A complaint against Thomas Johnson (son of Ashley Johnson) of Louisa Co of being guilty of defiling a daughter of Charles Johnson of Amelia Co. Moses Harris, Shadrack Stanly & John Harris appointed to make inquirey into complaint.

10/12/1768. Zachriah Stanly, membour of Newgarden, NC meeting, hath been guilty of some disorder. James Crew, Moses Harris & John Harris appointed to make inquiry into the matter.

11/2/1769. A report on Fork Creek that there appears several disorders subsisting amongst them. James Crew, Shadrack Stanly, Moses Harris, & Henary Terrell to visit them with John Davise and John Harris who was some time past appointed to that service.

11/2/1769. Sophia Harris produced a certificate from the meeting held at the Western Branch, Isle of White Co. Read and approved.

11/2/1769. John Davis, Pleasant Terrell, Henry Terrell & John Harris appointed to attend Fork Creek to treat with Thomas Johnson.

11/2/1769. John Davis, John Harris, Moses Harris, Samual Hargrove and Pleasant Terrell appointed to attend the Quarterly meeting.

11/2/1769. Yearly meeting quries read by which it appears John Cheadle an elder deceased ... last acct ... . John Harris, Moses Harris and Pleasant Terrell appointed to draw a memorial for John Cheadle deceased.

11/2/1769. Francis Clark of Louisa Co hath been guilty of some disorders such as using compliments and suffering himself to be joined in marriage to a woman of a defrent proswastion from us in matters of faith. We therefore disown him. Signed by: Daniel Harris, Chas Moorman, Jesse Johnson, Richd Blocksom, Pleasant Terrell, Shadrack Stanly, William Ratlive, Samual Hargrove, John Davis, John Harris, John Payne, Henry Terrell, John Barnett, James Crew, Archaldious Stanly.

11/3/1769. Report of Fork Creek that severall disorders still subsists, Bartlitt Haley and John Clark hath been fighting. A committee appointed to visit them.

11/3/1769. No acct from the friends appointed to visit the widow of Chas Johnson deceased. 20/5/1769 reported she moved out of the coloney.

8/4/1769. A paper was drawn up to send to the commanding offesor of the militia setting forth that Francis Clark (son of John Clark) hath been disown by this meeting.

8/4/1769. John Payne, his wife and children to wit Walter, Williams, Temple and Dolley Payne removed into this coloney from Newgarden, NC.

8/4/1769. Bartlit Haley with the friends at Fork Creek hath married by the hireling priest. James Crew, Shadrack Stanly & John Harris appointed to draw a paper of denial against him.

20/5/1769. David Terrell appointed to assist the committee to treate friends at Fork Creek.

20/5/1769. Friends appointed to spake with Elizabeth Johnson of the matter she charged Thos Johnson with report that she hath removed out of the coloney and hath not proved that fact laid to him. David Terrell, Pleasants Terrell, Richard Blocksom and John Harris appointed to make further inquirey into the matter.

20/5/1769. James Harris produced a certificate from the meeting at Newgarden, NC, reseved into membership.

20/5/1769. Christopher Johnson requested a certificate for himself and Elizabeth his wife and their children in order to joyne meeting at South River, Bedford Co. Richard Blocksom and David Terrell appointed to make inquirey into their lives, conversations and affairs.

20/5/1769. Henry Terrill, Pleasant Terrill, Nanthanual Winston, Daniel Harris and John Harris appointed to attend Quarterly meeting.

10/6/1769. Thomas Duglass (Doughless) wroat to this meeting and hath condemned the practice of marring by the hireling priest. Reseved as a membour.

8/7/1769. Friends appointed to visit Fork Creek is of the opinion that Frances Clark Junr, Edmond Clark and John Haley shall be disowned. John Harris, David Terrill and Moses Harris appointed to draw testifications against them.

8/7/1769. David Terrell presented Thomas Johnson with a minit but several things hath appeared in favour of the said Johnson since, the matter may be refered to give the young man an opportunity of clearing himself of the charge. David Terrill and John Davis to forward the matter.

8/7/1769. David Terrill and Richard Blocksom appointed with John Davis as overseers of Camp Creek meeting.

8/7/1769. Pleasant Terrell is appointed overseer in Caroline Co meeting in stead of Nichlous Stone.

8/7/1769. William Retliff request that his children be taken under the care of this meeting to wit Mary, Harrison, William, John & Gidion Ratliff. Taken under the care of this meeting accordingly.

12/8/1769. Sarah Johnson (widow of Charles Johnson deceased) request certificate for herself and three sons James, Thomas and Robert Johnson. Ashley and Jesse Johnson and John Harris to make the necessary enquirey into their lives, conversation and affairs.

12/8/1769. John Moore Senr requested to be taken under the care of friends. John Davis, Charles Moorman & Richard Blocksom appointed to make necessary inquirey into his life and conversation. The said Moore to send a letter condemning his former practice for which he was disowned. 14/10/1769 Received as a member.

12/8/1769. Strangmon Huching, John Davis, John Harris & Samual Hargrove appointed to attend Quarterly meeting.

14/10/1769. Ann Blocksom (wife of Richard Blocksom) requested to be reseved as a member. Referred to women's meeting.

14/10/1769. William Ratliff and his wife Elizabeth requested a certificate for themselves and children to wit Mary, Harrison, William, John and Gedion Ratliff in order to joyne meeting at Whiteoak Swamp, Henrico Co. Pleasant Terrell and Samual Hargrove to make inquery into his life, conversation and affairs.

14/10/1769. John Chiles and Mary Winston published their intentions of marriage. Pleasant Terrill and Henry Terrill appointed to inquire into his clearness.

14/10/1769. William Stanly and Ursley Stanly publish their intentions of marriage. John Harris and James Crew appointed to inquire into his clearness.

14/10/1769. Quarterly meeting extracts read respecting the many disorders subsisting amongst us. John Harris, ... Terrell, John Davis, Henery and Pleasant Terrell, Richard Blocksom and Samual Hargrove appointed to visit the several ... [blurred].

11/11/1769. Henry Terrel and Samual Hargrove appointed to attend the marriage of John Chiles and Mary Winston.

11/11/1769. John Harris and James Crew appointed to attend the marriage of William Stanly and Ursuly Stanly.

11/11/1769. James Harris and Mary Cheadles publish their intention of marriage. John Harris & Moses Harris appointed to inquire into his clearness.

11/11/1769. John Harris, James Crew, Henary Terrill and Thomas Harris appointed to attend the Quarterly meeting.

9/12/1769. John Payne and Moses Harris appointed to assist the committee to visit the preparative meetings.

9/12/1769. James Crew and Henry Terrill appointed to attend the marriage of James Harris and Mary Cheadle.

9/12/1769. Complaint from the preparitive meeting at Camp Creek that Thomas Clark Senr frequently in the practice of drinking to excess, and Thomas & John

Clark (sons of Thomas Clark) guilty of frequenting vaine company. Henry Terrell, James Crew, Jno Payne & John Harris to visit and treat with them.

10/2/1770. A paper was produced from under the hand of Elizabeth Johnson setting forth that Thomas Johnson was clear of scandol with her.

10/2/1770. Report that Daniel Harris Junr hath been guilty of marring out from amongst friends by a hireling priest to a woman of a defrent faith in matter of religion. Shadrack Stanly and Nichlous Huchins to draw a paper denial against him.

10/2/1770. Complaint that James Crew hath been guilty of bying several Negro slaves. Richard Blocksom, Moses Harris, Shadrack Stanly and John Harris to treat with him.

10/2/1770. John Davis, Richard Blocksom, Charles Moormon, Moses Harris, Shadrack Stanly, Archaldas Stanly, Nichlous Huchens and John Harris appointed to attend the Quarterly meeting.

10/3/1770. John and Thomas Harris to produce a testification against James Crew.

10/3/1770. John Johnson and Leda Hugings publish their intentions of marriage. John and Thomas Harris appointed to inquire into his clearness.

14/4/1770. Report that Nathanual Winston pay the hireing priest. John and Moses Harris and Henry Terrell to treat with him.

14/4/1770. John and Thomas Harris appointed to draw a testification against Thomas Clark Senr and his sons John and Thomas Clark.

14/4/1770. John Davis and Moses Harris appointed to attend the marriage of John Johnson and Cedey Huchings.

14/4/1770. John Barnett requested to be released from being overseer of Jeneto meeting.

14/4/1770. Thomas Pleasants is discontinued as overseer of Jeneto meeting as he hath neglected to attend preparative & monthly meetings.

14/4/1770. Moses Harris and Archaldus Stanly appointed overseer of Cedar Creek in the rum of James Crew and to have the oversight of Jeneto with John Harris.

12/5/1770. Micajah Davis request to be reseved a member of this meeting. David Terrell and Richard Blocksom appointed to make necessary inquirey. 14/7/1770 reseved as member.

12/5/1770. Samual Hargrove requested to be released from acting as clerk. Moses Harris appointed in his stead.

12/5/1770. John Harris, Moses Harris, David Terrel, Richard Blocksom and Samual Hargrove appointed to attend the Quarterly meeting.

20/5/1769. Bartlett Haley (son of John Haley) of Louisa Co hath been guilty of sundry disorders such as fighting and marring out by the hireling priest to a woman of a defrent proswation. We therefore disown him. Signed by: Nathanual Winston, Richard Blocksom, William Ratliff, Daniel Harris, John Harris, David Terrill, Henry Terrill, Moses Harris, Pleasant Terrill.

12/7/1769. John Haley (son of John Haley) of Louisa Co and Edmond Clark (son of Thomas Clark) of same co hath been guilty of sundry disorder such as using compliments and deveating from their plainness of speech and behaviour and frequenting places of deversion, dancing and by their own confession hath not been convinced in their own judgement of friends principles. We therefore disown them. Signed by: Pleasant Terrill, Shadrack Stanly, William Ratliff, Archelaus Stanly, Daniel Harris, Chas Moormon, Jesse Johnson, Richd Blocksom, Samual Hargrove, John Davis, Henry Terrill, John Harris, John Payne, John Barnett, James Crew.

James Harris (son of Benja Harris deceased) of Hanover Co and Mary Cheadle (daughter of Thomas Cheadle) of Caroline Co married the 10th da, 12th mo, 1769. Witnesses: George Cheadle, Henry Chiles, Samual Winston, Jesse Hargrove, Samual Hargrove Junr, Rachal Harris, Sarah Cheadle, Ann Chiels, Cagiah Wilding, Mary Gooch, Martha Hargrove, John Chiels, John Cheadle, Molley Winston, John ... [blurred] ... .

John Johnson (son of Ashly Johnson) of Amelia Co and Cedia Hutchins (daughter of Strangemon Hutchens) of Goochland Co married the 15th da, 4th mo, 1770. Witnesses: Edeth Harris, Sarah Hutchens, Sarah Harris, Rachal Harris, Edeth Watkins, Salley Cheadle, Rachal Harris, Susanah Stanly, Thomas Harris, Saml Persons, David Terrill, Micajah Terrill, Christa Antony, John Harris, Zacky Stanly, Samual Hargrove, Shadrack Stanly, Benjamin Johnson, Moses Harris, Joshua Stanly, John Davis, John Stanly Junr.

12/5/1770. John Clark (son of Thomas Clark) and Thomas Clark (son of John Clark) of Louisa Co hath been guilty of using complements, living in vain fashions and gruntways of the world and frequenting places of deverstion. We therefore disown him. Signed by: James Harris, Rich ... , Samual Winston, Richd Blonsom, Moses Harris, John Harris, Samual Hargrove, David Terrell, ...

9/6/1770. Nathan Stanly produced a certificate from the meeting at New Garden, NC. Reseved as a member.

9/6/1770. Samual Hargrove, Pleasant Terrell, Shadrack Stanly, John Harris & Moses Harris appointed to examine all the minits of this meeting.

14/7/1770. Application made by membours of Cain Creek meeting for a certificate for Niclios Stone and the children of Joseph Crew. Samual Hargrove appointed to prepare one.

11/8/1770. John Davis and David Terrill appointed to assist the friends appointed to treate with Nathanual Winston in refrence respecting Thos Clark.

11/8/1770. John Davis, John Harris, Pleasant Terrill & Moses Harris appointed to attend the Quarterly meeting.

8/9/1770. The clerk being absent through sickness Samual Hargrove acts in his stead.

10/11/1770. Clark Moormon and Rachal Harris published their intention of marriage. He is desired to produce a certificate form the meeting he belongs to setting forth his clearness. 8/12/1770 Clark Moormon produced a certificate from South River meeting.

10/11/1770. Henry Terrill, John Harris, Thomas Harris & Moses Harris appointed to attend Quarterly meeting.

8/12/1770. John & Moses Harris appointed to attend the marriage of Clark Moormon and Rachal Harris.

8/12/1770. Our esteamed friends Joseph Osley from Norwick, England and ... Neal from Cork, Irland were at this meeting.

12/1/1771. This meeting desires that those suffering for preasts wagers send in accts, Thos Clark to send a copy of the minits to each preparative meeting.

9/2/1771. Shadrack Stanly hath been guilty of breach of our disipline in buying a Negro. John Harris, Archalus Stanly and Moses Harris to treat with him.

9/2/1771. George Bell hath been guilty of buying a Negro contrary to our known discipline. John Davis, John Harris and Moses Harris to treat with him.

9/2/1771. Thomas Johnson (son of Ashley Johnson) of Louisa Co hath been guilty of fornication. Fact proved against him by a certificate from the Majestrats hand. John and Moses Harris appointed to prepare a paper of denial against him.

9/2/1771. Mary (daughter of Charles Moormon), Elizabeth (daughter of Charles Douglish), Lorana (daughter of James Johnson) and Ursule (daughter of John Haley) are marryed by the hireling preast. John and Moses Harris appointed to prepare a paper of denial against them. John Davis and Moses Harris appointed to speak to the parents of the young women to see if they were consenting to their marriage.

9/2/1771. John Harris, Archaldus Stanly, Pleasant Terrell and Moses Harris appointed to attend the Quarterly meeting.

13/4/1771. It appears that Charles Moorman and James Johnson were against their daughters marrying by the preast. Charles Duglish and John Haley to treat with them.

11/5/1771. Ursula Clark hath married from amongst friends. Refered to the womens meeting.

11/5/1771. John Harris, Pleasant Terrill, Archalus Stanly and Moses Harris appointed to attend the Quarterly meeting.

8/6/1771. A certificate given from meeting at New Garden, NC that William Ballard and his family was membours. Reseved as membours of this meeting.

8/6/1771. A certificate given from meeting at New Garden, NC that Mary Ballard is a membour. Reseved a membour of this meeting.

8/6/1771. James Crew gives a paper condemning the practice he was disowned for which was pretty much to the satisfaction of this meeting.

10/8/1771. John Davis, Pleasant Terrill and Henry Terrill joined with the friends appointed to treat with Shadrack Stanly.

10/8/1771. Charles Moorman and David Terrill appointed to assist the friends appointed to treat with George Bell.

10/8/1771. James Hunicutt gave a certificate from friends at Burley, Prince George Co. He is received as a membour.

10/8/1771. A certificate from meeting at Newgarden, NC setting forth that Susaner Stanley and her two children Elizabeth & John were membours of that meeting. Received as membours of this meeting.

10/8/1771. Agreeable to an order of last Quarterly meeting there was read an epistle written by Thomas Ellwood.

10/8/1771. Edward Terrill and Mary Johnson published their intentions of marriage. John Davis and Richard Brocksom appointed to inquire into his clearness.

10/8/1771. Samual Hargrove, John Davis, Ashley Johnson & John Harris appointed to attend Quarterly meeting.

12/10/1771. Dan Stockton made application for a certificate in relation to marriage to the meeting at South River, Bedford Co. Micajah Davis and Charles Moormon appointed to inquire into his clearness.

14/12/1771. A certificate from the meeting at Henrico Co setting forth that Mary Brooks was a membour. She is reseved a membour.

14/12/1771. Application being made for a certificate for Benjamin Terrell to joyne himself to the meeting at South River, Bedford Co. Charles Moorman appointed to make inquirey.

8/2/1772. John Harris, John Payne, Archaldus Stanly and Moses Harris appointed to attend Quarterly meeting.

14/3/1772. John and Thomas Duglish appointed to attend the marriage of Edward Terrell & Mary Johnson.

12/4/1772. Charles Moormon to treate with Benja Terrill.

12/4/1772. A certificate given from friends at New Garden, NC setting forth that Jahu Stewart and his family were membours. Received as membours.

12/4/1772. James Hunicutt applied for a certificate for the meeting at Blackewater, Surre Co in relation to marriage. Strangmon Hutchens & Benjamin Watkins appointed to make inquirey.

12/4/1772. Henry Chiles & Sarah Cheadle & Armsbe Crew and Luse Stone hath been married by the preast. John and ... Harris appointed to prepare papers of denial against them. Samual Hargrove and Pleasant Terrill to make inquirey of the parents of the young people to know if they consented to the marriage.

9/5/1772. John Harris and Henry Terrill appointed to attend the Quarterly meeting.

9/5/1772. Friends suffring at Camp Creek: Charles Moormon 3 pounds, John Davis 3 pounds 5 shillings, David Terrill 1 pound 10 shillings, George Bell for preasts wages 1 pound 18 shillings.

13/6/1772. A certificate from friends at Burley, Prince George Co setting forth that Benjamin Rusel was a membour. Reseved as a membour of this meeting.

13/6/1772. Richd Blocksom is appointed to assist the friends formerly appointed to treat George Bell.

13/6/1772. The parents of Henry Childes and his wife was not consenting to the marriage.

13/6/1772. A certificate was given from Newgarden, NC meeting that Elizabeth Stanly was a membour of that meeting. Reseved a membour of this meeting.

13/6/1772. A certificate was given from South River meeting setting forth that Ann Lain and three of her children viz Thomas, Margry & Mordicai were membours. They are received as membours.

11/7/1772. A certificate was given from meeting at Newgarden, NC setting forth that Zacha Stanly was a membour of our society. He also gives a paper condemning some misconduct he hath been guilty of. Consideration until next meeting.

8/8/1772. John Harris, Pleasant Harris and Moses Harris appointed to inquire into some matters conserning Zacha Stanly before he be reseved.

8/8/1772. Reported from Camp Creek preparative meeting that it appears that Moorman Ballard and David Ballard, Judeth Duglish and Elizabeth Bunch are married by the hireling preast. John and Moses Harris appointed to prepare paper of denial against them. John Davis appointed to inquire of the parents of the young women if they were consenting to the marriage.

8/8/1772. John Payne, John Harris & Moses Harris appointed to visit & inquire into the disorders among friends at Amelia Co preparative meeting.

8/8/1772. John Davis, Strangmon Hutchens, Pleasant Terrill, John Harris & Moses Harris appointed to attend the Quarterly meeting.

8/8/1772. Thomas Watkins Junr purchased a Negro slave contrary to the known rules of our discipline. Pleasant Terrill, Henry Terrill & John Harris appointed to treate with him.

Edward Terrill and Mary Johnson of Louisa Co married at the house of James Johnson, Louisa Co, the 17th da, 3rd mo, 1772. Witnesses: Thos Duglish, ... Duglish, ..., Lucy Johnson, Chas Moormon, Mary Moormon, Agness Johnson, David Terrill, James Johnson, Sarah Terrill.

10/10/1772. A certificate was given from meeting at White Oke Swamp setting forth that Mirim Pleasants, Miriam, Margit, Ann and Joseph Hunicutt, also Elizabeth Bates were membours. Received as members.

10/10/1772. John and Moses Harris appointed to prepare a paper of denial against Shadrack Stanly.

10/10/1772. John Davis reports that the parents of Judeth Douglish and Elizth Bunch say their marriage was contrary to their minds.

10/10/1772. Reported that Jane Watkins is married by the hireling preast. Refered to the womens meeting.

10/10/1772. John Harris, John Payne and Moses Harris appointed to visit Fine Creek, Cumberland Co about their application for a seprate meeting.

10/10/1772. Application made for a certificate to joine Jahu Start and his family to Newgarden, NC meeting. John Harris and Archalious Stanly appointed to prepare one.

14/11/1772. Benjamin Johnson gave this meeting a paper condemning his conduct for which he was formerly disowned as also a paper from several of the membours of South River meeting certifying that he behaves himself in an orderly manner. Richd Blocksom and John Harris appointed to make inquirey into his life and conversation.

14/11/1772. Joshua Stanly and Bettey Stanly declared their intentions of marriage. James Crew and John Harris appointed to make inquirey into his clearness.

14/11/1772. James Crew and John Harris appointed to attend the Quarterly meeting.

12/12/1772. Paper of denial sent from the womens meeting against Ann Duglish.

12/12/1772. Archaldus Stanly and Nichlous Hutchens appointed to attend the marriage of Joshua Stanly.

12/12/1772. Extract from last Quarterly meeting read directing 12 of Antony Benegats ... on slavry to be distributed.

12/12/1772. Maddox Stanly hath been for a long time past guilty of taking strong drink to excess and it appears by the oath of a young woman has of late been guilty of striving to defile her. Henry Terrill and Moses Harris appointed to treate with him.

13/2/1773. Thos Pleasants and John Barnett appointed overseers of the Jenetoe meeting.

13/2/1773. Thos Pleasants is added with the friends formerly appointed to visit Amelia meeting.

13/2/1773. Thos Pleasants and Richard Blocksom added with the former friends to treate with Maddox Stanly.

13/2/1773. Reported from the Jenetoe preparative meeting that Susanah Watkins hath joined herself in marriage by a hireling preast. Recommended to the womens meeting to take steps to disown her.

13/2/1773. Report from Camp Creek preparative meeting that John Davis requests to be releaved from being overseer. Charles Moorman appointed in his room.

13/2/1773. Report from South River preparative meeting that Sarah Ward, Richd Fillip and his wife requests to be membours of our society. Charles Moorman, Micajah Terrill, Byram Ballard and Christopher Antoney appointed to make inquirey concerning them.

13/2/1773. Shadrack Stanly motioned his intention of appeal to Quarterly meeting on his being disowned. Thos Pleasants, Samual Hargrove, Charles Moormon, David Terrill, Richard Blocksom, John Harris and Moses Harris appointed to prepare a coppe of all the minits concerning that matter and attend the Quarterly meeting.

13/2/1773. Thos Pleasants, Charles Moormon and Richard Blocksom appointed to attend Quarterly meeting.

13/3/1773. Thos Pleasants and Richd Blocksom report that Maddox Stanly confesses to his taking too much strong drink and also seems desirious that he may be preserved from that evil for the time to come, but denies the other charge, he's to git such proof and reasons to bear himself.

13/3/1773. Thomas Terrill and his wife made application to be reseved as membours. Samual Hargrove and Pleasant Terrill appointed to make inquirey respecting them.

13/3/1773. Geo Cheadle hath absented himself from attending our meeting and acted contrary to friends principles. Pleasant Terrill, Henry Terrill and Richd Lewis appointed to treate with him.

10/4/1773. A certificate given from the meeting held at Fairfax, Loudon Co, setting forth that Jane West hath settled within the compass of this meeting & is reseved as a membour.

10/4/1773. The matter concerning Richd Tilless is refered.

10/4/1773. Thos Hutchens and Patte Chiles published their intentions of marriage. Archaldus Stanly and John Payne appointed to make inquirey respecting preengagement.

10/4/1773. Thos Pleasants, Benja Russell, John Payne, Samual Hargrove & John Harris appointed to attend the Quarterly meeting.

8/5/1773. Pleasant Terrill and Henary Terrill appointed to attend the marriage of Thos Hutchens and Patte Chiles.

8/5/1773. Pleasant Terrill and Henry Terrill added with the friends formerly appointed to examine the minits.

8/5/1773. Thos Ridell requests to be reseved a membour. John and Moses Harris appointed to enquire into his life & conversation.

8/5/1773. John Davis an elder belonging to Camp Creek meeting departed this life the 16th of the 3rd last.

8/5/1773. Rebeck Terrill hath been reseved by convinsment.

8/5/1773. Samual Hargrove, John Harris, Clarke Moormon & Moses Harris appointed to attend the Quarterly meeting.

12/6/1773. Thos Clark appointed to send coppes of such munits that is necessary to South River meeting, in matter of Benja Johnson and Richd Tilless.

12/6/1773. Pleasant Terrill and Benja Russell added to friends formerly appointed to treate with Maddox Stanly.

12/6/1773. Matter respecting Geo Cheadle is continued as he hath removed out of the parts where he formerly lived.

12/6/1773. John Barnett added with friends before appointed to make inquirey with respect to Thos Ridell.

12/6/1773. Information from Jenetoe meeting it appears that Benja Watkins hath purchased a Negro. Benja Rusell and John Barnett appointed to inquire into the nature of the purchase.

12/6/1773. It appears that Nichlious Huchens hath bought a Negro. John Harris and Moses Harris appointed to inquire of him what was his reasons for buying the said Negro.

From Camp Creek Monthly meeting:

Mary Moormon (daughter of Thos Moormon & Rachael his wife) b. 19/12/1732; Zacariah Moormon b. 2/2/--; Micajah Moormon b. 28/6/--; Elizabeth Moormon b. 2/2/- - d, 1740; Thos Moormon b. 6/6/174-; Mildred Moormon b. 25/11/174-; Pleasant Moormon b. 19/3/17--.

Christopher Clark (son of Micajah Clark & Judith his wife) b. 20/2/173-; Robert Clark b. 15/6/1735; Mourning Clark b. 6/6/1740; Micajah Clark b. 27/12/174-; John Clark b. 26/10/--; Edward Clark b. 12/10/--.

Christopher Clark (son of Boling Clark & ... his wife) b. 30/2/--; Elizabeth Clark b. 21/11/--.

Moley Clark (daughter of Francis Clark & ... his wife) b. 17/9/--; Betty Clark b. 22/11/-- ; Nicklous Clark b. 6/2/--; Francis Clark b. 7/2/--.

Thos Clark (son of John Clark & Ann his wife) b. 30/7/1746; Francies Clark b. 5/8/174-; John Clark b. 3/11/1750.

Elizabeth Moormon (daughter of Charles Moormon & Mary his wife) b. 9/2/1737; Lucey Moormon b. 20/2/174-; Agge Mormon b. 26/2/1743; Charles Moormon b. 28/6/1746; Jude Moormon b. 26/--/1748; Molley Mormon b. 25/--/1750; Robert Moormon b. 16/--/1753; Thomas Moormon b. 25/--/1756.

Zachreas[?] Johnson (son of William Johnson) d, 2/--/--.

Mary Ballard (daughter of William Ballard) d. 7/9/17--.

... (wife of Madox Stanly) d. 6/9/177-.

16/11/1747. Arther Bardin is desirious to be taken under the care of friends.

16/11/1747. Charles Moormon Senr appointed to take the collection and inspect into the state of the poor friends.

16/11/1747. Thomas Clark appointed to inspect to the wants of the poor.

19/12/174-. Jane Hoggitt and William Hoggitt taken under the care of this meeting.

..argit (daughter of Robt Johnson and Sarah his wife) b. 5/8/1752.

James Philups Hart (son of Henry Philups Hart & Mary his wife) was b. 20/6/1741; William Hart b. 13/2/1743; John Hart b. 18/3/1746; Joseph Hart b. 3/12/1748; Elizabeth Hart b. 3/2/1751.

Chas Dougless (son of John Douglas & Judeth his wife) b. 29/4/1732; Elizabeth Doughliss b. 18/12/1733; Thomas Dugliss b. 3/7/1740; Polly Dugliss b. 12/6/1744; Judeth Dougliss b. 18/7/1746; John Dugliss b. 8/8/1748; Anne Duglless b. 10/2/1750; Archillss Doughless b. 22/2/1752; Darkass Dughliss b. 9/10/1755.

Thos Ballard (son of William Ballard & Mary his wife) b. 12/11/1735; Frances Ballard b. 12/12/1737; Byram Ballard b. 27/2/1740; Delphin Ballard b. 1/5/1742; David Ballard b. 9/4/1750; Moorman Ballard b. 16/3/1742 [sic].

Sarah Johnson (daughter of Benja Johnson & Agness his wife) b. 30/1/1729; Christopher Johnson b. 22/11/1731; William Johnson b. 25/4/1734; Benja Johnson b. 24/8/1736; Penelope Johnson b. 27/2/1739; Collings Johnson b. 28/6/1741; Edward Johnson b. 23/2/1744; Agness Johnson b. 11/12/1746.

19/--/--. Charles Moormon Senr, Benjmon Johnson, Francis Clark, Thomas Clark & Charles Moormon Junr appointed to attend the Quarterly meeting.

10/--/--. Edmond Colley desires to come under the care of friends.

16/2/1748. John Mucdanald requested being under the care of friends.

16/2/1748. Richard Henderson is taken under the care of friends.

16/5/1748. Friends taken under the care of this meeting: Charles Moormon and his family, Sarah Ballard, Charles Clark and his family, John Moore and his family, Charles Moormon Senr and his wife, Benjmon Johnson and his family, Edward Clark, Achillias Moormon and his family, Samual Bunch and his family, James Johnson and his family, William Callard and his family, William

Haley and his family, Francis Clark and his family, Francis Clark Junr & his wife & children, Christopher Clark Junr.

16/5/1748. George Taylor desires to be taken under the care of friends.

17/7/1748. Benjmon Johnson and Mary Moormon declare their intention of marriage. Ann Moore and Agness Johnson to examine into Mary Moormons clearness.

15/8/1748. Christopher Clark and Charles Moormon appointed to attend the above marriage.

15/8/1748. Christopher Clark appointed overseer in the room of Micajah Clark.

15/8/1748. Henary Hart is taken under the care of friends.

Benjmon Johnson of Hanover Co and Mary Moormon of Louisa Co married the 19th da, 8th mo, 1748. Witnesses: Thos Moormon, Chas Moormon, Xpher Clark, ... Clark, Charles Moormon, John Moore, James Johnson, Benj Johnson, David Terrell, Edward Clark, Chas Dugless, Rachal Moormon, Ann Moor, Agness Johnson, Penelope Clark, Elizabeth Moormon, Sarah Johnson.

17/10/1748. John Moore, Thomas Moormon, James Johnson, Thomas Clark & William Hale Junr appointed to attend the Quarterly meeting.

17/10/1748. Christopher Clark in behalf of the friends at the Mountains requested a meeting house to be built at the Mountains.

18/12/1748. David Terrill and Sarah Johnson declared their intentions of marriage. Ann Moore and Patte Johnson appointed to examine into her clearness. David Terrill is ordered to bring a certificate.

18/1/1749. Christopher Clark and Charles Moormon appointed to attend the above marriage.

18/1/1749. John Moore, Nathanual Winston, Thos Clark & William Haley appointed to attend the Quarterly meeting.

15/2/1749. Benjmon Johnson and his wife taken under the care of this meeting.

David Terrell of Caroline Co and Sarah Johnson of Louisa Co married the 19th da, 1st mo, 1749. Witnesses: David Terrill, Aggatha Terrill, Benjmon Johnson, Agness Johnson, Thos Moormon, Rachal Moormon, James Stanly, Chas Moormon Junr, Xpher Clark, Penelop Clark, Mary Johnson, John Moore, Benja Johnson, Sarah Lynch, Ann Moor, Charles Moormon, Boling Clark.

17/4/1749. John Moore, Benjmin Johnson, Ashly Johnson, William Haley, Francis Clark & Thos Moormon appointed to attend Quarterly meeting.

15/5/1749. Expher Clark and Charles Moormon appointed to make enquirey into the clearness of Nathanual Winston for certificate relating to marriage.

19/6/1749. John Moore Junr requests to be taken under the care of this meeting. Charles Moormon Junr, James Johnson & Thos Moormon appointed to enquire into the occations lade against John Moore Junr.

16/7/1749. Ashly Johnson, William Haley, Francis Clark Junr, Thomas Clark & Thomas Moormon appointed to attend Quarterly meeting.

21/8/1749. Christopher Clark & Boling Clark appointed overseers of meeting near the Sugerlofe Mountain.

21/8/1749. Benjmin Johnson Senr appointed overseer in room of Christopher Clark.

21/8/1749. James Tate and his family taken under the care of friends.

16/10/1749. Charles Moorman, Charles Moormon Junr, William Haley, Thos Clark & Benjmin Johnson appointed to attend Quarterly meeting.

20/11/1749. John Moore Junr requests certificate in relation to marriage. James Johnson and Thos Moormon appointed to make inquiery into his clearness.

20/11/1749. Jane Hoggits certificate from friends at Perquemons read. She acquainted this meeting of her conserns to travel to MD or elsewhere on truths account.

17/1/1749. Jane Hoggit acquainted this meeting of her consern of traveling to Carolina or elsewhere on truth.

21/2/1750. Francis Clark & William Haley appointed to treat with Edmond Lalley in this matter of his out going.

19/3/1750. Sarah Lynch requested to be taken under the care of friends.

16/4/1750. Edmon Lylley shall be testified against.

16/4/1750. Stephen Scott's certificate from the meeting in Pospatank Co was read & approved.

16/4/1750. William Moore's certificate from the meeting at Perquimons Co, NC read & excepted.

16/4/1750. William Haley desired to be acquitted of being overseer of Fork Creek meeting.

21/5/1750. Edmond Lilly having married contrary to the advice of friends is denied.

18/6/1750. Richard Henderson requests a certificate on occation of traveling to Carolina.

18/6/1750. Robert Davis desires to be taken under the care of friends.

15/7/1750. James Take, Phillup Hoggit, Francies Clark & James Johnson appointed to attend the Quarterly meeting.

15/7/1750. Francis Clark is ordered a certificate.

15/7/1750. William Hoggitt is ordered a certificate.

15/7/1750. John Moore is ordered a certificate.

17/9/1750. Joseph White a publick friend of Bucks Co, PA, his certificate was read and approved.

15/10/1750. Thomas Moormon desires to be acquitted as overseer.

19/11/1750. Francis Clark appointed overseer of Fork Creek meeting in room of William Haley.

16/1/1751. Francis Clark, Philup Hoggitt, John Dugless & Charles Moormon appointed to attend the Quarterly meeting.

20/2/1751. The certificate of Easter White a publick friend from Philadelphia was read & approved.

20/2/1751. John Davis is taken under the care of friends.

18/3/1751. John Moore request a certificate on occation of going to Great Britton.

18/3/1751. Thomas Moormon, Chas Moormon Junr, Rachal Moormon, Agness Johnson & Winiford Clark appointed to inquirer into the perpetors conserning the disorder in Fork Creek meeting and indeavour to reconsile.

15/4/1751. Charles Moormon Senr, James Tate, James Johnson, Sarah Lynch, Winifred Clark appointed to make inquirey into the differences at Fork Creek & reconcile them.

17/6/1751. William Moore a publicke friend from Pirquimons Co, NC, his certificate was read & approved.

21/7/1751. Jane Hoggitt acknowledgments in a disorder between her and Francis Clark seems to give satisfaction.

21/7/1751. Boling Clark, William Haley & Francis Clark appointed to attend Quarterly meeting.

21/7/1751. John Moormen taken under the care of friends.

21/7/1751. John Moormon and Tabitha Clark declare their intentions of marriage. William Haley and Francis Clark Junr appointed to seek into his clearness. Christania Clark and Mary Moormon to see into her clearness.

19/8/1751. Charles Moormon and Benjamin Johnson appointed to attend the above marriage.

19/8/1751. The acknowledgment of Francis Clark seems to give satisfaction to this meeting.

19/8/1751. Benjmon Moormon requests being taken under the care of friends.

16/9/1751. Richard Davis request to be taken under the care of friends.

20/10/1751. George Taylor request to be taken under the care of friends.

John Moormon of Louisa Co and Tabitha Clark of same co married the 20th da, 8th mo, 1751. Witnesses: John Sanders, Joseph Crew, John Moore, John ..., Samual Bunch, Susanar Johnson, John Robberts, Sarah Harris, Mary Johnson, Agness Johnson, Rachal Moormon, James Tate, Ursule Clark, Xper Clark, Thomas Moormon, William Haley, Benjmon Johnson, Charls Moormon, Boling Clark, William Ballard, James Bunch, Charls Mormon Junr.

18/11/1751. Christopher Clark request a certificate in relation to marriage.

18/11/1751. William Hoggitt is ordered a certificate to NC.

18/11/1751. Benjmin Clark is ordered a certificate to NC.

18/11/1751. Benjamin Johnson request being released as overseer.

15/12/1751. Charles Moormon and Benjamin Johnson appointed to examine into the clearness of Christopher Clark.

21/1/1752. John Davis appointed overseer in stead of Benjamin Johnson.

21/1/1752. Boling Clark, John Moor, Chas Moormon, Philup Hoggitt & Francis Clark Junr appointed to attend Quarterly meeting.

15/8/1752. Those appointed to attend the marriage of Charles Dougless report that things was carried on in an orderly manner.

15/8/1752. Christopher Johnson and Bettey Moormon in a publick manner declare their intention of marriage. John Moore and Ashley Johnson appointed to enquire into the mans clearness. Mary Bunch and Matthew Johnson to enquire to the womans clearness.

15/8/1752. William Haley and Francis Clark requested a certificate to Cain Creek.

21/11/1752. Charles Moormon and Samual Bunch appointed to attend the marriage of Christopher Johnson and Bettey Moormon.

18/2/1753. Request of Anne Addoms to be taken under the care of friends is referred to next meeting. Charles Moormon appointed to enquire of Moring Addoms to know if she is agreeable to her request.

20/4/1753. Ashley Johnson, John Moore, Charles Moormon & Benjamon Johnson appointed to attend Quarterly meeting.

20/4/1753. The request of Charles Clark of being aquid [sic] of being overseer is refered to next meeting.

20/4/1753. Charles Dugless and Anne Addoms declare their intentions of marriage. William Ballard and Benjamin Johnson appointed to examine into his clearness. Ann Moor and Martha Johnson to examine into her clearness.

18/5/1753. Henry Hart and Chas Moormon Junr appointed to attend the above marriage.

18/8/1753. Request of John Roberds and likewise William Diggs to be taken under the care of friends is refered.

18/8/1753. Christopher Clark is ordered a certificate to Caroline.

18/8/1753. Boling Clark and his family on their request to be taken under the care of friends.

21/7/1753. John Moore hath gone away to his own appetites so far as drink strong liquers to excess to be often disguised. We theretore disown him. Signed by: Jon Davis Boling Clark, William Ballard, Charles Moormon, Benja

Johnson, Benja Johnson, Charles Moormon Junr, Xpher Clark, Thomas Moormon.

21/7/1753. Francis Clark hath gone away to his passions so far for some time. Appointed by our meeting to reconsile with Jane Hoggitt as he spake disrespectfully against her. Therefore we disown him. Signed by: John Davis, Henry Philip Hart, Boling Clark, Charles Moormon, Expher Clark, Ashley Johnson, Charles Moorman clk, Thos Moormon, Benjaman Johnson.

19/5/1753. Philip Hoggitt request a certificate on occation of traveling to NC. A certificate is ordered for him and one for Jane Hoggitt for meeting at Western Branch or elsewhere.

16/6/1753. Thos Moormon, John Davis & Charles Moormon Junr appointed to attend the Quarterly meeting.

20/1/1753. William and Anttony Hoggitt ordered certificates on their requests.

20/1/1753. Ashley Johnson and his family are taken under the care of this meeting.

17/2/1753. John Moormon is ordered a certificate on condition he gives satisfaction in some perticlers.

17/3/1753. The certificate of Mical Lightfoot a publick friend from PA was read and approved.

17/3/1753. Charles Moormon and John Davis appointed to treat with those that are the cause of disorder at Fork Creek.

17/3/1753. Ashly Johnson, James Johnson, Thomas Clark & Willm Haley appointed to attend the Quarterly meeting.

End of Camp Creek Meeting.

13/5/1775. The matter concerning James Bunch is again continued.

13/5/1775. A certificate was produced on behalf of Edward Terrell and his wife & approved.

13/5/1775. Friends appointed to attend the marriage of Benjamin Hutchings and Judith Mcgehee report that it was conducted in an orderly manner.

13/5/1775. Richard Bloxsom appointed to read justification against Robert Mooreman.

13/5/1775. Madox Stanly hath ... at his daughter marrying from among friends. John Payne and Archiles Stanly appointed to treat with him.

13/5/1775. The following lines were wrote by direction of Stanly Harriss a few hours before his death. "28/4/1775 To the monthly meeting I formerly belonged, I have stood disowned by you many years past, now believing my time near expired, I should begin to be reunited to my friends ... I heartily condemn every part of my conduct that ever has been contrary to truth."

13/5/1775. Jessee Hargrave requested a certificate to the meeting at Blackwater in relation to marriage. Pleasants Terrell and Thomas Terrell appointed to make necessary enquirey.

13/5/1775. Micajah Terrell, John Payne, John Harriss, Moses Harriss & Pleasants Terrell appointed to attend Quarterly meeting.

13/5/1775. Susanah Pleasants an elder of Jeneto deceased, no memorial as yet.

10/6/1775. Micajah Davis appointed to know of them the reasons of the failure of the friends appointed to treat with James Bunch.

10/6/1775. Money ordered to be raised towards the charge of enlarging and repairing the meeting house at Blackwater paid into the hand of Anselm Bailey.

10/6/1775. Madox Stanly acknowledges he consented to his daughters marriage out. Pleasants Terrell and Samuel Hargrave appointed to treat with him.

10/6/1775. Jessee Hargrave doth not need a certificate for reasons given by Samuel Hargrave which was satisfactory.

10/6/1775. Shadrack Stanley made application for advice in a certain matter of controversy between him and Daniel Harriss. John Payne, Pleasants Terrell, James Crew and Samuel Hargrave appointed to take the matter under their consideration and give such advice therein.

10/6/1775. Micajah Davis made application for a certificate to Henrico meeting signifying his clearness with respect to marriage. Achillas Douglas and James Crew appointed to make the necessary enquiry.

12/8/1775. A committee appointed to enquire into the conduct of each friend concerned in the estate of Stanly Harriss.

12/8/1775. John Payne, James Crew, John Harriss, Pleasants Terrell, Thomas Terrell & Micajah Terrell appointed to attend the Quarterly meeting.

12/8/1775. Samuel Hargrave requested to be released from acting as clerk. John Payne appointed in his stead.

12/8/1775. The committee appointed to examine the minutes from the beginning of Henery Terrill's clerkship to this time viz Micajah Terrell, Pleasants Terrell, Thomas Terrell, John Payne & John Harriss.

9/9/1775. The committee appointed to the matter relative to Stanly Harris' last will have not as yet treated with & advised Daniel Harriss & other friends concerned. Micajah Terrell and Thomas Terrell are added to the former committee.

14/10/1775. A complaint against John & Thomas Harriss that on their affirmation as witness to Stanly Harriss' will, added some particulars groundless. Micajah Terrell, Pleasants Terrell, Henry Terrell, Clark Moorman, John Barnett & Micajah Davis appointed to enquire into the foundation of the said charge. Also against Moses Harriss for proceeding in diverse measures to make void Stanly Harriss' will.

14/10/1775. Micajah Crew requests a certificate to the meeting of White Oak Swamp, Henrico Co in relation to marriage. Clark Terrell, Moorman & Shadrack Stanly appointed to make the necessary enquiry.

21/11/1775. Report: John & Thomas Harris have acted indiscreetly and Shadrack Stanly hath also behaved in a manner unbecoming a person in unity with us, and hath proceeded against the accused with too much warmth and ill will ... they ought to make satisfaction by condemning their conduct ... we recommend that neither of them be employed in any publick service of the meeting. Signed by: John Barnett, Henry Terrell, Pleasants Terrell, Clark Terrell, Moorman & Micajah Terrell. Micajah Davis, Pleasants Terrell & Achillis Douglas to procure a coppy of the report & produce to the next Quarterly meeting.

21/11/1775. Moses Harriss found not guilty of the whole of the charges laid against him but has in some instances acted indiscreetly. Signed by: Henry Terrell, John Barnett, Pleasants Terrell, Micajah Davis and Clark Terrell Moorman. Moses Harriss condemned the same to the satisfaction of this meeting.

21/11/1775. Micajah Moorman from South River meeting produced a certificate for himself and family.

21/11/1775. Archabald Pleasants of the Geneto preparative meeting hath married by an hireling priest contrary to the rules of our disipline. Thomas Pleasants & Benjamin Watkins appointed to produce a testification against him.

21/11/1775. Micajah Davis, Achillis Douglas, Pleasants Terrell & Micajah Terrell appointed to attend Quarterly meeting.

21/12/1775. A certificate from the meeting in Henrico on behalf of Mary Davis on which she is received and recommended to the care of the overseer of Camp Creek meeting.

13/1/1776. David Brooks attended this meeting on a religious visit and produced a certificate from Newgarden meeting. Obediah Harriss attended this meeting as companion to David Brooks from Newgarden.

13/1/1776. Bartlett Ballard of South River meeting & Judith Johnson declare their intentions of marriage.

13/1/1776. Soloman Stanly married from among friends. Archilous Stanly & Clark Terrill Moorman appointed to produce a testification against him.

13/1/1776. Thomas Moorman (son of Micajah) hath married from among friends. Pleasants Terrell & Thomas Terrell appointed to produce a testification against him.

23/2/1776. Representatives for Cedar Creek preparative meeting: James Crew, John Payne & Archilous Stanly; from Camp Creek David Terrill & Micajah Davis; from Caroline Thomas Terrell & Samuel Winston.

23/2/1776. The women friends requests the advice of this meeting with respect to the request of Obdiance Harding to be received as a member. Micajah Terrell & John Payne appointed to visit her.

23/2/1776. James Bunch appeared at this meeting and produced a paper of condemnation for his past misconduct.

23/2/1776. Ashley Johnson & Benjamin Johnson appointed to attend the marriage of Bartlett Ballard & Judith Johnson.

23/2/1776. Henry Childs requests to be reunited with his friends. Micajah Terrell & Thomas Terrell appointed to visit him.

23/2/1776. Archilous Stanly & William Ballard are about to remove within the verge of New Garden, NC meeting and requests certificates for themselves and families. James Crew & Clark Terrell Moorman appointed to make the necessary enquirey.

23/2/1776. Samuel Hargrave, Pleasants Terrell & James Harriss request certificates as they purpose travilling to the southward province. Micajah Terrell & Thomas Terrell appointed to make necessary enquiry.

23/2/1776. Samuel Hargrave, James Harriss & Micajah Terrell appointed to attend the Quarterly meeting.

9/3/1776. Representatives appointed to attend the monthly meeting are for Cedar Creek, James Crew, Clark Terrell Moorman & Moses Harriss who were present.

9/3/1776. A certificate was produced from meeting at South River informing us that Archilles & Andrew Moorman removed within the verge of our meeting.

9/3/1776. Byrom Ballard made application on behalf of David Ballard who requests to be reunited to his friends. Micajah Davis & Achilles Douglass appointed to visit him.

9/3/1776. Agreeable to the minutes of the quarterly meeting for ministers and elders Henrico Co 26/11/1775 Samual Hargrave & Micajah Terrell are appointed to nominate such members as elders as they think proper.

13/4/1776. Representatives from Jeneto are James Hunnicutt & John Barnett; from Caroline Micajah & Pleasant Terrell; from Cedar Creek Thomas Hutchings & Clark Terrell Moorman, who were present.

13/4/1776. Samuel Bell (son of George Bell) stands charged with something of a scandalous nature. Arcchillas Duglesh to enquire into the said report and treat with said Bell, and if it appears true to prepare a testification against him.

13/4/1776. James Crew and Moses Harriss appointed to draw a certificate for Nicholas Stone agreeable to act of assembly and direct same to the chief commanding officer in Goochland Co, also for James Hunnicutt, John Hunnicutt & Joseph Hunnicutt to be directed to the Col of Cumberland Co, Samuel Hargrave and Pleasants Terrell to do the same for Micajah & Archilles Moorman in Caroline Co.

11/5/1776. Representatives from the preparative meetings: for Caroline Pleasant Terrill & Samuel Hargrave, from Cedar Creek Jerimiah Harriss, James Crew & Clark Terrill Mooreman, from Amelia John Johnson, who were present.

11/5/1776. Clark T. Mooreman appointed overseer in place of Archelous Stanly who is removed from out the verge.

Barckly (Barcklay) Ballard (son of William Ballard) of Bedford Co & Judith Johnson (daughter of John Johnson) of Amelia Co married the 27th da, 2nd mo, 1776. Witnesses: Ashly Johnson, Jesse Johnson, Mary Johnson, Elizabeth Johnson, John Johnson Senr, Lydia Johnson.

11/5/1776. Pleasant Terrill, Samuel Hargrave, James Crew & Moses Harriss appointed to attend Quarterly meeting.

8/6/1776. Representatives from the preparative meetings: for Cedar Creek Jeremiah Harriss & Joshua Stanly, from Camp Creek Charles Mooreman & Micajah Davis, from Amelia Ashly Johnson & William Johnson, from Caroline Thomas Terrell who were present except for Charles Moorman who is required to give his reason.

8/6/1776. Henry Chiles offered a paper of condemning his conduct for which he was disowned, but not satisfactory.

8/6/1776. Thomas Pleasants, Strangman Hutchings, Ashley Johnson, Jessee Johnson, Charles Moorman, David Terrell, Clark T. Moorman & James Crew are added to those formerly appointed for the nomination of elders.

8/6/1776. Soloman Stanly (son of John Stanly) gave a paper of condemnation for marrying a wife contrary to the rules of our dicipline.

8/6/1776. Jonathan Terrell & Margreat Hunnicutt published their intentions of marriage. Thomas Terrell & Samuel Winston appointed to make the needful inquierie.

8/6/1776. A request made for certificates to the commanding officer of Amelia Co certifying their being members of our society by Benjamin Johnson (son of Ashly), James Johnson (son of John), Andrew Mooreman, John Johnson Senr, Gerrad Johnson (son of Ashly).

13/7/1776. Representatives from preparative meetings: for Cedar Creek James Crew & Jeremiah Harriss, from Caroline Pleasants Terrell & James Harriss, from Camp Creek Micajah Davis.

13/7/1776. Henry Chiles requests to be received a member of our society is continued. Pleasants Terrell appointed to inform him friends reasons.

13/7/1776. Request of Soloman Stanly is again deferd. Micajah Davis & Charles Moorman appointed to take some opportunity with him.

13/7/1776. Samuel Winston and Robert Terrell appointed to attend the marriage of Jonathan Terrell & Margreat Hunnicutt.

13/7/1776. Charles Moorman & Micajah Davis appointed to assist the women friends relative to the request of Ursley Mosby in being again received a member of our society.

13/7/1776. Jessee Hargrave requests a certificate to the meeting at Whiteoak Swamp, Henrico Co signifying his clearness relative to marriage. Pleasants & Thomas Terrell appointed to make needful enquirey.

23/8/1776. Representatives from the several preparitive meetings: for Cedar Creek Clark T. Moorman & James Crew, from Caroline Thomas & Pleasants Terrell, from Jeneto James Hunnicutt, Benjamin Watkins & Thomas Pleasants, from Amelia Jesse Johnson & Ashley Johnson, from Camp Creek Archillis Douglass & Micajah Davis, they appeared except James Hunnicutt.

23/8/1776. Margreat Crew's certificate from the meeting at White Oak Swamp was produced.

23/8/1776. Peter Fitz Garrald of Jeneto requests to be taken under the notice of friends. Thomas Pleasants & Strangman Hutchings appointed to make enquirey into his life, conduct and motives for said request.

23/8/1776. Henry Terrell of Caroline hath joined himself with those of a different persuasion in matters of faith from us. Micajah Terrell & Samuel Hargrave to visit him on the occation.

23/8/1776. Pleasants Terrell, Jesse Johnson, Clark T. Moorman, Micajah Terrell & Strangman Hutchings appointed to attend the Quarterly meeting.

14/9/1776. Representatives from the several preparative meetings: for Cedar Creek Thomas Harris & James Crew, from Camp Creek Acchilles Douglass & Micajah Davis, from Caroline Pleasants Terrell & Thomas Terrell, from Amelia John Johnson, Jesse Johnson who were present.

14/9/1776. Friends appointed to nominate & addition of elders have complied, names are Jesse Johnson, Jesse Johnson [sic], Pleasants Terrell, Thomas Terrell, John Payne, Acchillas Douglass, Byrom Ballard, Susanah Moorman, Rebecak Terrell, Miriam Pleasants, Elizabeth Winston, Mary Payne & Elizabeth Pleasants, who were approved.

14/9/1776. Micajah Davis requests to be released from treating with Ursly Mosby. Byrom Ballard appointed in his stead.

14/9/1776. Samuel Hargrave & Micajah Terrell produced a testification against Henry Terrell. Pleasant Terrell to read the same.

12/10/1776. Representatives from the several preparative meetings: for Cedar Creek Micajah Crew & Clark T. Moorman, from Caroline Pleasant Terrell & Thomas Terrell, from Amelia Jesse Johnson & Ashley Johnson, who were present.

12/10/1776. Acchillis Moorman of Caroline hath acted in several matters contrary to friends dicipline. Samuel Hargrave, James Harris, Samuel Winston & Micajah Terrell to treat with him.

21/11/1776. Representatives from the several preparative meetings: for Cedar Creek Nicholas Hutchings & James Crew, from Caroline Pleasant Terrell & Samuel Hargrave, from Amelia Jesse Johnson Junr & Benjamin Johnson, from Jeneto John Barnet & Strangman Hutchings, from Camp Creek Charles Moorman & Micajah Davis, who were present.

21/11/1776. Soloman Stanly condemns his misconduct for which he was disowned to their satisfaction, on which he was again received a member of our society.

21/11/1776. Strangman Hutchings, James Crew & John Payne added to friends to assist in treating with Ursly Mosby.

21/11/1776. Charles Moorman of Camp Creek requests to be released from the service of overseer which is granted.

21/11/1776. Jemimah Chouning hath joined herself in society with the Baptists. Charles Moorman & George Bell to make some conversation with her on the account.

21/11/1776. Obediah Stanly married by a hireling priest to one not of our society. John Payne appointed to produce a testification against him.

21/11/1776. Madox Stanly of late hath kept a woman in his house under pretents of being married & acknowledged to have lived with her as his wife, and since confesses they were not lawfully married. Pleasants Terrell & Micajah Davis to treat with him.

21/11/1776. Micajah Davis, Achilles Douglass, Samuel Hargrave, John Barnard, James Crew & Benjamin Johnson Junr appointed to attend Quarterly meeting.

14/12/1776. Representatives from Camp Creek are Richard Bloxsom & Micajah Davis, for Ceder Creek Clark Terrell Moorman & Thomas Harriss, from Caroline Pleasant Terrell, who were present.

14/12/1776. Hannah Bunch is received a member.

14/12/1776. Micajah Terrell informed this meeting that he had drawings on his mind to visit a few friends in Brunswick Co.

11/1/1777. Representatives from the preparitive meetings: from Cedar Creek James Crew & Moses Harris, from Caroline Thomas & Pleasants Terrell, who were present.

21/2/1777. Representatives from the preparative meetings: for Cedar Creek Clark Terrel Moorman, Moses Harris & James Crew, for Caroline Thomas Terrel & Pleasants Terrel, for Camp Creek David Terrel & Micajah Davis, for Amelia Jesse Johnson & Ashly Johnson, for Jeneto Strangman Hutchings, John Barnet & Benjamin Watkins, who were present.

21/2/1777. Thomas Ballard sent a paper of condemnation for marrying out of the society. Also a letter from Toms Creek, Surry Co, NC on his behalf. David Terrel & Acchillis Douglass appointed to make some further enquiry into his affairs.

21/2/1777. Micajah Moorman & family having removed within the virge of Bedford meeting, Samual Hargrave & Pleasants Terrell appointed to make the needful enquirey into his affairs & produce certificate.

21/2/1777. Thomas Harlow of Camp Creek requests being received a member of our society.

21/2/1777. Charles Douglass of Camp Creek is in the practice of drinking spirituous liquors to excess. David Terrell & Micajah Davis appointed to take the necessary steps on such occations.

21/2/1777. Micajah Terrell, Samuel Hargrave, Pleasants Terrell & James Hunnicutt appointed to attend the Quarterly meeting.

8/3/1777. Representatives from the several preparative meetings: for Cedar Creek Jerimiah Harris & Thomas Harris, for Caroline Micajah Terrell & Samuel Hargrave, who were present, except Micajah Terrell.

12/4/1777. Representatives from the several preparative meetings: for Cedar Creek James Crew, John Johnson & Moses Harris, for Camp Creek Robert Bell, in Caroline Micajah Terrell & Thomas Terrell, who were present.

12/4/1777. Jemimah Chouning hath desented from us and by thus absenting herself from our meetings and the society, hath forfeited her birth right of membership amongst us, we therefore disown her.

12/4/1777. David Terrell & Micajah Davis sent account of their proceedings in assisting the women friends in matter relative to James Bunch's daughter, which was not to satisfaction. John Payne appointed to assist the women to accomplish the same .

12/4/1777. James Bunch of Camp Creek is in the practice of taking spirituous liquor to excess. John Payne & James Crew appointed to visit him on the occation.

12/4/1777. Pleasants Terrell, Thomas & Elizabeth Pleasants, Arcillis Douglass, Byrom Ballard, John Payne, Thomas Terrill & Rebeccak Terrill appointed elders.

10/5/1777. Representatives from the several preparative meetings: for Cedar Creek Moses Harris & Shadrack Stanly, for Amelia Jesse & Jarrad Johnson, for Caroline Thomas Terrill & Pleasants Terrill, for Camp Creek Micajah Davis, were mostly present.

10/5/1777. Ursly Mosby is received as a member.

10/5/1777. William Davis & Mary his wife of Camp Creek requests to be received members of our society. Micajah Davis to inform them to attend next meeting.

10/5/1777. Samuel Hargrave, Micajah Terrell, Pleasants Terrell, James Crew, James Harris & Jesse Johnson appointed to attend Quarterly meeting.

14/6/1777. Representatives appointed by Cedar Creek preparative meeting are James Crew, Clark Terrel Moorman, for Camp Creek David Terrell, for Caroline Samuel Hargrave & Thomas Terrell, who were present.

14/6/1777. William Davis & Mary his wife received as members.

14/6/1777. Samual Hargrave is released from acting as an overseer of Caroline meeting & Thomas Terrell appointed in his place.

14/6/1777. John Peatross requests to be joined in membership with us. Thomas & Pleasants Terrell appointed to take an opportunity with him.

14/6/1777. James & Micajah Johnson have removed to Whiteoak Swamp, Henrico Co meeting without certificates. George Bell & David Terrell appointed to make necessary inquirey into each of their situations.

12/7/1777. Representatives appointed by Cedar Creek preparative meeting are: James Crew & John Johnson, for Caroline Pleasants Terrell & Thomas Terrell, who are present.

12/7/1777. John Peatross received into membership with us.

22/8/1777. Representatives appointed by the several preparative meetings: for Cedar Creek Clark Terrill Moorman & Micajah Crew, for Caroline Pleasants Terrell & Thomas Terrell, for Amelia Jesse Johnson, for Camp Creek David Terrell & Micajah Davis, for Jeneto Strangman Hutchings, John Barnet, Benjamin Watkins & Thomas Pleasants, who were all present.

22/8/1777. The case of Thomas Harlow is continued and David Terrell & Samuel Bunch appointed to have the care thereof.

22/8/1777. A certificate was produced from the meeting of Pipe Creek in MD on behalf of Sarah Harris signifying her clearness of marriage.

22/8/1777. Micajah Terrell, Samuel Hargrave, Pleasants Terrell & John Payne appointed to visit the Jeneto meeting.

22/8/1777. John Moore of Camp Creek appeared to stand in need of the assistance of his friends. 6 pounds 6 shillings raised and put into the hand of Samuel Bunch to be appropriated toward his maintenance.

22/8/1777. Pleasant Terrell, Thomas Terrell & Acchillis Douglass appointed to joine with the quarterly meetings committee in visiting those who hold Negroes in bondage.

22/8/1777. Clark Terrel Moorman, James Crew, Thomas Terrell, Pleasants Terrell, David Terrell, Samuel Bunch, Thomas Pleasants, Strangman Hutchings & Jessee Johnson appointed to attend Quarterly meeting.

13/9/1777. Shadrack Stanly requests a certificate to New Garden, NC.

11/10/1777. Representatives appointed by the preparative meetings: for Cedar Creek James Crew & Moses Harris, for Caroline Pleasants Terrell, for Amelia John Johnson.

11/10/1777. Robert Terrell, Micajah Davis & John Payne inform this meeting that they purpose attending the Yearly meeting to be held in NC and request certificates.

8/11/1777. Representatives appointed by the preparative meetings: for Cedar Creek Micajah Crew & Thomas Harris, for Caroline Thomas Terrell & Pleasants Terrell, for Jeneto James Hunnicutt, John Barnard & Thomas Pleasants.

8/11/1777. Armsby Crew and wife request to be reinstated among friends and sent a paper of condemnation for their past misconduct. Thomas Pleasants, James Hunnicutt & John Barnet appointed to take an opportunity with them.

8/11/1777. Micajah Terrell, Shadrack Stanly & John Payne appointed to attend Quarterly meeting.

13/12/1777. Representatives appointed by the preparative meeting: for Cedar Creek Clark Terrill Moorman & Thomas Harris, for Caroline Pleasants Terrill, for Camp Creek Achillis Douglas.

13/12/1777. James Moorman of Camp Creek hath so far acted in the military service as to furnish a substitute soldier. Micajah Terrill & Accillis Douglass appointed to take the necessary care in that matter.

13/12/1777. Charles Douglass hath been contributing money for the purpose of raising men to go to war and is in other respects disorderly. David Terrell, Pleasants Terrell & Micajah Terrell appointed to take the necessary care in that case.

13/12/1777. Thomas Moorman of Camp Creek stands charged by Mary Terrell of a marriage engagement and refuses to consummate the marriage & that she is with child by him. Acchillis Douglass and Byrom Ballard to take the necessary care in that case.

13/12/1777. James Bunch is still in the practice of taking spirituous liquor to excess. Acchillis Douglass and David Terrell appointed to inform him it is the mind of this meeting a testification should be prepared against him.

13/12/1777. Richard Bloxsom is discontinued as overseer of Camp Creek friends. George Bell appointed in his stead.

10/1/1778. Representatives appointed by the preparative meetings: for Cedar Creek Zachariah Stanly & Thomas Harriss, for Caroline Pleasants Terrell & Thomas Terrell, for Camp Creek Elijah Johnson.

10/1/1778. Armsby Crew & wife reinstated as members of our society.

10/1/1778. Samuel Winston of Caroline hath removed within the virge of Henrico meeting and requests a certificate for himself & family. Thomas Terrell & Pleasants Terrell appointed to make the necessary inquirey.

10/1/1778. Micajah Terrill requests a certificate to the meeting at New Garden, NC signifying his clearness of marriage engagements. James Crew & John Payne appointed to make the needful inquirey.

27/2/1778. Representatives appointed by the preparative meetings: for Cedar Creek Nicholus Hutchings & Jeremiah Harris, for Camp Creek David Terrell & William Davis, for Amelia Jesse Johnson, Benjamin Johnson & Jesse Johnson Junr, for Geneto James Hunnicutt, who are mostly present.

27/2/1778. A certificate from South River meeting was produced on behalf of James Johnson & family, they are received.

27/2/1778. Moorman Ballard sent a paper condemning the disorderly conduct for which he stands disowned together with a paper of recommendation from the friends of Toms Creek, NC.

27/2/1778. Byrom Ballard, James Hunnicutt, James Crew & Jesse Johnson appointed to attend Quarterly meeting.

14/3/1778. Representatives appointed by the preparative meeting: for Cedar Creek James Crew & John Johnson, for Caroline Pleasants Terrill & Thomas Terrill.

14/3/1778. The clerk not being present, Moses Harris appointed to act in his stead for this time.

14/3/1778. A paper of denial was presented from the womens meeting against Mary Terrell.

14/3/1778. Moses Harriss appointed to prepare a certificate for Moorman Ballard.

14/3/1778. Acchillis Moorman of Caroline hath married contrary to the rules of our society. Pleasants Terrell appointed to prepare a testification against him.

11/4/1778. Representatives appointed by the preparative meetings: for Cedar Creek Joshua Stanly, Thomas Harris & Nicholas Hutchings, for Camp Creek David Terrell, for Caroline Thomas Terrill & Pleasants Terrill.

11/4/1778. James Moorman hath produced in writing his condemnation for his misconduct, which being satisfactory is recorded.

11/4/1778. John Barnett of Camp Creek requests to be taken into membership with friends. David Terrill & Elijah Johnson appointed to take the case.

10/5/1778. Representatives appointed by the preparative meetings: for Cedar Creek John Johnson & Micajah Crew, for Caroline Samuel Hargrave & Pleasants Terrell, for Camp Creek Robert Bell.

10/5/1778. David Terrell requests to be released from the service of an overseer. William Davis appointed in his stead.

10/5/1778. Pleasants Terrell, Thomas Harris, John Harris & Moses Harris appointed to attend Quarterly meeting.

13/6/1778. Representatives appointed by the preparative meetings: for Cedar Creek John Johnson, Shadrack Stanly & Moses Harris, for Caroline Micajah Terrell, for Camp Creek Elijah Johnson & William Davis.

13/6/1778. Micajah & William Davis added to the friends formerly appointed to enquire into a late charge against Charles Douglass.

13/6/1778. Deborah Terrell produced a certificate from meeting at New Garden, NC, she was received.

11/7/1778. Representatives appointed by the preparative meetings: for Cedar Creek James Crew & John Johnson, for Caroline Thomas Terrell.

11/7/1778. Gamm Moore requests a certificate to meeting at New Garden signifying his birth right of membership. Micajah Davis appointed to produce the same.

11/7/1778. John Moore of Camp Creek stands in need of friends assistance. Micajah Davis appointed to furnish him with the necessaries his present situation calls for.

24/8/1778. Representatives appointed by the preparative meetings: for Cedar Creek John Johnson & Nicholas Hutchings, for Camp Creek William Davis & Micajah Davis, for Jeneto Thomas Pleasants & Strangman Hutchings.

24/8/1778. Strangman Hutchings, James Crew, John Payne, Pleasants Terrell & Micajah Crew appointed to visit Amelia preparative meeting on their repeated neglect of sending accounts.

24/8/1778. Micajah Davis, William Davis, Micajah Crew, Pleasants Terrell & Strangman Hutchings appointed to attend Quarterly meeting.

12/9/1778. Representatives appointed by the preparative meetings: for Cedar Creek John Johnson & Thomas Harris.

12/9/1778. John Stanly having some time past removed from this meeting within the limits of New Garden. John Payne to produce a certificate.

12/9/1778. The certificate granted Samuel Pleasants Junr dated 8/4/1775 directed to the meeting of friends in Philadelphia never got to hand before his removal again within the virge of this, it is returned.

--/10/1778. Representatives appointed by the preparative meetings: for Cedar Creek James Crew & Nicholas Hutchings, for Camp Creek Byrom Ballard & Micajah Davis, for Caroline Pleasants Terrell & Thomas Terrell.

--/10/1778. The money to be raised to repay John Harris and to purchase the book to record births & deaths is complyd with.

--/10/1778. John Douglass of Camp Creek is frequently in the practice of taking spirituous liquor to excess. Micajah Davis, Micajah Terrell, Thomas Terrell & Pleasants Terrell appointed to take opportunity with him.

--/10/1778. John Douglass Junr having married from among friends & requests this meeting not to testify against him but to indulge him for another month.

--/10/1778. Our esteemed friend Abraham Griffith attended this meeting & produced his certificate from Rednor meeting Philadelphia Co.

24/11/1778. Representatives from Cedar Creek preparative meeting are John Johnson & Thomas Harris, from Caroline Micajah Terrell, from Camp Creek Elijah Johnson & Micajah Davis.

24/11/1778. Mary Hargrave late of White Oak Swamp meeting removed within these limits, whose certificate was read and received.

24/11/1778. Micajah Crew, Elijah Johnson, John Harris & Thomas Harris appointed to attend Quarterly meeting.

12/12/1778. Representatives from Cedar Creek preparative meeting are Moses Harris & James Crew, from Caroline Thomas Terrell.

12/12/1778. Samuel Hargrave & Lucy Terrell declared their intentions of marriage. Micajah Terrell & James Harris appointed to make the needful inquirey.

9/1/1779. Micajah Terrell appointed to attend the marriage of Samuel Hargrave & Lucy Terrell.

26/2/1779. Representatives from Cedar Creek preparative meeting are Nicholas Hutchings & Micajah Crew, from Camp Creek William Davis, Achillis Douglass & Micajah Davis, from Amelia William Johnson & Jesse Johnson, from Jeneto Strangman Hutching & Thomas Pleasants, from Caroline Thomas Terrell & Pleasants Terrell, who were mostly present.

26/2/1779. John Douglass still continues in the practice of taking spirituous liquor to excess. Byrom Ballard appointed to the care and oversight of him.

26/2/1779. John Douglass Junr sent a paper of condemnation for his outgoing in marriage, which was to the satisfaction of this meeting.

26/2/1779. Robert Douglass of Camp Creek married contrary to the rules of our society. Micajah Davis & William Davis appointed to prepare a paper of denial against him.

26/2/1779. Nicholas Hutchings appointed overseer in place of John Johnson who removed to Amelia meeting.

26/2/1779. Micajah Terrell, Thomas Pleasants, William Davis & James Crew appointed to attend Quarterly meeting.

13/3/1779. Representatives from Cedar Creek preparative meeting are Micajah Crew & John Stanly, from Camp Creek David Terrill, who were mostly present.

10/4/1779. Representatives from Cedar Creek preparative meeting are Nicholas Hutchings & Moses Harris, from Caroline Thomas Terrell, from Amelia John Johnson, who were present.

8/5/1779. Representatives from Cedar Creek preparative meeting are Shadrack Stanly & James Crew, from Caroline Thomas & Pleasants Terrell, from Camp Creek Byrom Ballard, who were present.

8/5/1779. The womens meeting presented a certificate to joine Jean West to South River meeting.

8/5/1779. Charles Woodson Junr and Ann his wife of Jenito hath for several years past neglected to attend our meetings and he has been concerned in hireing a man to go into the army. Strangman Hutchings & Thomas Pleasants appointed to visit & treat with them.

8/5/1779. Isaac Pleasants hath of late taken up arms to guard prisoners in Albermarle Co. Strangman Hutchings & James Hunnicutt appointed to treat with him.

8/5/1779. James Moorman of Camp Creek is in the practice of gameing & frequenting places of diversion. Byrom Ballard & William Davis appointed to treat with him.

8/5/1779. Charles Moorman & elder of Camp Creek deceased since last account. No memorial as yet.

8/5/1779. Pleasants Terrell, Thomas Terrell & John Harris appointed to attend Quarterly meeting.

12/6/1779. Representatives appointed by Cedar Creek preparative meeting are Nicholass Hutchings & James Crew, from Caroline Thomas Terrill & Pleasants Terrill, from Camp Creek Acchillis Douglass.

12/6/1779. Charles Linch Terrell & Anthony Winston hath entered voluntarily into the military service. Also Samuel Hargrave, Thomas Cheadle & John Chiles have been in some degree active therein. Clark Terrell Moorman, John Pettross, Thomas Terrell & John Payne appointed to visit each of them.

10/7/1779. Representatives from Cedar Creek preparative meeting are Nicholas Hutchings & Micajah Crew, from Caroline Thomas Terrell & Pleasants Terrell.

10/7/1779. Zachariah Stanly of Caroline hath lately been in the practice of drinking spirituous liquor to excess and gameing. He appearing at this meeting offered a paper condemning such practices.

27/8/1779. Representatives for Cedar Creek preparative meeting are Nicholas Hutchings & Shadrack Stanly, for Amelia Jesse Johnson & John Johnson, for Camp Creek Acchillis Douglas & William Davis, for Jenito James Hunnicutt & Strangman Hutchings, for Caroline Thomas Terrell & Pleasants Terrell, who were all present.

27/8/1779. James Hunnicutt is added to the assistance of friends appointed in the case of Charles Woodson & wife.

27/8/1779. A paper of condemnation from Samual Hargrave was produced, which is to the satisfaction of this meeting.

27/8/1779. Anthony Winston, Charles Lynch Terrell, & John Chiles, do not appear to be in a dispostion to make satisfaction yet. Pleasants Terrell and

Micajah Crew added to the committee formerly appointed to take another opportunity with them.

27/8/1779. Samuel Pleasants of Jeneto hath acted in the capacity of a soldier voluntarily, also married contrary to the rules of our dicipline. James Hunnicutt & Jesse Johnson appointed to visit him.

27/8/1779. Samuel Bunch Junr of Camp Creek is in the practice of exercising in military duty. William Davis & Acchillis Douglass appointed to treat with him.

27/8/1779. Walter Payne has removed to Philadelphia. Micajah Terrell, James Hunnicutt, Moses Harris & Micajah Davis appointed to prepare a certificate for him.

27/8/1779. Micajah Terrell, Micajah Crew, Strangman Hutchings, Jesse Johnson & William Davis appointed to attend Quarterly meeting.

11/9/1779. Representatives from Cedar Creek preparative meeting are Joshua Stanly & Nicholas Hutchings, from Caroline James Harris & Thomas Terrell, from Camp Creek Byrom Ballard.

11/9/1779. Moses Harris & James Hunnicutt appointed to prepare a paper of denial against Isaac Pleasants.

11/9/1779. Byrom Ballard & Acchilles Douglass appointed to prepare paper of disunion against Samual Bunch.

11/9/1779. Acchilles Douglass & Elizabeth Terrell declare their intentions of marriage. Byrom Ballard & William Davis appointed to make the needful inquirey.

9/10/1779. Representatives from Cedar Creek preparative meeting are Nicholas Hutchings & Moses Harris, from Camp Creek Elijah Johnson.

9/10/1779. Benjamin Watkins is added to the assistance of those formerly appointed in case of Charles Woodson & wife.

9/10/1779. John Petross & Thomas Terrell appointed to prepare a paper of disunion against John Chiles.

9/10/1779. Thomas Terrell & John Pettross appointed to attend the marriage of Acchilles Douglass & Elizabeth Terrell.

9/10/1779. John Harris, Micajah Terrell, John Payne & Miriam Pleasants informed this meeting that they propose attending the yearly meeting in NC.

126

13/11/1779. Representatives from Cedar Creek preparative meeting are Nicholas Hutchings & Thomas Harris, from Amelia John Johnson, from Caroline Micajah Terrell & Thomas Terrell, from Jeneto Strangman Hutchings & James Hunnicutt.

13/11/1779. James Hunnicutt & Benjamin Watkins appointed to prepare a paper of disunion against Charles Woodson.

13/11/1779. Pleasants Terrell & Thomas Terrell appointed to prepare a paper of disunion against Anthony Winston.

13/11/1779. David & James Johnson of Camp Creek request certificates, the former to South River meeting, the latter to Deep Creek, NC. Acchillis Douglas & Micajah Davis appointed to make the needfull inquiry.

13/11/1779. Thomas Terrell, John Payne, John Harris & John Pettross appointed to attend the Quarterly meeting.

11/12/1779. Representatives from Cedar Creek preparative meetings are Moses Harris & Joshua Stanly.

11/12/1779. Jonathan Stanly hath married with one not professing with us. John Payne & Shadrack Stanly appointed to prepare paper of disunion against him.

--/1/1780. Thomas Hutchings requests a certificate to Henrico meeting setting forth his clearness of marriage. Shadrack Stanly & John Harris appointed to make the needfull enquiry.

25/2/1780. Representatives from Cedar Creek preparative meeting are Shadrack Stanly & John Harris.

25/2/1780. Micajah Crew & Moses Harris appointed to accompany the overseers in a visit to Zachariah Stanly.

25/2/1780. Nicholas Hutchings, William & Micajah Davis, Shadrack Stanly & Moses Harris appointed to attend the Quarterly meeting.

11/3/1780. Representatives from Cedar Creek preparative meeting are Shadrack Stanly and Moses Harris, from Caroline Thomas Terrell, from Camp Creek William Davis.

11/3/1780. Thomas Johnson (son of Ashley of Camp Creek) sent in a paper condemning his past misconduct for which he was disowned, which was to general satisfaction. John Payne appointed to draw him a few lines certifying his being reunited to friends directed to meeting at South River.

8/4/1780. Representatives appointed from Cedar Creek preparative meeting are John Harris & Shadrack Stanly, from Caroline Thomas Terrell, from Camp Creek Samuel Bunch.

8/4/1780. John Moore & wife of Camp Creek need the assistance of friends. 112 pounds 10 shillings to be raised and commit it to the care of Samuel Bunch to be laid out as he shall think best for the said friends.

13/5/1780. Representatives appointed from Cedar Creek preparative meeting are Shadrack Stanly & Micajah Crew, from Camp Creek Micajah Davis, from Caroline Micajah Terrell & Samuel Winston, from Amelia Jesse Johnson & James Johnson, from Jeneto Strangman Hutchings & James Hunnicutt, who were present.

13/5/1780. Micajah Davis, Thomas Terrell, John Harris & Thomas Harris appointed to attend the Quarterly meeting.

10/6/1780. Representatives appointed from Cedar Creek preparative meeting are Thomas Stanly & Shadrack Stanly, from Caroline Micajah Terrell.

10/6/1780. Nicholas Crew hath removed within the virge of South River meeting. John & Moses Harris to make the necessary enquirey into his affairs and produce a certificate.

9/7/1780. Representatives appointed from Cedar Creek are Shadrack Stanly & Moses Harris.

25/8/1780. Representatives appointed from Cedar Creek are Nicholas Hutchings & Joshua Stanly, from Caroline Thomas Terrell & Pleasants Terrell, from Camp Creek Acchillis Douglass & William Davis, from Jeneto Thomas Pleasants, Benjamin Watkins & James Hunnicutt, from Amelia Jesse Johnson, Jesse Johnson Junr & John Johnson, who were present.

25/8/1780. Samuel Winston removed within the limits of this meeting with his family viz his wife, her children James and Ann Bates, their children John, Elizabeth & Issac Winston, and produced a certificate from Henrico meeting, and are received.

25/8/1780. Mildred Madox who for some time past hath resided within the limits of this meeting and hath been pretty diligent in the attendance thereof produced a few lines from Henrico meeting that she had made satisfaction for her misconduct in marrying contrary to our dicipline, received as a member.

25/8/1780. Joseph Watkins of Jenito hath been purchasing slaves and hireing men for military services. James Hunnicutt & Thomas Pleasants appointed to treat with him.

25/8/1780. Benjamin Johnson (son of Ashly) of Amelia Co requests a certificate to the meeting at Deep River, NC. Jesse Johnson Senr and John Johnson appointed to make the necessary enquiery.

25/8/1780. Christopher Johnson (son of James Johnson) hath removed within the limits of South River meeting. Jesse Johnson & John Johnson to prepare a certificate for him.

25/8/1780. Moorman Johnson hath married contrary to the dicipline and also to a woman too near of kin. Micajah Terrell & Pleasants Terrell appointed to treat with him.

25/8/1780. Thomas Moorman sent a paper condemning his outgoing in marriage. Micajah Terrell & Pleasant Terrell appointed to enquire if his life & conversation correspond therewith.

25/8/1780. Micajah Terrell is recommended to the Quarterly meeting as a minister.

25/8/1780. Thomas Terrell, Pleasants Terrell, Acchillis Douglass, Thomas Pleasants, John Harris & Jesse Johnson appointed to attend the Quarterly meeting.

14/10/1780. Representatives from the preparative meeting from Ceder Creek Nicholas Hutchins & Thomas Harris, from Caroline Thomas & Pleasants Terrell, from Camp Creek William Davis, who were present.

14/10/1780. The committee continued to visit John Wilson, Maddox Littlebury, Stanley & Waddy Stanly to inquire into their motives for requesting to be received members of our society. 7/12/1780 received as members.

11/11/1780. Representatives from the preparative meetings: for Caroline Thos & Pleasants Terrell, for Cedar Creek Nicholas Hutchins & Shadrack Stanly, for Jenito Benjamin Watkins, who were mostly present.

11/11/1780. Thomas Stanley (son of John Stanley) & Unity Crew published their intentions of marriage. John Harris & John Payne appointed to enquire into his clearness.

11/11/1780. David Brooks & Seth Goffin from Deep River, NC meeting attended our meeting.

11/11/1780. Pleasants Terrel & John Harris appointed to attend the Quarterly meeting.

7/12/1780. Representatives from the preparative meetings are: for Cedar Creek Shadrack Stanley & Moses Harris, for Caroline Pleasant Terrell.

7/12/1780. James Hunnicutt & Thos Pleasants are to prepare a paper of disunion against Joseph Watkins.

7/12/1780. James Hunnicutt to accompany the women friends on a visit to Ann Woodson.

7/12/1780. Micajah Crew & John Payne appointed to attend the marriage of Thomas Stanley & Unity Crew.

13/1/1781. Representatives from the preparative meetings are: for Cedar Creek Nicholas Hutchins & Moses Harris, for Caroline Thomas Terrell & Pleasants Terrell, for Camp Creek Acchillis Douglas, who were present.

13/1/1781. Thomas Douglas is in the practice of attending places appointed for military exercise & the intemperate use of spirituous liquors. Thomas Terrell & Accillas Douglas appointed to treat with him.

13/1/1781. Charles Linch Terrell of Caroline has agreed to take the place of a soldier in military capacity & also has been active in horse racing. Micajah Crew & John Payne appointed to use their endeavours to convince him of the evil of those practices.

13/1/1781. Mary Payne proposed in some short time a journey to Philadelphia and requests a certificate. John & Moses Harris appointed to draw & sign a certificate.

23/2/1781. Representatives appointed by the preparative meetings are: for Cedar Creek Nich Hutchings & Thomas Stanley, for Camp Creek Elijah Johnson & Accillis Douglas, for Caroline Thomas & Pleasant Terrell, for Amelia Ashley Johnson & Jesse Johnson Junr, for Jenito Thos Pleasants & Strangeman Hutchings, who were present.

23/2/1781. Certificates from White Oak Swamp meeting for Elizabeth Edmond & Susana Hutchins were received.

23/2/1781. Sarah & Priscilla Bunch of Camp Creek have lately had each a bastard child born. Elijah Johnson & George Bell appointed to assist in drawing testifications against them.

23/2/1781. John Cheadle of Jenito hath lately appeared in arms with the military. John Payne & Moses Harris appointed to treat with him.

23/2/1781. Zachariah Stanley hath again been in the practice of drinking spirituous liquors to excess & gaming. John Payne & Moses Harris appointed to treat with him.

23/2/1781. Jemima Zachary sent a condemnation of her conduct in marrying contrary to our dicipline, which is satisfactory. She is received a member. John & Moses Harris appointed to draw a certificate for her to the meeting at Deep River, NC.

23/2/1781. Catlet Jones of Camp Creek requests to be received a member of our society. Thomas Terrell & Pleasants Terrell appointed to inform themselves of his motive & of his life & conduct. 10/3/1781 received a member.

23/2/1781. Nicholas Crew some time past obtained a certificate to meeting at South River, but before it got to their hands he was guilty of some disorders. Micajah Terrell & Ashley Johnson appointed to visit him.

23/2/1781. James Johnson (son of John) requests a certificate to South River in clearness from marriage engagements. Ashley Johnson & John Johnson appointed to make the necessary enquiry.

23/2/1781. Accillias Douglas, Micajah Terrell, Thomas Pleasants, Micajah Crew, Strangeman Hutchins & Moses Harris appointed to attend Quarterly meeting.

10/3/1781. Representatives appointed by the preparative meeting: for Cedar Creek Shadrack Stanley & Thomas Harris, for Amelia John Johnson.

10/3/1781. Benjamin Watkins is added to the formerly appointed to treat with John Cheadle.

10/3/1781. James Johnson hath removed within the limits of South River meeting and requests our certificate for himself & family. John Johnson & Benjamin Watkins appointed to make needful inquiry.

10/3/1781. Strangeman Hutchins, Pleasant Terrell, & Thomas Terrell appointed to visit friends who still hold their fellow creatures in bondage.

14/4/1781. Representatives appointed by the preparative meetings: for Cedar Creek Nicholas Hutchins & Shadrack Stanley, for Camp Creek Elijah Johnson, for Caroline John Peatross & Jesse Hargrave.

14/4/1781. Elijah Johnson is added to the assistance of friends in the case of Zachariah Stanley.

14/4/1781. Robert Bell of Camp Creek requests our certificate to joine him to Deep River, NC meeting. Elijah Johnson, Acchillis Douglas & Byrom Ballard appointed to make the needful inquiry.

14/4/1781. Wm Davis and his family removed within the verge of South River meeting & requested our certificate. Elijah Johnson, Acchillis Douglas & Byrom Ballard appointed to make the needful inquirey.

12/5/1781. Representatives appointed by the preparative meetings: for Cedar Creek Micajah Crew & Moses Harris, for Caroline Micajah Terrell & Thomas Terrell, for Amelia Ashley Johnson & And Johnson.

12/5/1781. Micajah Davis requested a certificate for himself & family to join to South River meeting. Micajah Terrell & Thomas Terrell appointed to make the necessary enquirey.

12/5/1781. Davis Cobbs of Caroline hath married contrary to our dicipline. Pleasant & Thomas Terrell appointed to prepare a testimony of disunion against him.

12/5/1781. Micajah Terrell, James Hunnicutt, Micajah Crew & Thomas Terrell appointed to attend the Quarterly meeting.

9/6/1781. Representatives appointed by the preparative meetings: for Caroline Pleasant Terrell, for Cedar Creek Shadrack Stanley & Thomas Harris, for Camp Creek Byrom Ballard.

9/6/1781. Charles Linch Terrell hath again been acting disorderly. Thomas Terrell is added to the friends formerly appointed to treat with him.

9/6/1781. Byrom Ballard is added to the friends formerly appointed to treat with Zachariah Stanley.

9/6/1781. Elizabeth Easting sent a paper condemning her past misconduct in marrying contrary to our dicipline and requests to be taken under the care of friends. She is received a member.

9/6/1781. Thomas Coppage & Gideon Lay of Camp Creek request to be received as members of our religious society. Byrom Ballard & Acchilles Douglas appointed to inform themselves of their motives. 14/7/1781 Thomas Coppage received as a member. Gideon Lay's request discontinued.

9/6/1781. Richard Bloxom of Camp Creek has been acting in military service. Byrom Ballard & Acchillas Douglas appointed to visit him.

14/7/1781. Representatives appointed by the preparative meetings: for Cedar Creek Nicholas Hutchings & Micajah Crew, for Camp Creek Catlett Jones & Achilias Douglas, for Caroline Micajah Terrell & Thomas Terrell, who were present.

14/7/1781. Charles Lynch Terrell gave a paper condemning his misconduct.

14/7/1781. Thomas Stanley Junr requests to be received a member. Micajah Crew & Moses Harris appointed to visit him and inform themselves of his motives.

14/7/1781. David Terrell & his family request a certificate to join them to South River meeting. Accillis Douglas & Catlet Jones appointed to make necessary enquiry.

14/7/1781. Moorman Johnson (of South River of late) sent a condemnation of his misconduct in marrying contrary to our dicipline, which is satisfactory & received as member.

11/8/1781. Representatives appointed by the preparative meetings: for Cedar Creek John Wilson Maddox & James Crew, for Caroline Thomas Terrell & James Harris, for Amelia Jesse Johnson & John Johnson, for Camp Creek Catlet Jones & Elijah Johnson, who were present.

11/8/1781. A certificate for Elizabeth Pleasants from White Oak Swamp meeting was received.

11/8/1781. Accillis Douglas, Thomas Terrell, Jesse Johnson, Strangeman Hutchins & Moses Harris appointed to attend Quarterly meeting.

8/9/1781. Representatives appointed by the preparative meetings: for Cedar Creek Moses Harris & Thomas Stanley, for Camp Creek Zachariah Stanley, for Caroline Samuel Winston.

8/9/1781. Benjamin Johnson of South River & Mary Hargrave publish their intentions of marriage. He is requested to produce a certificate.

13/10/1781. Representatives appointed by the preparative meetings: for Cedar Creek Moses Harris & Micajah Crew, for Camp Creek Accillis Douglas, for Caroline Pleasant Terrell & Thos Terrell, for Amelia Jesse Johnson & John Johnson, who were present.

13/10/1781. Thomas Terrell & Pleasant Terrell appointed to prepare a testimony of disunion against Charles Linch Terrell.

13/10/1781. Richard Bloxom appeared and verbally condemned his past disorderly conduct, which appeared to general satisfaction. His case discontinued.

13/10/1781. Thomas & Pleasants Terrell appointed to attend the marriage of Benjamin Johnson & Mary Hargrave.

13/10/1781. The children of John Wilson Maddox & Mildred his wife are received members viz Thomas, William, Griffin & Wilson Maddox.

13/10/1781. Robert Bell of Camp Creek requests certificate to join him to Deep River, NC meeting. Accillis Douglas appointed to make the necessary enquiry.

10/11/1781. Representatives appointed by the preparative meetings: for Cedar Creek Nicholas Hutchins & Shadrack Stanley, for Caroline Samuel Winstone, for Jenito Thomas Pleasants & Strangman Hutchins, for Camp Creek George Bell & Richard Bloxom.

10/11/1781. John Cheadle hath late been in the practice of bearing arms in a military way and hireing a substitute contrary to our known rules. Therefore we disown him.

10/11/1781. Charles Linch Terrell (son of Micajah Terrell) late of Caroline Co hath been in the practice of sundry disorders such as frequenting places of diversion, horse racing, wagering & offering to act in the military service. We certify that we disown him. John Payne clerk.

10/11/1781. Micajah Terrell requests our certificate for himself & family to join them to South River meeting. James Harris & Samuel Winston appointed to make necessary inquiry.

10/11/1781. Richard Bloxom requests our certificate for himself & family to join them to South River meeting. Elijah Johnson & George Bell appointed to make the necessary enquiry. 8/6/1782 he declined moving, returned his certificate.

10/11/1781. Pleasant Terrell, John Harris, Micajah Crew & James Hunnicutt appointed to attend the Quarterly meeting.

8/12/1781. Representatives appointed by the preparative meetings: for Cedar Creek John & Moses Harris.

8/12/1781. Nicholas Stone hath married contrary to our dicipline. Micajah Crew & Armsbee Crew appointed to visit him. 12/1/1782 he shall be discontinued from being a member.

12/1/1782. The representatives appointed by the preparative meetings: for Cedar Creek Shadrack Stanley & Moses Harris, for Caroline Thomas Terrell, Pleasant Terrell & John Peatross.

12/1/1782. Moses Harris, James Hunnicutt & Micajah Crew appointed to assist the Yearly & Quarterly meetings in respecting the freedom of Negroes and in establishing schools.

22/2/1782. Representatives appointed by the preparative meetings: for Cedar Creek Shadrack Stanley & Moses Harris, for Caroline Thomas Terrell & Pleasant Terrell, for Jenito Strangman Hutchins & James Hunnicutt, for Camp Creek Byrom Ballard & Catlet Jones, for Amelia Jesse Johnson & Ashley Johnson, who were present.

22/2/1782. Micajah Crew, John Peatross & Byrom Ballard are added to the committee formerly appointed to Micajah Terrell, as his affairs remains unsettled.

22/2/1782. Ashley Johnson & Milley Johnson declare their intentions of marriage. He produced a certificate from South River.

22/2/1782. Elijah Johnson appointed overseer of Camp Creek preparative meeting.

22/2/1782. Moses Harris, Byrom Ballard, Pleasant Terrell, James Hunnicutt & Jesse Johnson appointed to attend Quarterly meeting.

9/3/1782. Representatives appointed by the preparative meetings: for Amelia Joseph Johnson, for Cedar Creek Micajah Crew & Littleberry Stanley, for Caroline Pleasant Terrell, for Camp Creek Zachariah Stanley.

9/3/1782. Ashley Johnson Senr & John Johnson appointed to attend the marriage of Ashley Johnson & Milley Johnson.

9/3/1782. The women produced a certificate for Mary Johnson to South River meeting.

9/3/1782. The women produced a minute of disunion against Judith Cheadle (daughter of Thomas Cheadle) of Caroline.

9/3/1782. Micajah Terrell of Camp Creek requests our certificate for himself & family to join them to South River meeting. Zachariah Stanley & Elijah Johnson appointed to make the necessary enquiry.

13/4/1782. Representatives appointed by the preparative meetings: for Cedar Creek Nicholas Hutchins & Moses Harris, for Camp Creek Catlet Jones & Richard Bloxom, for Caroline Thomas Terrell.

13/4/1782. Byrom Ballard & Accillis Douglas appointed to prepare a testification against Nicholas Crew.

13/4/1782. Charles Eastin of Camp Creek requests to be received a member. Byrom Ballard, Accillis Douglas & Catlet Jones appointed to visit him.

11/5/1782. Representatives appointed by the preparative meetings: for Cedar Creek Micajah Crew & John Harris, for Jenito James Hunicutt, for Camp Creek Armsbee Crew & Catlet Jones, who were mostly present.

11/5/1782. Mordecai Payne removed within the virge of Deep River, NC meeting. John Harris & Moses Harris appointed to enquire into his conduct & affairs, & prepare certificate.

11/5/1782. Thomas & Pleasant Terrell appointed to assist the women on a visit to Dorcus Bennet.

11/5/1782. Thomas Terrell, John Peatruss, Catlet Jones, John Harris & Moses Harris appointed to attend the Quarterly meeting.

8/6/1782. Representatives appointed by the preparative meetings: for Cedar Creek John Harris & Moses Harris, for Camp Creek Byram Ballard & Zachariah Stanley, for Amelia John Johnson & Jesse Johnson, for Jenito Strangman Hutchins & Peter Fitz Garrald, for Caroline Thomas Terrell & Pleasant Terrell, who were present.

13/7/1782. Representatives appointed by the preparative meetings: for Cedar Creek Shadrack Stanley & Moses Harris, for Caroline Thomas Terrell & Pleasant Terrell, for Camp Creek Accillis Douglas & Jonathan Terrell, for Jenito Strangman Hutchins & James Hunnicutt.

13/7/1782. Thomas Terrell, James Hunnicutt & Thomas Pleasants added to the committee appointed to prepare a certificate for Micajah Terrell & his family, as certificate produced appears not to be to general satisfaction.

13/7/1782. Strangman Hutchins & James Hunnicutt appointed to join the Quarterly meeting committee on the freedom of Negroes & establishment of schools.

14/7/1782. Certificate provided for Micajah Terrell and his wife & children namely Agatha, Sarah, Ann, Micajah & Mary.

23/8/1782. Representatives appointed by the preparative meetings: for Cedar Creek Moses Harris & Joshua Stanly, for Jenito Strangman Hutchins & James Hunicutt, for Amelia John Johnson & Jesse Johnson, for Caroline Thomas Terrell & John Peatruss, for Camp Creek Catlet Jones, Elijah Johnson & Richard Bloxom.

23/8/1782. James Hunnicutt, Strangman Hutchins & John Payne appointed to assist the women in a visit to Mary Pleasants who has married contrary to our dicipline.

23/8/1782. James Hunnicutt, Moses Harris, Thomas Terrell, Richard Bloxom, Jesse Johnson & Accillis Douglas appointed to attend the Quarterly meeting.

14/9/1782. Representatives appointed by the preparative meetings: for Cedar Creek John Harris & Nicholas Hutchins, for Caroline Thomas Terrell, for Jenito Strangman Hutchins & Thomas Pleasants, who were present.

12/10/1782. Representatives appointed by the preparative meetings: for Cedar Creek Shadrack Stanley & Waddey Stanley, for Camp Creek Byrom Ballard & Jonathan Terrell, for Caroline Pleasant Terrell, for Jenito Strangman Hutchins & James Hunnicutt.

12/10/1782. Charity Cook, Mary Pearson, Henry Steadham & James Brooks from Bush River, SC attended this meeting on a religious visit.

12/10/1782. Thos Douglas of Camp Creek has again been in the practice of drinking spirituous liquors to excess. 14/12/1782 Catlet Jones & Byrom Ballard appointed to revisit him.

12/10/1782. John Moore & his family stand in need of friends assistance. Jonathan Terrell, Pleasant Terrell & James Hunnicutt to raise corn, port, salt, seed & cotton for that purpose.

12/10/1782. At the request of John Peatruss his children are received as members.

9/11/1782. Representatives appointed by the preparative meetings: for Cedar Creek John Harris, for Jeneto Strangman Hutchins & James Hunnicutt.

9/11/1782. James Hunnicutt & Jesse Johnson are recommended to the consideration of the Quarterly meeting as suitable persons to be appointed elders.

9/11/1782. Thomas Terrell, James Hunnicutt, John Payne & Moses Harris appointed to attend Quarterly meeting.

14/12/1782. Representatives appointed by the preparative meetings: for Cedar Creek Moses Harris & Shadrack Stanly, for Caroline Thomas Terrell, for Camp Creek Accillis Douglas & Catlet Jones, for Jenito James Hunnicutt.

14/12/1782. Accillis Douglas requests our certificate for himself & family to join them to South River. Catlet Jones & Jonathan Terrell appointed to make the necessary enquiry.

14/12/1782. David Brooks and his companion Joel Saunders attended this meeting on a religious visit & produced certificate from Deep River, NC.

11/1/1783. Representatives from Cedar Creek preparative meeting are John Harris & Moses Harris.

21/2/1783. Representatives appointed by the preparative meetings: for Cedar Creek Micajah Crew & Thomas Stanley, for Jenito Thomas Pleasants & James Hunnicutt, for Camp Creek Byrom Ballard & Elijah Johnson, for Caroline Thomas Terrell & Jonathan Terrell.

21/2/1782. John Payne requests our certificate for himself & family to join friends in Philadelphia. Micajah Crew & Moses Harris appointed to make necessary inquiry.

21/2/1782. John Hutchins requests our certificate for himself & family to join them to Deep River, NC meeting. Thomas Pleasants & James Hunnicutt appointed to make necessary enquiry.

21/2/1782. Jonathan Hutchins of Jenito has married contrary to our dicipline. Thomas Pleasants & James Hunnicutt appointed to visit him.

21/2/1782. Thomas Terrell, Byrom Ballard, John Harris & Thomas Pleasants appointed to attend Quarterly meeting.

8/3/1783. Representatives appointed by the preparative meetings: for Cedar Creek Moses Harris & Shadrack Stanley, for Caroline Pleasant Terrell, who were present.

12/4/1783. James Hunnicutt appointed clerk, as John Payne is about to remove without the verge of this meeting.

12/4/1783. Chiles Terrell of Camp Creek hath joined himself in marriage contrary to the rules of friends to a woman of a different persuasion from us. We do therefore disown him.

12/4/1783. James Crew is appointed to receive the estate of Elizabeth Elmore deceased from John Payne, executor. Micajah Crew, James Harris & James Hunnicutt are appointed to assist him in dividing the said Elizabeth Elmore's cloths & give their advice in settling all other matters.

12/4/1783. A certificate for Mary Logan & her children James & Sarah from Philadelphia meeting being produced was received.

12/4/1783. The following friends are appointed to collect the sufferings of friends in their respective neighbourhoods, to wit for Caroline Thos and Pleasant Terrell, for Jenito John Barnett & James Hunnicutt, for Cedar Creek Moses Harris & Micajah Crew, for Camp Creek Catlet Jones.

10/5/1783. Representatives appointed by the preparative meetings: for Cedar Creek Moses Harris & Shadrack Stanley, for Caroline Thomas Terrell & Pleasant Terrell, for Camp Creek Zachariah Stanley.

10/5/1783. Jonathan Hutchins of Jenito hath joined himself in marriage to a woman of a different persuation from us. Therefore we disown him.

10/5/1783. Nicholas Hutchins and his family have removed to Deep River, NC meeting. Micajah Crew & John Wilson Maddox appointed to make the necessary enquiry and produce a certificate.

10/5/1783. Elizabeth Elmore an elder deceased the 11th da, 11th mo, 1782, but no memorial concerning her or other deceased friend.

10/5/1783. Pleasant Terrell, Thomas Terrell, John Harris & James Hunnicutt appointed to attend Quarterly meeting.

14/6/1783. Representatives appointed by the preparative meetings: for Cedar Creek John Wilson Maddox & Thomas Stanley, for Caroline Jonathan Terrell & Thomas Terrell, for Camp Creek Richard Bloxom, who were present.

14/6/1783. Samuel Parsons produced a certificate from Whiteoak Swamp meeting for himself, his wife & their children viz John Scott Pleasants, Elizabeth Tucker Pleasants, Thomas Exum Pleasants & Sarah Pleasants Parsons which is received.

14/6/1783. Samuel Parsons, Micajah Crew & James Hunnicutt appointed to examine & correct the minutes of this meeting.

12/7/1783. Representatives appointed by the preparative meetings: for Cedar Creek Joshua Stanley & Shadrack Stanley, for Caroline Thomas Terrell & Pleasant Terrell, for Camp Creek Richard Bloxom, for Genito James Hunnicutt, who were present.

12/7/1783. Byrom Ballard informed this meeting of his intention to go into NC to visit his relations.

22/8/1783. Representatives appointed by the preparative meetings: for Cedar Creek Micajah Crew & John Harris, for Amelia Joseph Johnson & Jesse Johnson Junr, for Caroline Thos Terrell & Pleasant Terrell, for Camp Creek Catlet Jones & Elijah Johnson, for Jenito Thomas Pleasants & James Hunnicutt, who were present except Pleasant Terrell who was prevented by sickness.

22/8/1783. Mary Bunch consented at her daughters marrying contrary to our dicipline. Richard Bloxom & Catlet Jones appointed to join the women in a visit to her. 11/10/1783 found Mary Bunch disposed to condemn her conduct, her case is discontinued.

22/8/1783. John Johnson Junr of Amelia hath removed with his family to Deep River, NC without a certificate. Thomas Pleasants, Jesse Johnson & James Hunnicutt appointed to make the necessary inquiry, and prepare one for them.

22/8/1783. Benjamin Johnson (son of Jesse) and Mary Johnson (daughter of Ashley) have joined themselves to each other by marriage contrary to our dicipline. John Harris & James Hunnicutt appointed to prepare a minute of disunion against them, and to inform themselves whether the parents were clear of consenting to their said marriage.

22/8/1783. George Bunch has given himself a loose to several dishonourable practices, such as fighting, swaring & other lewd disorders. Catlet Jones & George Bell appointed to treat with him.

22/8/1783. Thomas Terrell, Micajah Crew, John Harris & Richard Bloxom appointed to attend the Quarterly meeting.

140

13/9/1783. Representatives appointed by the preparative meetings: for Cedar Creek Thomas Harris & Joshua Stanley, for Caroline Pleasant Terrell, who were present.

11/10/1783. Representatives appointed by the preparative meetings: for Camp Creek Catlet Jones & Richard Bloxom, for Genito John Barnett, who were present.

8/11/1783. Representatives appointed by the preparative meetings: for Caroline Thomas Terrell & Pleasant Terrell, for Cedar Creek Moses Harris & Thomas Stanley, for Jeneto Strangeman Hutchings & Thos Pleasants, who were present except Thos Stanley.

8/11/1783. Thomas Pleasants, Thomas Terrell, James Harris, Samuel Parsons & James Hunnicutt are appointed overseers.

8/11/1783. Shadrack Stanley requests a certificate for him & his family to join them to meeting at Newgarden, NC. James Crew & Jno Wilson Maddox appointed to make needful enquiry and produce one.

8/11/1783. Thomas Terrell, John Harris, Micajah Crew & James Hunnicutt appointed to attend Quarterly meeting.

13/12/1783. Representatives appointed by the preparative meetings: for Cedar Creek Micajah Crew & John Harris, for Caroline Pleasant Terrell & Jonathan Terrell, for Jenito Strangman Hutchins & Samuel Parsons, who were present.

13/12/1783. The following friends are appointed (instead of the former committee) to revisit all those who continue to hold slaves: Pleasants Terrell, Clark T. Moorman, Samuel Parsons & Strangman Hutchins.

13/12/1783. In the case of Benjamin & Mary Johnson, it appears that Ashley & Jesse Johnson & wives consented to their childrens disorderly marriage. The clerk is directed to furnish the parties a copy of the minute of disunion.

13/12/1783. Christopher Johnson of South River & Sarah Hargrave published their intentions of marriage. Christopher is requested to produce a certificate of clearness.

10/1/1784. Moses Harris is appointed to act as clerk this time.

10/1/1784. Representatives appointed by the preparative meetings: for Cedar Creek Shadrack Stanley & James Crew, for Caroline Thomas Terrell & Pleasant Terrell.

10/1/1784. Obadiah Harris attended this meeting and produced a minute of concurrence from Deep River, NC meeting.

10/1/1784. Thomas Terrell & Pleasant Terrell appointed to attend the marriage of Christopher Johnson & Sarah Hargrave.

28/2/1784. Representatives appointed by the preparative meetings: for Cedar Creek Thomas Stanley & Moses Harris, for Camp Creek Catlet Jones & Elijah Johnson, for Caroline Thos Terrell & Pleasant Terrell, for Amelia Ashley Johnson & Thomas Johnson, who were present except Ashley Johnson.

28/2/1784. Richard Bloxom of Camp Creek has removed within the limits of South River meeting and requests a certificate for himself & family. Catlet Jones & Elijah Johnson appointed to make the necessary enquiry and prepare certificate.

28/2/1784. Zachariah Stanley requests a certificate for his three children Elizabeth, John & Bulah to join them to Bradford meeting in Chester Co, PA. The above named friends are also requested to make the necessary enquiry and prepare certificate.

28/2/1784. Elijah Johnson, Clark T. Moorman, Pleasant Terrell, James Hunnicutt and Micajah Crew appointed to attend Quarterly meeting.

13/3/1784. Representatives appointed by the preparative meetings: for Cedar Creek John Wilson Maddox & Joshua Stanley, for Camp Creek Catlet Jones.

13/3/1784. Moses Harris, Micajah Crew & John Harris appointed as overseers.

13/3/1784. Shadrack Stanley produced an account of ... which he expended in endeavouring to prove Stanley Harris' will.

13/3/1784. James Crew has paid the sum of 7 pounds 10 shillings into the hands of Elijah Johnson.

13/3/1784. Pleasant Terrell & James Crew laid before the meeting that they had a prospect of traveling into NC on their lawfull business. No objection appeared.

14/3/1784. Shadrack Stanley cannot have a certificate until he condemns some reflections which he has oust on this meeting. Pleasant Terrell, Clark Terrell Moorman & James Hunnicutt appointed to treat with him.

10/4/1784. Representatives appointed by the preparative meeting: for Cedar Creek Thos Stanley & Moses Harris, for Camp Creek Catlet Jones, for Jenito

Strangman Hutchins & Saml Parsons, who were present except Thos Stanley, Strangman Hutchins & Saml Parsons.

8/5/1784. Representatives appointed by the preparative meeting: for Caroline Thomas Terrell & Clark T. Moorman, for Cedar Creek Moses Harris & John Harris, for Jenito Strangman Hutchins & John Barnett, who were present.

8/5/1784. A minute of disunion against Huldah Sanley was produced by the women and approved.

8/5/1784. Eleanor Ballard was recommended by the select meeting as a minister, who was approved & submitted to the Quarterly meeting.

8/5/1784. James Hunnicutt & Micajah Crew appointed to attend Quarterly meeting.

12/6/1784. Representatives appointed by the preparative meetings: for Camp Creek Elijah Johnson & Catlet Jones, for Cedar Creek John W. Maddox & Thomas Harris, for Caroline Jonathan Terrell & Pleasant Terrell, for Jenito Strangman Hutchens & Saml Parsons, who were present.

12/6/1784. Micajah Crew appointed to assist the committee appointed to treat with Shadrack Stanley. A certificate to be prepared for his wife & children.

12/6/1784. Zachariah Stanley having placed his children at different meetings, returned their certificate & requests one for his son John to Bradford meeting, Chester Co, PA. Catlet Jones & Elijah Johnson appointed to prepare one.

12/6/1784. Byrom Ballard of Camp Creek has removed with his family within the limits of South River, Campbell Co, meeting and requests certificate. Catlet Jones & Elijah Johnson appointed to make necessary enquiry, and prepare one.

10/7/1784. Representatives appointed by the preparative meetings: for Camp Creek Zachariah Stanley & Catlet Jones, for Caroline Thomas Terrell & Pleasants Terrell, for Cedar Creek John Harris & Micajah Crew, for Jenito Peter Fitz Garrald & Samuel Parsons, who were present.

10/7/1784. Jeremiah Harris hath sold a Negro. Pleasant Terrell, Samuel Parsons & James Hunnicutt appointed to treat with him.

10/7/1784. Thomas Hutchins hath sold a Negro woman and child after having manumitted them. Catlet Jones & Micajah Crew appointed to treat with him.

10/7/1784. Benjamin & Mary Johnson sent written condemnations of their conduct in marrying contrary to our dicipline accompanied with a recommendation from friends at Deep Creek, NC which being to satisfaction, they are reinstated in the society. John & Moses Harris appointed to draw a certificate directed to Deep River, NC meeting.

10/7/1784. Zachariah Stanley informed this meeting that he had it in view to travel into NC on his lawfull business, and no objection appearing.

28/8/1784. Representatives appointed by the preparative meetings: for Caroline John Peatruss & Thos Terrell, for Amelia William & Jesse Johnson, for Cedar Creek John Wilson Maddox & John Harris, for Camp Creek Catlet Jones & Elijah Johnson, for Jenito Strangman Hutchins & Samuel Parsons, who were present except Thos Terrell who was prevented by sickness.

28/8/1784. Our esteemed friends Aron Lancaster from New York & Thomas Massey from PA attended this meeting on a religious visit, and produced certificates.

28/8/1784. Catlet Jones & Zachariah Stanley informed this meeting that they had a desire to attend the yearly meeting in Philadelphia, no objection appearing.

28/8/1784. Charles Bunch of Camp Creek is in the practice of gaming and neglects the attendance of our religious meetings. Zachariah Stanley & Elijah Johnson appointed to treat with him.

28/8/1784. Pleasant Terrell, John Harris, James Hunnicutt, Catlet Jones, Jesse Johnson & Moses Harris appointed to attend the Quarterly meeting.

11/9/1784. Representatives appointed by the preparative meetings: for Cedar Creek Micajah Crew & Moses Harris, for Caroline Jonathan Terrell who were present except Jonathan Terrell.

11/9/1784. John Harris, Micajah Crew, Samuel Parsons, Pleasant Terrell, Moses Harris & James Crew to have the care & management of repairing this meeting house and providing a stove agreeable to the will of Elizabeth Elmore deceased.

9/10/1784. Representatives appointed by the preparative meetings: for Caroline Pleasant Terrell, for Cedar Creek Moses Harris & John W. Maddox, who were present except Moses Harris.

9/10/1784. Pleasants Terrell & Samuel Parsons appointed to prepare a minute of disunion against Jeremiah Harris.

9/10/1784. Maddox Stanley of Camp Creek hath married contrary to our dicipline. John Harris & Thomas Stanley appointed to treat with him, and produce a paper of disunion against him.

9/10/1784. Nathaniel Winston & Samuel his son of Caroline have been concerned in selling a Negro. Pleasant Terrell & James Hunnicutt appointed to treat with them. Also Nathaniel Winston is slack in discharging a debt due to Benjamin Russell.

13/11/1784. Moses Harris appointed to act as clerk this time.

13/11/1784. Representatives appointed by the preparative meetings: for Caroline Thomas Terrell & Pleasant Terrell, for Camp Creek Zachariah Stanley, for Amelia Jesse Johnson, for Cedar Creek John Harris & John Wilson Maddox, who were present except Thomas Terrell who was prevented by indisposition.

13/11/1784. Jacob Cheadle of Caroline hath married a woman nearer of kin than is allowable by our dicipline by a hireling priest. Pleasant Terrell appointed to prepare a minute of disunion against him.

13/11/1784. John Harris & Samuel Harris appointed to attend the Quarterly meeting.

13/11/1784. Pleasant Terrell informs this meeting that he intended to travel into the upper parts of NC to visit his relations, this meeting concurs.

11/12/1784. Representatives appointed by the preparative meetings: for Cedar Creek Moses Harris & Thomas Harris, for Caroline Jonathan Terrell & Thomas Terrell, who were present.

11/12/1784. As there are several of the preparative meetings that have sent no account, John Harris & Micajah Crew appointed to visit the several preparative meetings and endeavour to stir them to more deligence in future.

11/12/1784. Elizabeth Walker hath requested to be received as a member of our society. Thomas Terrell, Pleasant Terrell & Micajah Crew appointed to join the women friends in a visit to her.

11/12/1784. Jeremiah Harris hath sold a slave which we believe to be iniquitous practice & contrary to our dicipline. This is to certify that we disown him. James Hunnicutt clerk.

11/12/1784. Pleasant Terrell & Thomas Terrell are appointed to visit friends who still hold slaves.

145

8/1/1785. Representatives appointed by the preparative meetings: for Camp Creek Catlett Jones & Robert Bell, for Cedar Creek John Harris & Richard Harris, who were present.

26/2/1785. Representatives appointed by the preparative meetings: for Cedarcreek Thomas Stanley & John Harris, for Genito Samuel Parsons, for Caroline Clark Terrell Moorman & Thomas Terrell, for Amelia William Johnson & Jesse Johnson, for Campcreek Elijah Johnson & Thomas Coppedge, who were present.

26/2/1785. Catlet Jones & Thomas Pleasants appointed to join the former committee to treat with Elizabeth Walker.

26/2/1785. Elisha Johnson & Jane Johnson published their intentions of marriage. He produced a certificate from Deep River, NC meeting of his right of membership & clearness from marriage engagements.

26/2/1785. Samuel Winston wrote signifying he was ready to pay part of his debt to Benjamin Russell. James Hunnicutt is requested to receive & convey it to Benjamin Russell. 9/4/1785 Samuel Winston discharged his debt to Benjamin Russell.

26/2/1785. Samuel & Joseph Johnson removed within the virge of South River meeting and request our certificate. Jesse & William Johnson appointed to make the necessary enquiry & prepare one.

26/2/1785. Charles Eastin requests a certificate to South River meeting. Catlet Jones is appointed to make the necessary enquiry & prepare one.

26/2/1785. Thomas Pleasants, Pleasant Terrell, John Harris, Catlet Jones & Jesse Johnson appointed to attend the Quarterly meeting.

12/3/1785. Representatives appointed by the preparative meetings: for Cedar Creek Moses Harris & Micajah Crew, for Camp Creek Arthanatious Barnett, for Caroline Thomas Terrell & Pleasant Terrell, who were present except Arthanatious Barnett & Pleasant Terrell.

12/3/1785. Thomas Copage sent satisfactory reason for not attending last meeting.

12/3/1785. Jesse Johnson Senr & William Johnson appointed to attend the marriage of Elisha Johnson & Jane Johnson.

12/3/1785. Zachariah Stanley of Camp Creek is in the practice of drinking to excess and is concerned in gaming. John Harris & Micajah Crew appointed to treat with him.

9/4/1785. Representatives appointed by the preparative meetings: for Caroline Pleasant Terrell, for Cedar Creek Moses Harris & Thomas Harris, for Camp Creek Catlet Jones, for Jenito Saml Parsons, who were present.

9/4/1785. Jonathan Terrell appointed to assist the former committee on the case of Thomas Hutchins.

14/5/1785. Representatives appointed by the preparative meetings: for Caroline Pleasant Terrell & Jonathan Terrell, for Cedar Creek Micajah Crew & Thomas Stanley, for Camp Creek Catlet Jones & Armsbee Crew, for Jenito Samuel Parsons, who were present except Samuel Parsons.

14/5/1785. Pleasant Cobbs & Amy Terrell declared their intention of marriage. Clark Terrell Moorman & Jonathan Terrell appointed to inquire into his clearness.

14/5/1785. Peter Fitz Garrald of Genito is in the practice of drinking spirituous liquors to excess. Catlett Jones & Armsbee Crew appointed to treat with him.

14/5/1785. Clark T. Moorman, Catlet Jones, Thomas Harris, Pleasant Terrell & Moses Harris appointed to attend the Quarterly meeting.

11/6/1785. Representatives appointed by the preparative meetings: for Caroline Jonathan Terrell & Clark T. Moorman, for Cedar Creek Thomas Harris & John W. Maddox.

11/6/1785. Jonathan Terrell & Clark T. Moorman appointed to attend the marriage of Pleasant Cobbs & Amy Terrell.

9/7/1785. Representatives appointed by the preparative meetings: for Caroline Thomas Terrell & Pleasant Terrell, for Camp Creek Catlet Jones, for Jenito Strangman Hutchins, who were present.

9/7/1785. Elizabeth Walker hath not arrived to a state of experience sufficient to qualify her for a usefull member of our society. Her request is discontinued.

27/8/1785. Representatives appointed by the preparative meetings: for Caroline Thomas Terrell & Jonathan Terrell, for Cedar Creek Thomas Stanley & Thomas Harris, for Camp Creek Elijah Johnson, for Amelia William Johnson & Jesse Johnson, for Jenito Strangman Hutchins & Thomas Pleasants, who were present.

27/8/1785. James Hunnicutt appointed to assist the former committee on assisting Thomas Hutchins in procureing the freedom of the slaves which he sold.

27/8/1785. Catlet Jones informed this meeting of his intention to attend the ensuing yearly meeting at Philadelphia, no objection appearing.

27/8/1785. John Scott Pleasants has removed and settled within the limits of Fairfax, Loudon Co without a certificate. Thomas Pleasants & James Hunnicutt appointed to prepare one.

27/8/1785. Moses Harris hath married contrary to our dicipline. Samuel Parsons & James Hunnicutt appointed to treat with him & prepare a minute of disunion against him.

27/8/1785. Robert Bell produced a certificate from Deep River, NC, received a member.

27/8/1785. John Harris, Thomas Terrell, Samuel Parsons, Jesse Johnson & Catlet Jones appointed to attend Quarterly meeting.

10/9/1785. Representatives appointed by the preparative meetings: for Caroline Thomas Terrell, for Cedar Creek Micajah Crew & Thos Harris, for Jenito Samuel Parsons & James Harris, who were present.

10/9/1785. Micajah Crew, Samuel Parsons & Thomas Harris Junr appointed to visit Orrange meeting having for some time been without overseers.

8/10/1785. Representatives appointed by the preparative meetings: for Jenito Samuel Parsons, for Caroline Clark T. Moorman & Pleasant Terrell, for Amelia Ashley Johnson & Benjamin Johnson, for Cedar Creek John Wilson Maddox & Joshua Stanley, for Camp Creek Elijah Johnson, who were present except Clark T. Moorman.

8/10/1785. Thomas Terrell & Thomas Harris Junr appointed to unit with the Yearly & Quarterly meetings on a visit to all those members that still own slaves.

8/10/1785. Moses Harris hath joined in marriage with a woman not of our society, therefore we disown him. James Hunnicutt clerk.

8/10/1785. Strangman Hutchins requests a certificate for himself and his wife & granddaughter Elizabeth Hutchins (daughter of Thomas) also Thos Hutchins for his wife and children and Benjamin Hutchins for himself & family to join them to Deep River, NC meeting. Micajah Crew & Samuel Parsons appointed to make the needful enquirey and produce certificates.

12/11/1785. Representatives appointed by the preparative meetings: for Cedar Creek Thomas Stanley & Thomas Harris, for Caroline Thomas Terrell & Clark T. Moorman, who were present except Thos Terrell.

12/11/1785. Pleasants Terrell, John Harris, Thomas Harris & Samuel Parsons appointed to attend Quarterly meeting.

10/12/1785. Representatives appointed by the preparative meetings: for Caroline Thomas Terrell & Pleasant Terrell, for Cedar Creek Micajah Crew & Thomas Stanley, for Camp Creek Elijah Johnson, for Jenito James Hunnicutt, who were present.

10/12/1785. Ann Moore of Camp Creek stands in need of some assistance. The preparative meetings are directed to raise 4 pounds 10 shillings.

10/12/1785. James Candler & Agness Johnson published their intentions of marriage. He is desired to produced a certificate of clearness.

10/12/1785. Ashley Johnson sent a written condemnation of his misconduct for which he was disowned accompanied by a recommendation from meeting at Muddy Creek, Surry Co, NC, which were satisfactory. He is therefore reinstated in membership. Micajah Crew & James Hunnicutt appointed to prepare a certificate for him to Deep River, NC meeting.

14/1/1786. Representatives appointed by the preparative meetings: for Cedar Creek John Wilson Maddox & Joshua Stanley, for Camp Creek Catlet Jones, for Caroline Pleasant Terrell, for Jenito Thomas Pleasants & Samuel Parsons, who were present.

14/1/1786. James Candler produced a certificate from South River meeting. Catlet Jones appointed to attend the marriage of James Candler & Agness Johnson.

25/2/1786. Representatives appointed by the preparative meetings: for Cedar Creek Thomas Harris & Waddey Stanley, for Jenito Saml Parsons, for Caroline Thomas Terrill, Clark T. Moorman & Pleasant Terrell, for Amelia Jesse Johnson Senr & Benjamin Johnson, for Camp Creek Catlet Jones, George Bell Senr & Arthanatious Barnett, who were present except for Geo Bell & Arthas Barnett.

25/2/1786. Clark T. Moorman & Thomas Terrell added to the assistance of the former committee appointed to treat with Nathl & Samuel Winston.

25/2/1786. Catlet Jones appointed overseer for Orrange meeting.

25/2/1786. James Crew hath disposed of a slave and also alloweth the practice of gaming in his house. Pleasant Terrell, Samuel Parsons & Thomas Terrell appointed to treat with him.

25/2/1786. At the request of James Hunnicutt he is released as clerk, Micajah Crew appointed in his stead.

25/2/1786. Catlet Jones, Edith Harris & Rachel Moorman recommended as elders.

25/2/1786. Pleasant Terrell, John Harris, Thos Harris Junr & Catlet Jones appointed to attend Quarterly meeting.

11/3/1786. Representatives appointed by the preparative meetings: for Cedar Creek Thomas Stanley & Thomas Harris Junr, for Caroline Clark T. Moorman & Thomas Terrell, for Jenito James Hunnicutt & Samuel Parsons, who were present.

11/3/1786. Littlebury Crew is about to remove within the virge of Wrights Borough, GA and requests our certificate. John Harris, Thomas Harris, Samuel Parsons, James Hunnicutt, Thomas Stanley & Micajah Crew appointed to make necessary inquiry and prepare one.

11/3/1786. Benjamin Watkins Junr of Jenito hath married out of the unity of friends and therefore disown him.

8/4/1786. Representatives appointed by the preparative meetings: for Cedar Creek Thomas Stanley & Jno W. Maddox, for Caroline Thomas Terrell & Jonathan Terrell.

8/4/1786. A minute of disunion against Obedience Barnett was produced by the women which was approved & signed.

13/5/1786. Representatives appointed by the preparative meetings: for Cedar Creek John Harris & Thomas Stanley, for Jenito James Hunnicutt & Samuel Parsons, for Camp Creek Catlet Jones & Elijah Johnson, for Amelia Gerrard Johnson & Ashley Johnson, for Caroline Pleasant Terrell & Clark T. Moorman, who were present.

13/5/1786. Robert Bell of Camp Creek removed within the verge of Deep River, NC meeting and requests our certificate. Catlet Jones & Elijah Johnson appointed to make necessary enquiry and prepare one.

13/5/1786. 9 barrels of corn taken from Pleasant Terrell by the sheriff for military charges.

13/5/1786. Pleasant Terrell, Catlet Jones, John Harris, James Hunnicutt, Samuel Parsons and Thomas Harris Junr appointed to attend Quarterly meeting.

10/6/1786. Representatives appointed by the preparative meetings: for Cedar Creek Micajah Crew & John W. Maddox, for Jenito Samuel Parsons, for Caroline Clark T. Moorman & Jonathan Terrell.

10/6/1786. Thomas Terrell & Pleasant Terrell appointed to furnish Nathl & Samuel Winston a copy of the minute of disunion against them.

10/6/1786. John Barnett of Jenito hath married contrary to our dicipline. Samuel Parsons is desired to take an opertunity with him and prepare a minute of disunion against him.

10/6/1786. Samuel Parsons & Micajah Crew appointed to settle with James Crew respecting Elizabeth Elmore's estate, pay him for his trouble therein, take the papers into their hands and produce a proper state of all matters.

8/7/1786. Representatives appointed by the preparative meetings: for Cedarcreek Thomas Harris & Thomas Stanley, for Jenito Samuel Parsons, for Caroline Thomas Terrell & Pleasant Terrell, for Campcreek Catlet Jones, who were present.

8/7/1786. A paper of testification against James Crew was approved. Micajah Crew appointed to read it.

21/8/1786. Representatives appointed by the preparative meetings: for Jenito Thomas Pleasants, for Caroline Clark T. Moorman & John Peatross, for Cedar Creek Thomas Stanley & Micajah Crew, for Camp Creek Catlet Jones, Elijah Johnson & Thomas Coppage, for Amelia Jesse Johnson Senr, who were present.

21/8/1786. A certificate for Joseph Anthony was produced from South River meeting which is received.

21/8/1786. A certificate for Benjamin & Mary Johnson was produced from Deep River, NC meeting which was received.

21/8/1786. Catlet Jones, Clark T. Moorman, Samuel Parsons, Pleasant Terrell, Thomas Harris Junr & Jesse Johnson Senr appointed to attend Quarterly meeting.

9/9/1786. Representatives appointed by the preparative meetings: for Cedar Creek Thomas Stanley & John W. Maddox, for Caroline Pleasant Terrell & Jonathan Terrell, for Jenito Samuel Parsons, who were present except Samuel Parsons.

9/9/1786. A minute of disunion against Elizbeth Brooks was produced by the women which was approved.

9/9/1786. Mary Brooks of Jenito stands in need of assistance. The preparative meetings requested to the sum of 6 pounds 5 shillings for that purpose.

9/9/1786. Isaac Stanley of Jenito hath married his first cousin contrary to our dicipline. Thomas Stanley & John Harris appointed to speak with him & prepare a minute of disunion against him.

14/10/1786. Representatives appointed by the preparative meetings: for Cedar Creek Waddy Stanley & Thomas Harris, for Caroline Thomas Terrell, for Camp Creek Catlet Jones.

14/10/1786. Samuel Parsons appointed to keep a record of the births and deaths of the members.

11/11/1786. Representatives appointed by the preparative meetings: for Cedar Creek Thomas Stanley & Micajah Crew, for Jenito Samuel Parsons, for Caroline Thomas Terrell & Pleasant Terrell, for Amelia Garrard Johnson, for Camp Creek Elijah Johnson & Catlet Jones, who were present.

11/11/1786. Isaac Stanley had been guilty of defiling the young woman before he married her. A paper of disunion was produced and approved. Samuel Parsons appointed to read it.

11/11/1786. William Crew from Camp Creek requests to be received a member. Catlet Jones, Thomas Harris Junr & Micajah Crew appointed to visit him.

11/11/1786. Thomas Stanley Junr request our certificate to Wright Borough, GA meeting. John Harris & Thomas Stanley appointed to enquire into his affairs and prepare one.

11/11/1786. Thomas Terrell, Elijah Johnson, Pleasant Terrell, Thomas Harris, John Harris & Micajah Crew appointed to attend Quarterly meeting.

13/1/1787. Representatives appointed by the preparative meetings: for Cedarcreek Thomas Stanley & Micajah Crew, for Caroline Thomas Terrell & Jonathan Terrell, for Jenito Samuel Parsons, for Camp Creek Catlett Jones, who were present.

152

13/1/1787. Littlebury Stanley and Aggatha Stanley published their intention of marriage. John Harris & Micajah Crew appointed to enquire into his clearness.

13/1/1787. A minute of disunion against Ann Woodson was produced by the women which was approved.

13/1/1787. James Brook Pleasants from Jenito has been concerned in racing and that his general deportment has been inconsistent with our profession. He sent a writing acknowledging a sence of his misconduct and importing a wish to live a different life in future. For proof of his sincerity the matter is continued under the care of John Harris & Samuel Parsons.

13/1/1787. Thomas Harris Junr requests our certificate to White Oak Swamp, Henrico Co meeting of his right of membership and clearness from marriage engagements. John Harris & John W. Maddox appointed to make necessary enquirey and prepare one.

13/1/1787. Friends have endeavoured to convince Shadrack Stanley of his disorderly conduct but he still persists in a spirit of opposition, therefore we disown him.

24/2/1787. Representatives appointed by the preparative meetings: for Caroline Clark T. Moorman & Pleasant Terrell, for Cedar Creek Thomas Harris Junr & John W. Maddox, for Camp Creek Catlet Jones & Elijah Johnson, for Jenito Samuel Parsons & James Bates, for Amelia John Johnson Junr, who were present.

24/2/1787. John Harris & Micajah Crew appointed to attend the marriage of Littlebury Stanley & Aggatha Stanley.

24/2/1787. A paper of condemnation from Nancy Barksdale was handed in by the women which friends appear satisfied with, she is therefore received a member.

24/2/1787. Jesse Terrell requests a certificate to the meeting at White Oak Swamp, Henrico Co showing his clearness from marriage engagements. Clark T. Moorman & Jonathan Terrell appointed to make necessary enquiry & produce one.

24/2/1787. Clark T. Moorman, Catlet Jones, Samuel Parsons, Thomas Stanley & Pleasant Terrell appointed to attend Quarterly meeting.

11/3/1787. Representatives appointed by the preparative meetings: for Cedar Creek Thomas Stanley & Micajah Crew, for Caroline Clark T. Moorman & Pleasant Cobbs, who were present except Clark T. Moorman & Thomas Stanley.

11/3/1787. Friends appointed in the case of James B. Pleasants report he has been for some time past in MD.

14/4/1787. Representatives appointed by the preparative meetings: for Cedar Creek Thomas Stanley & Thomas Harris Senr, for Caroline Clark T. Moorman & Matthew P. Terrell, for Jenito Samuel Parsons, for Camp Creek Catlet Jones & Elijah Johnson, for Amelia Garrard Johnson, who were present except Thos Harris & Samuel Parsons.

14/4/1787. William Crew received as a member of our religious society.

14/4/1787. Zachariah Stanley has again been in the practice of drinking to excess and encouraging gaming, therefore a testification against him was read which was approved & signed. Elijah Johnson appointed to read.

14/4/1787. A paper of condemnation from Robert Douglas of Camp Creek was read, which being to pretty general satisfaction, received a member.

12/5/1787. Representatives appointed by the preparative meetings: for Cedar Creek Thomas Harris & Micajah Crew, for Caroline Pleasant Terrell & Thomas Terrell, for Jenito Samuel Parsons, for Camp Creek Catlet Jones, who were present.

12/5/1787. Thomas Terrell, Thomas Stanley, Samuel Parsons & Catlet Jones appointed to attend Quarterly meeting.

9/6/1787. Representatives appointed by the preparative meetings: for Cedar Creek Thomas Stanley & John W. Maddox, for Caroline Clark T. Moorman & Pleasant Cobbs, for Jenito Samuel Parsons, who were present.

9/6/1787. Jemima Winston hath in an unfair manner obtained her husbands last will out of the care of the person he had intrusted with it, and contrary to the repeated advice of friends refuses to suffer it to be proved according to law, by which means it is apprehended a number of Negroes who by the said will are left to be free after his widow's death. Thomas Harris Junr, Jonathan Terrell & Micajah Crew appointed to united with the women in a further visit to her.

14/7/1787. Representatives appointed by the preparative meetings: for Cedar Creek Thomas Harris Senr & Joshua Stanley, for Caroline Clark T. Moorman

& Pleasant Terrell, for Jenito Samuel Parsons & William Henry Pleasants, for Camp Creek Catlet Jones & George Bell, who were present.

14/7/1787. James Hunnicutt appointed to assist the friends appointed to treat with James B. Pleasants.

14/7/1787. John Scott Pleasants has lost or mislaid a certificate granted by this meeting some time past to join him to Fairfax meeting and requests another. Samuel Parsons & Micajah Crew appointed to prepare one.

14/7/1787. Richard Lewis of Caroline has neglected the attendance of our meetings for several years past. Pleasant & Thomas Terrill & Clark T. Moorman appointed to treat with him.

14/7/1787. Shadrack Stanley gave a letter of his intention of appealing from the judgment of this to the Quarterly meeting respecting his being disowned. James Hunnicutt, Thomas Terrell, Pleasant Terrell, Clark T. Moorman, Catlet Jones, Samuel Parsons & Thomas Stanley appointed to attend the meeting with a copy of all minutes relative to the matter.

25/8/1787. Representatives appointed by the preparative meetings: for Cedar Creek Thomas Stanley & Waddy Stanley, for Caroline Clark T. Moorman & Thomas Terrell, for Jenito Thomas Pleasants & James Hunnicutt, for Amelia William Johnson & Jesse Johnson, for Camp Creek Robert Douglass & William Crew, who were present except Jesse Johnson.

25/8/1787. A testimony of disunion against Mary Bunch (daughter of Samuel Bunch) was presented by the women, which was approved.

25/8/1787. The preparative meeting at Amelia requested assistance to settle a dispute between Ashley & William Johnson. Thomas Pleasants, Samuel Parsons, Micajah Crew & John Harris appointed to that service.

25/8/1787. Thomas Terrell, Thomas Pleasants, Pleasant Terrell, John Peatross, Samuel Parsons & Robert Douglass appointed to attend the Quarterly meeting.

25/8/1787. Elijah Johnson informed the meeting that he had it on his mind to attend the ensuing Quarterly meeting at Fairfax, no objection appeared.

8/9/1787. Representatives appointed by the preparative meetings: for Caroline Jonathan Terrell & Pleasant Terrell, for Cedar Creek Thomas Stanley & Waddy Stanley, for Jenito Samuel Parsons, for Camp Creek Elijah Johnson, who were present.

155

8/9/1787. A testification against Richard Lewis was produced & approved. Clark T. Moorman appointed to read it.

13/10/1787. Representatives appointed by the preparative meetings: for Caroline Clark T. Moorman & Pleasant Terrell, for Jenito Thomas Pleasants & James Hunnicutt, for Camp Creek Elijah Johnson & Catlet Jones, for Amelia Garrard Johnson.

13/10/1787. Sarah Stanley (wife of Zachariah) requests our certificate for herself and children viz Susanah, Abraham, Abigal & Zachariah. Elijah Johnson appointed to join the women in making the necessary enquiry and prepare one.

13/10/1787. A testification against Jemima Winston was produced and approved. Jonathan Terrell appointed to read it.

13/10/1787. Ann Moore will likely need farther assistance. The preparative meetings requested to raise 10 pounds.

10/11/1787. Representatives appointed by the preparative meetings: for Cedar Creek Thomas Stanley & Thos Harris Junr, for Jenito James Hunnicutt, for Caroline Thos Terrell & Jonathan Terrell, for Camp Creek Peter Fitz Garrald, who were present except Jonathan Terrell.

10/11/1787. Pleasant Terrell, Clark T. Moorman, Thomas Harris Junr & Micajah Crew appointed to attend Quarterly meeting.

10/11/1787. Armsbee Crew requests our certificate for himself his wife & daughters (Frances & Agness) to join them to Cane Creek, NC meeting. John Harris & Thomas Stanley appointed to enquire into his affairs.

8/12/1787. Representatives appointed by the preparative meetings: for Cedar Creek Thomas Stanley & Waddy Stanley, for Jenito James Hunnicutt, for Caroline Thos Terrell & Pleasant Terrell, who were present.

12/1/1788. Representatives appointed by the preparative meetings: for Cedar Creek Thos Stanley & Thos Harris Junr, for Caroline Thomas Terrell & Mathew P. Terrell, for Jenito James Hunnicutt & Samuel Parsons, for Camp Creek Catlet Jones & Elijah Johnson, who were present.

23/2/1788. Representatives appointed by the preparative meetings: for Jenito James Hunnicutt & Saml Parsons, for Cedar Creek Joshua Stanley & John W. Maddox, for Camp Creek Elijah Johnson & Robt Douglass, for Caroline Clark T. Moorman & Pleasant Terrell, who were present.

23/2/1788. A certificate for Agness Candler (formerly Johnson) to join her to South River, Campbell Co, meeting was handed in by the women & approved.

23/2/1788. Margery Bunch (daughter of James Bunch) hath married contrary to our dicipline. John Harris & Micajah Crew appointed to assist the women in preparing a minute of disunion against her.

23/2/1788. James Hunnicutt, Catlet Jones, Clark T. Moorman, Samuel Parsons & Thos Harris Junr appointed to visit the Amelia preparative meeting to stir them up to more deligence in sending accounts to the monthly meetings.

23/2/1788. Catlet Jones, Pleasant Terrell, James Hunnicutt, Thomas Harris Junr & Clark T. Moorman appointed to unite with the overseers & other concerned friends in a visit to the friends who hold slaves and are deficient in other branches of our testimony.

23/2/1788. Pleasant Terrell, Robert Douglas, Samuel Parsons & Thomas Stanley appointed to attend Quarterly meeting.

8/3/1788. Representatives appointed by the preparative meetings: for Cedar Creek Thomas Stanley & Thomas Harris Senr, for Jenito Joseph Anthony & Thomas S. Pleasants, for Caroline Jonathan Terrell & Matthew P. Terrell, for Amelia Garrard Johnson, who were present.

8/3/1788. Nicholus Johnson from South River and Martha Hargrave published their intentions of marriage.

8/3/1788. Ashley Johnson & Jesse Johnson Senr of Amelia preparative meeting requested to be released from acting as overseers of that meeting. John Johnson, Garrard Johnson & Benjamin Johnson Senr appointed to that station in their stead.

12/4/1788. Representatives appointed by the preparative meetings: for Cedar Creek Thos Harris Junr & Jno W. Maddox, for Caroline Thomas Terrell & John Peatross, for Jenito Benjamin Watkins & James Hunnicutt, for Camp Creek Catlet Jones & Elijah Johnson, for Amelia Ashley Johnson & John Johnson Senr, who were present except Benjamin Watkins & Elijah Johnson.

12/4/1788. Pleasant Terrell & Thomas Terrell appointed to attend the marriage of Nicholus Johnson & Martha Hargrave.

12/4/1788. Matthew P. Terrell & Salley Moorman published their intentions of marriage. Pleasant Terrell & John Peatross appointed to enquire into his clearness.

12/4/1788. Martha Winston (daughter of Nathl Winston deceased) hath married contrary to the dicipline of friends. Clark T. Moorman appointed to join the women on a visit to her and assist them to prepare a minute of disunion against her.

12/4/1788. Mary Logan & Caroline Matilda Bates of Jenito have for some time past totally neglected the attendance of our religious meetings and that their conduct in other respects is inconsistent with our profession. Micajah Crew appointed to join the women on a visit to them on the subject.

12/4/1788. James Bates of Jenito removed within the limites of Henrico meeting and requests our certificate. Thomas Pleasants & Samuel Parsons appointed to make necessary enquiry and prepare one.

12/4/1788. Micajah Crew requests to be released from acting as overseer and Thomas Stanley appointed to that station in his stead.

10/5/1788. Representatives appointed by the preparative meetings: for Caroline Clark T. Moorman & John Peatross, for Cedar Creek Thomas Harris Junr & Thomas Stanley, for Jenito James Hunnicutt & Thomas Pleasants, for Camp Creek Elijah Johnson, for Amelia John Johnson, who were present.

10/5/1788. Pleasant Terrell, Thos Harris Junr, John Harris & Micajah Crew appointed to attend the Quarterly meeting.

10/5/1788. John Peatross & Pleasant Terrell appointed to attend the marriage of Matthew P. Terrell & Salley Moorman.

10/5/1788. Joseph Anthony requests our certificate to join him to South River meeting. Thomas Pleasants & James Hunnicutt appointed to make necessary enquiry and prepare one.

14/6/1788. Representatives appointed by the preparative meetings: for Caroline Clark T. Moorman & Matthew P. Terrell, for Cedar Creek Thomas Harris Senr & Thomas Stanley, for Jenito James Hunnicutt & Samuel Parsons, for Camp Creek Peter Fitz Garrald & Catlet Jones, who were present.

14/6/1788. Certificates from Whiteoak Swamp meeting for Chlotilda Harris & Mary Terrell were produced and approved.

14/6/1788. A paper of disunion to be prepared against Mary Logan & Caroline Matilda Bates.

14/6/1788. Thos Terrell, Thomas Pleasants, Thomas Stanley, John Peatross & Micajah Crew appointed to assist the preparative meeting in revisiting such members that hold slaves.

12/7/1788. Representatives appointed by the preparative meetings: for Cedar Creek Joshua Stanley & Thomas Harris Junr, for Caroline Thomas Terrell & Pleasant Terrell, for Jenito James Hunnicutt & Thos S. Pleasants, for Camp Creek Catlet Jones, who were present.

12/7/1788. Minutes of disunion against Caroline Matilda Bates & Mary Logan were produced & approved.

23/8/1788. Representatives appointed by the preparative meetings: for Cedar Creek Thomas Stanly & John Harris, for Caroline Jonathan Terrell & Pleasant Cobbs, for Jenito Samuel Parsons, for Camp Creek Robert Douglas & Elijah Johnson, for Amelia Jesse Johnson Senr, who were present.

23/8/1788. Clark T. Moorman, Samuel Parsons, Jesse Johnson, Thomas Stanley & Catlet Jones appointed to attend Quarterly meeting.

23/8/1788. Rebecca Winston (daughter of Nathl Winston deceased) hath had a bastard child. Pleasant Terrell appointed to assist the women in preparing a testimony of disunion against her.

13/9/1788. Representatives appointed by the preparative meetings: for Jenito James Hunnicutt & Samuel Parsons, for Cedar Creek Thos Harris Senr & Thos Harris Junr, for Caroline Clark T. Moorman & Thos Terrell, for Camp Creek Elijah Johnson & Catlet Jones, who were present.

13/9/1788. Pleasant Terrell, Samuel Parson, Micajah Crew & Thomas Harris Junr appointed to have Queries and Books of Dicipline prepared for each preparative meeting.

13/9/1788. We have visited all those members who hold slaves, yet there are divers who still continue to hold them. We have but little prospect of anything further for ourselves with them, therefore have annexed their names viz John Hunnicutt, Wm Stanley, Jesse, Saml & Thomas Hargrave, Judith & Ursla Cheadle, John Douglas, James Johnson, Soloman Stanley, George Winstone for hireing and overseeing slaves, Milley Machgeehee & Nancy Bates, we also may add that several of those who signed manumissions have since demanded them back we thought it best to bring up their names viz John Stanley, Ann Mackgeehee & Elizabeth Cheadle. Signed: Thomas Terrell, Thomas Stanley, John Peatross, Micajah Crew.

13/9/1788. Clark T. Moorman, Catlet Jones, James Hunnicutt, Pleasant Terrell, Thomas Terrell, Thomas Harris Junr & Micajah Crew appointed to visit the friends named in the [above] report.

13/9/1788. Charles Douglas Junr of Camp Creek is living in the corrupt practices of cursing & swaring and that his general deportment is inconsistant with our profession. Catlet Jones & Elijah Johnson appointed to treat with him.

13/9/1788. Ann Moor is like to need assistance. The preparative meetings are requested to raise 6 pounds. The meeting being informed that she has property, Catlet Jones & Elijah Johnson to inform her that tis the judgment of the meeting that she ought to make it over to friends in such manner that after her death it may be applied to the use of supporting the poor in the society.

11/10/1788. Representatives appointed by the preparative meetings: for Caroline Matthew P. Terrell, Jonathan Terrell, Cedar Creek Thomas Stanley & Thomas Harris Junr, for Jenito James Hunnicutt & Samuel Parsons, for Camp Creek Robert Douglas & Peter Fitz Garrald, who were present.

11/10/1778. Clark T. Moorman appointed to assist the women to prepare a certificate for Martha Johnson (daughter of Saml Hargrave deceased) to join her to South River meeting where she has removed by marriage.

11/10/1778. The committee appointed to visit several persons named in a report given last meeting, produced a minute of disunion against Solomon Stanley, John Douglas, James Johnson, William Stanley & testimonys of disunion against John Stanley, Jesse, Samuel & Thomas Hargrave, which were approved. Clark T. Moorman & Thomas Harris Junr appointed to have the testimonies read.

11/10/1778. A testimony of disunion was produced against Charles Douglas Junr and approved. Catlet Jones to have it read.

11/10/1778. Samuel Chiles hath married contrary to our dicipline. Pleasant Terrell & Thomas Terrell appointed to visit him and prepare a minute of disunion against him.

11/10/1778. Pleasant Terrell of Caroline requested to be released from the station of overseer. Clark T. Moorman appointed in his stead.

11/10/1778. Robert Douglas appointed overseer of the Orrange meeting.

8/11/1788. Representatives appointed by the preparative meetings: for Cedar Creek Thomas Stanley & Micajah Crew, for Caroline Thos Terrell & Pleasant Terrell, for Camp Creek Catlet Jones, who were present.

8/11/1788. Clark T. Moorman & Thomas Harris Junr recommended to the consideration of the Quarterly meeting as sutable persons to be appointed elders.

8/11/1788. The committee continued to finish a visit to several persons named in a report given to a former meeting, & brought up minutes of disunion against Judith Cheadle, Ursla Cheadle & Milley Mackgeehee, & testimonies against Ann Mackgeehee & John Hunnicutt, which were approved. Pleasant Terrell & Micajah Crew appointed to have the testimonies read.

8/11/1788. William Crew appointed to join the women on a visit to Ann Moore on account of her conduct respecting her property.

8/11/1788. A minute of disunion against Saml Chiles was produced and approved.

8/11/1788. A condemnation from Shadrack Stanley was handed to the meeting which was satisfactory. He is reinstated a member of our society. Thomas Harris Junr & Pleasant Terrell appointed to inquire into his affairs & prepare certificated for him.

8/11/1788. Pleasant Terrell, Catlet Jones, James Hunnicutt, Thomas Terrell & Thomas Harris Junr appointed to attend Quarterly meeting.

13/12/1788. Representatives appointed by the preparative meetings: for Cedar Creek Thomas Harris Senr & John W. Maddox, for Caroline Clark T. Moorman & John Peatross, for Camp Creek Peter Fitz Garrald, for Jenito Thomas Pleasants & James Hunnicutt, who were present.

13/12/1788. James B. Pleasants sent a letter confirming his former paper of condemnation and professing an earnest desire to conduct himself in future so as to give no further uneasiness to friends, which was recorded. Committee to prepare a certificate for him to join him to friends where he now lives.

10/1/1789. Representatives appointed by the preparative meetings: for Caroline Thomas Terrell & Clark T. Moorman, for Cedar Creek Thomas Stanley & John Harris, for Jenito Thomas Pleasants & Samuel Parsons, for Camp Creek Robert Douglas & Elijah Johnson, for Amelia John Johnson, who were present.

10/1/1789. A certificate for Daniel Clark from Goos Creek meeting and one for Charles Eastin from South River meeting were produced and received.

10/1/1789. Catlet Jones & Ann Barksdale published their intentions of marriage. Wm Crew & Elijah Johnson appointed to inquire into his clearness.

10/1/1789. Samuel Parsons & Thomas Stanley added to the committee to visit deficient members.

10/1/1789. Thomas Terrell, Pleasant Terrell, Catlet Jones, Thomas Stanley, Robert Douglas, Elijah Johnson & Samuel Parsons appointed to hear the reasons of the objections made to the friends recommended as sutable persons to be appointed elders.

10/1/1789. Elizabeth Johnson (daughter of William Johnson) hath married contrary to our dicipline. Clark T. Moorman appointed to join the women in a visit to her and assist them to prepare a minute of disunion against her.

10/1/1789. The women produced a paper of condemnation from Nanney Bunch with a recommendation from New Garden, NC preparative meeting, which are received and she reinstated a member of our religious society. Micajah Crew & Elijah Johnson appointed to assist the women to make the necessary enquiry and prepare a certificate for her.

28/2/1789. Representatives appointed by the preparative meetings: for Cedar Creek Thomas Stanley & Wm Eley Harris, for Caroline Thomas Terrell & Pleasant Terrell, for Jenito Thos Pleasants & James Hunnicut, who are present.

28/2/1789. Elijah Johnson & Thos Terrell appointed to attend the marriage of Catlet Jones & Ann Barksdale.

28/2/1789. A minute of disunion against Elizabeth Johnson was produced and approved.

28/2/1789. A certificate from White Oak Swamp, Henrico meeting for Thomas & Sarah Hatton & their children was produced which is recorded.

28/2/1789. Thomas Pleasants, Thomas Stanley, Thomas Terrell & Catlet Jones appointed to attend Quarterly meeting.

14/3/1789. Representatives appointed by the preparative meetings: for Caroline Clark T. Moorman & Pleasant Terrell, for Cedar Creek Thomas Harris Senr & Samuel Harris, for Jenito James Hunnicutt & Samuel Parsons, for Camp Creek Peter Fitz Garrald, who were present.

14/3/1789. Margaret Stanley hath married out of the unity of friends. Thomas Stanley & Micajah Crew appointed to join the women on a visit to her and prepare a minute of diounion against her.

14/3/1798. Mary Bunch requests a certificate for herself, daughter Ann & son James, to join them to South River, Campbell Co meeting. Samuel Parsons & Micajah Crew appointed to make the necessary enquiry and prepare a certificate for them.

14/3/1798. A complaint against Sarah Douglas was given by the women. William Crew appointed to join them on a visit to her and prepare a minute of disunion against her.

14/3/1798. In the case of James B. Pleasants, the committee produced a certificate to join him to Indian Spring, MD meeting.

11/4/1789. Representatives appointed by the preparative meetings: for Cedar Creek Thomas Hatton & Thomas Stanley, for Caroline Pleasant Terrell & Pleasant Cobbs, for Jenito James Hunnicutt & Thomas S. Pleasants, for Camp Creek Catlet Jones, for Amelia Garrard Johnson Senr & Benjamin Johnson Senr, who were present.

11/4/1789. William Stabler & Deborah Pleasants published their intentions of marriage. He is to produce a certificate of his clearness.

11/4/1789. John & William Johnson of Amelia requests our certificates for themselves & families to join them to South River, Campbell Co, meeting. Garrard Johnson & Micajah Crew appointed to make necessary enquirey and prepare certificates.

11/4/1789. Sarah Crew (daughter of James Crew) hath married contrary to our dicipline. Thomas Harris Senr appointed to assist the women to prepare a minute of disunion against her.

11/4/1789. Thomas S. Pleasants, Clark T. Moorman, Thomas Harris Senr, Catlet Jones, John Johnson & Elijah Johnson are appointed to collect subscriptions agreeable to the plan of the Yearly meeting for the purpose of establishing a school.

13/1/1776. Archabald Pleasants hath lately been married by a hireling priest to a person not of our society, we do therefore disown him. John Payne clerk.

23/2/1776. Soloman Stanly (son of John Stanley Junr) hath taken a wife of a different persuasion of faith, we therefore disown him.

25/2/1776. Thomas Moorman (son of Micajah Moorman) hath married to a woman of another persuasion in matters of faith by a hireling priest, we therefore disown him.

13/7/1776. Samuel Bell (son of George Bell) hath suffered himself to be baptised and drawn a side into certain scandulous lascivious practices to the great dishonour of our holy profession, we therefore disown him. John Payne clerk.

14/9/1776. Henry Terrell (son of Henry Terrell deceased) deviated in many things from what truth requires was disowned by us. Since which he hath condemned his former misconduct pretty well to the satisfaction of friends ... but hath of late absented himself from attending meetings and joined in membership with another society of people using the extarnal in religion and vain complimenting of men which we believe to be wrong, we therefore disown him. Signed by: John Payne clerk, Pleasant Terrell, Clark T. Moorman, Shadrack Stanly, Strangman Hutchings, Micajah Terrell, Thomas Harris, James Crew, Micajah Davis, Samuel Hargrave, Byrom Ballard, John Barnett, Moses Harris, John Harris, Acchillis Douglass, Athanasius Barnett.

11/1/1777. Obediah Stanly (son of Madox Stanly) hath been joined in marriage by a hireling priest to a woman not of our society, we therefore disown him. John Payne clerk.

11/9/1779. James Moorman give himself alosse to frequent taverns, and unnecessary places of diversion & gaming, we therefore disown him. John Payne clerk.

10/1/1778. James Bunch hath drawn a side into the practice of intemperance in the use of spirituous liquor, to the great scandal of our profession, we therefore disown him. John Payne clerk.

11/4/1778. Acchillis Moorman (son of Thomas Moorman deceased) hath of late married by a hireling priest, we therefore disown him. John Payne clerk.

11/4/1778. Thomas Moorman is guilty as appears to us of being father of a child without being lawfully married to the woman by whom he is accused of that gross evil & now refuses to accomplish his engagement of marriage with her, we therefore disown him. John Payne clerk.

11/7/1778. Charles Douglass of Albemarle Co deviated from our principles in drinking strong drink to excess & subscribing money for the purpose of war, and that he hath unlawfully kept company with a young woman which charge he doth not deny, we therefore disown him. John Payne clerk.

13/3/1779. Robert Douglass (son of Charles) of Albemarle Co hath by giving too much aloose to the inclination of his own will swerved from our known principles by taking to himself a wife of a different profession in matters of faith, we therefore disown him. John Payne clerk.

13/3/1779. Milley Hutchings (daughter of Strangman Hutchings) of Goochland Co hath suffered herself to be joined in marriage to a man of a different persuasion from us in matters of faith by a hireling priest, we therefore disown her. John Payne clerk, Mary Payne clerk.

9/10/1779. Samuel Bunch Junr hath deviated so far as to engage in military service, we therefore disown him. John Payne clerk.

9/10/1779. Samuel Pleasants hath volenterily taken part in military duty & suffered himself to be joined in marriage by a hireling priest contrary to the known rules of our dicipline, we therefore disown him. John Payne clerk.

9/10/1779. Isaac Pleasants acted contrary to our peaceful principles in joining with the militia as a military man in guarding prisoners which misconduct he justifies, we therefore disown him. John Payne clerk.

13/11/1779. John Chiles (son of Menoak Chiles deceased) hath of late joined himself with the spirit of war contrary to the known principles of friends, we therefore disown him. John Payne clerk.

11/12/1779. Anthony Winston (son of Nathaniel Winston) of Caroline Co of late hath voluntarily inlisted in the militia service contrary to the known principles of friends, we therefore disown him. John Payne clerk.

16/3/1781. I heartily condemn all such practices of going out in marriage, much desiring to be received again which am willing to submit to friends consideration. Moorman Johnson

11/11/1780. Moorman Johnson (son of James Johnson) of Bedford Co hath married to one of too near of kin and contrary to the good order used amongst friends, we therefore disown him. John Payne clerk.

8/4/1780. Charles Woodson Junr of Powhatan Co hath so far deviated from our principles as to absent himself from our religious meetings and likewise taken part in military duty contrary to the known rules of our dicipline, we therefore disown him. John Payne clerk.

8/4/1780. Jonathan Stanley hath not abide in the rules of our dicipline in that importon point of marriage we do therefore disown him. John Payne Clerk.

14/7/1781. David Cobbs (son of Robert Cobbs) of Caroline Co hath married contrary to the method of our society and hath been active in military services, we therefore disown him. Moses Harris clerk this time.

6/6/1782. Nicholas Crew hath suffered himself to be drawn aside into the intemperate use of spirituous liquor and also absented himself from the attendance of our religious meetings, we therefore disown him. James Hunnicutt clerk this time.

11/12/1774. Madox Stanly of Hanover Co hath of late taken to him a woman and by his own confession lives with her as tho she was his wife, before they were lawfully married, therefore we disown him. Saml Hargrave.

13/12/1783. Benjamin Johnson (son of Jesse Johnson) of Amelia Co hath suffered himself to be joined in marriage to a woman too nearer kin then is allowable by friends, we therefore disown him. James Hunnicutt clerk.

13/12/1783. Mary Johnson (daughter of Ashley Johnson) of Amelia Co hath suffered herself to be joined in marriage to a man of nearer kin then is allowable by friends, therefore we disown her. James Hunnicutt clerk.

13/12/1783. George Bunch hath suffered himself to be drawn aside into contentious practices, we therefore disown him. James Hunnicutt clerk.

Jonathan Hutchings hath suffered himself to be joined in marriage to a woman of a different persuasion from us, we therefore disown him. James Hunnicutt clerk.

28/8/1784. Thomas Douglass of Orange Co hath suffered himself to be drawn aside by the intemperate use of spirituous liquor, we therefore disown him. James Hunnicutt clerk.

11/12/1784. Jeremiah Harris hath sold a Negro as a slave which we believe to be an ... practice and contrary to our dicipline, we therefore disown him. James Hunnicutt clerk.

8/1/1785. Madox Stanly (son of Madox Stanly) of Hanover Co hath married out contrary to the rules of our dicipline to a woman nearer of kin than is allowed of amongst us, we therefore disown him. James Hunnicutt clerk.

8/1/1785. Jacob Cheadle of Caroline Co hath married a woman of too near kin & by a hireling priest contrary to the good order of friends, we therefore disown him. James Hunnicut clerk.

26/2/1785. Charles Bunch (son of Samuel Bunch deceased) hath gone out into several disorderly practices such as gaming, cursing & swearing, we therefore disown him. James Hunnicutt clerk.

--/10/1789. Representatives appointed by the preparative meetings: for Caroline Matthew P. Terrell & Clark T. Moorman, for Cedar Creek Thos Stanley & Waddy Stanley, for Jenito Thomas Pleasants & Saml Parsons, for Camp Creek Wm Crew & Peter Fitz Garrald, for Amelia Garrard Johnson & Benja Johnson, who were present except Benja Johnson.

--/10/1789. One of the friends ... on a visit to Ann Harris ... of disunion ... was approved.

--/10/1789. Friends requested to inform James Harris of the judgment, not having complied.

--/10/1789. Garrard Johnson requests our certificate for himself & family to join them to South River meeting. Saml Parsons & Thos Pleasants appointed to make the necessary enquiry.

--/10/1789. A certificate granted to Robert Bell to join him to Deep River, NC meeting was returned accompanied by a letter from David Brooks informing that said Bell had returned before his certificate got to hand.

--/10/1789. Thos Harris, Pleasants Terrell, Clark T. Moorman, John Harris, Thos Pleasants, Saml Parsons, Elijah Johnson & Micajah Crew appointed to view & consider if repairs were necessary to be made to the meeting house.

14/11/1789. Representatives appointed by the preparative meetings: for Caroline Thos Terrell & Jonathan Terrell, for Cedar Creek Jno Harris & Micajah Crew, for Jenito Thos Pleasants & Saml Parsons, for Camp Creek Peter Fitz Garrald & Catlet Jones, who were present except Saml Parsons.

14/11/1789. Milley Stanley sometime past signed a manumission for some Negroes which she now refuses to suffer to take effect. John Harris & Jonathan Terrell appointed to accompany the women on a visit to her.

14/11/1789. Thos Pleasants of Camp Creek complains that Arthanatious Barnett is indebted to him and neglects payments. Thos Harris Junr, Catlet Jones & Clark T. Moorman appointed to give their assistance in the matter.

14/11/1789. Thos Harris Junr, Clark T. Moorman, Jno Harris, Obadiah Crew & Saml Harris appointed to attend Quarterly meeting.

12/12/1789. Representatives appointed by the preparative meetings: for Caroline Pleasant Terrell & Pleasant Cobbs, for Cedar Creek Thos Harris Senr & Waddy Stanley, for Jenito Saml Parsons, who were present except Saml Parsons.

12/12/1789. James Hunnicutt & Pleasants Terrell added the assistance of friends appointed in the matter of difference between Thos Pleasants & Arthanatious Barnett.

12/12/1789. George & Edmond Winstone & James Harris' wife & children from Caroline are now residing within the limits of White Oak Swamp meeting. Clark T. Moorman & Micajah Crew appointed to enquire into their affairs & produce certificates.

9/1/1790. Representatives appointed by the preparative meetings: for Caroline Thos Terrell & Matthew P. Terrell, for Cedar Creek Thos Harris Junr & Jno Harris, for Camp Creek Catlet Jones, for Jenito Saml Parsons, who were present.

9/1/1790. A certificate for Mary Harris (wife of James Harris) and her children viz Benjamin, Judith, Elizabeth, Mary, Thos, Lucy & James to join them to White Oak Swamp meeting approved.

27/2/1790. Representatives appointed by the preparative meetings: for Cedar Creek Thos Harris Junr & Thos Stanley, for Caroline Pleasant Terrell & Clk T. Moorman, for Jenito Saml Parsons & Robt Watkins, for Camp Creek Catlet Jones & Elijah Johnson, for Amelia Jesse Johnson Junr, who were present.

27/2/1790. Joseph Hargrave & Rachal Terrell published their intentions of marriage. John Peatrus & Clarke Terrell Moorman appointed to enquire in to his clearness.

27/2/1790. Thos Terrell & John Harris added to the former committee appointed to use their endeavours to have the business of Thos Pleasants & Arthanatious Barnett finished.

27/2/1790. Nathan Winston of Caroline is in the practice of hireing slaves, offering to fight & other disorders, such as dancing, vain complements & a neglect of the attendance of our meetings. Jonathan Terrell, John Peatruss & Thos Harris Junr appointed to visit him.

27/2/1790. Thos Terrell, Thos Stanley, Saml Parsons, Micajah Crew, Matthew P. Terrell & Catlet Jones appointed to attend Quarterly meeting.

13/3/1790. Representatives appointed by the preparative meetings: for Caroline John Peatrus & Pleasant Terrell, for Cedar Creek Wm Eley Harris & Peter Fitz Garrald, who were present.

13/3/1790. Thos Terrell & John Peatrus appointed to attend the marriage of Joseph Hargrave & Rachel Terrell.

13/3/1790. A testification against Milley Stanley was produced and approved.

10/4/1790. Representatives appointed by the preparative meetings: for Caroline Jonathan Terrell & Thos Terrell, for Cedar Creek Peter Fitz Garrald & Thos Stanley, for Jenito Thos S. Pleasants, who were present.

10/4/1790. John Hargrave of Caroline is in the practice of slave holding. Thos Terrell & Thos Harris appointed to visit him.

10/4/1790. Jesse Johnson Senr appointed to overseer of Amelia meeting in the room of Garrard Johnson who was removed.

8/5/1790. Representatives appointed by the preparative meetings: for Caroline Jonathan Terrell & Clk T. Moorman, for Cedar Creek Thos Harris Junr & Joshua Stanley, for Jenito Ben Watkins, for Camp Creek Catlet Jones, who were present.

8/5/1790. Our esteemed friends Mary Ridgeway & June Watson from Ireland on a religious visit to America and their companion Casper Wister Haines from Philadelphia attended this meeting.

8/5/1790. A testimony of disunion against Nathan Winston produced and approved. Matthew P. Terrell appointed to read it.

8/5/1790. Thos Harris Junr, Clk T. Moorman, Thos Pleasants & Matthew P. Terrell appointed to attend Quarterly meeting.

8/5/1790. Jesse Johnson an elder of Amelia meeting departed this life the 12th da, 4th mo, last in the 62nd year of his age.

12/6/1790. Representatives appointed by the preparative meetings: for Caroline Pleasant Terrell & Clk T. Moorman, for Jenito Thos S. Pleasants & Saml Parsons, for Cedar Creek Thos Stanley & Petar Fitz Garrald, who were present.

12/6/1790. Saml Parsons & Elijah Johnson added to the committee appointed in matter in dispute between Thos Pleasants & Arthanitious Barnett.

12/6/1790. Anne Bates has married contrary to our dicipline. Thos Pleasants appointed to assist the women to prepare a minute of disunion against her.

10/7/1790. Representatives appointed by the preparative meetings: for Jenito Thos Pleasants & Saml Parsons, for Caroline Thos Terrell & Clark T. Moorman, for Cedar Creek Wm. E. Harris & Micajah Crew, who were present.

10/7/1790. The committee appointed to assist in the dispute between Thomas Pleasants & Arthanatious Barnett, as security for Charles Thomas, for the rent of the Byrd ordinary ... for the year 1787, are of opinion that Arthanatious Barnett is still liable as security, and there appears to be due Thos Pleasants 20 pounds 13 shillings 6 pence with interest.

28/8/1790. Representatives appointed by the preparative meetings: for Caroline Thos Terrell & Clk T. Moorman, for Jenito Saml Parsons & Joseph Hunnicutt, for Cedar Creek Peter Fitz Garrald & Thos Harris Senr, for Camp Creek Elijah Johnson & Jno W. Maddox, who were present except Thos Terrell.

28/8/1790. Isaac & Elizabeth Stanley requested to be reinstated in our religious society and their condemnation. Catlet Jones & Jonathan Terrell appointed to visit with them on the subject.

28/8/1790. Micajah Crew of Cedar Creek requests to be released from acting as overseer. Thos Stanley appointed in his stead.

28/8/1790. A certificate from Guinedd, PA meeting for John Stanley was received as it appears he is residing within the limits of South River meeting is directed forward.

28/8/1790. Thomas Harris Junr, Clk T. Moorman, Jno W. Maddox & Catlet Jones appointed to attend the Quarterly meeting.

11/9/1790. Representatives appointed by the preparative meetings: for Caroline Clark T. Moorman & Matthew P. Terrell, for Cedar Creek Thos Stanley & Wm E. Harris, for Camp Creek Catlet Jones, for Jerito Thos S. Pleasants & Joseph Hunnicutt, who were present.

11/9/1790. A testimony of disunion against John Hargrave was produced & approved.

9/10/1790. Representatives appointed by the preparative meetings: for Caroline Pleasant Terrell & Jonathan Terrell, for Cedar Creek Thos Stanley & Obadiah Crew, for Jenito Thos Pleasants & Daniel Clark, for Camp Creek Elijah Johnson & William Crew, who were present.

9/10/1790. Clark T. Moorman & Thos Terrell added to the friends appointed to visit Isaac & Elizabeth Stanley.

13/11/1790. Representatives appointed by the preparative meetings: for Caroline Jonathan Terrell & Matthew P. Terrell, for Cedar Creek Thos Hatton & Waddy Stanley, for Jenito Saml Parsons & Joseph Hunnicutt, for Camp Creek Catlet Jones & John W. Maddox, who were present.

13/11/1790. John Johnson & Nancy Hunnicutt published their intentions of marriage. Joseph Hunnicutt & Saml Parsons appointed to enquire into his clearness.

13/11/1790. Thomas S. Pleasants & Elizabeth T. Pleasants published their intentions of marriage. Micajah Crew & Jno Harris appointed to enquire into his clearness.

13/11/1790. John Heirst from Goos Creek & his companion James Rattikin from Fairfax attended this meeting on a religious visit to South River meeting.

13/11/1790. Ben Stanley (son of Wm) has married contrary to our dicipline. Thos Harris Junr & Thos Stanley appointed to have the matter under their care & prepare a minute of disunion.

13/11/1790. Clark T. Moorman, Saml Parsons, Jno Harris, Thos Harris Junr & Thos Stanley appointed to attend Quarterly meeting.

11/12/1790. Representatives appointed by the preparative meetings: for Cedar Creek Thos Stanley & Micajah Crew, for Caroline Pleasant Terrell & Clark T. Moorman, for Jenito Joseph Hunnicutt & Daniel Clark, who were present.

11/12/1790. Danl Clark & Thos Stanley appointed to attend the marriage of John Johnson & Nancy Hunnicutt.

11/12/1790. Thos Harris Junr & Jno Harris appointed to attend the marriage of Thomas S. Pleasants & Elizabeth T. Pleasants.

8/1/1791. Representatives appointed by the preparative meetings: for Cedar Creek Wm E. Harris & Micah Crew, for Caroline Pleasant Terrell, Clark T. Moorman & Joseph Hargrave, for Jenito Thos Pleasants & Danl Clark, who were present.

8/1/1791. Thos Johnson of South River meeting & Milecent Hargrave published their intentions of marriage. He is requested to produce a certificate of clearness.

8/1/1791. Thos Pleasants, Saml Parsons, Thos Terrell, Clark T. Moorman & Elijah Johnson appointed to assist Cedar Creek preparative meeting in settling a matter now before them.

26/2/1791. Representatives appointed by the preparative meetings: for Cedar Creek Thos Harris Junr & Obadiah Crew, for Jenito Thos Pleasants & Joseph Hunnicutt, for Camp Creek Elijah Johnson & Robt Douglas, who were present except Robert Douglas who was prevented from attending by sickness.

26/2/1791. Benjamin Vaughan produced a certificate from Henrico meeting which is received & recorded.

26/2/1791. Jonathan Terrel & Micajah Crew appointed elders.

26/2/1791. Thos Harris Junr, Catlet Jones, Thos Pleasants & Clark T. Moorman appointed to attend Quarterly meeting.

12/3/1791. Representatives appointed by the preparative meetings: for Cedar Creek Thomas Hatton & Micajah Crew, for Caroline Thos Terrell & Clark T. Moorman, who were present.

12/3/1791. Thos Johnson having failed to produce a certificate & the meeting being informed that he & Melicent Hargrave were married contrary to the rules of friends.

12/3/1791. Our esteemed friends Joseph Potts from PA & his companion John McKin... from Baltimore attended this meeting on a religious visit.

12/3/1791. Lucy Chiles (daughter of John Chiles) married out of the unity of friends. Pleasant Terrell appointed to assist the women to prepare a minute of disunion against her.

9/4/1791. Representatives appointed by the preparative meetings: Caroline Jonathan Terrell & Pleasant Cobbs, for Cedar Creek Thos Stanley & Obadiah Crew, for Jenito Thos Pleasants & Joseph Hunnicutt, who were present.

9/4/1791. Joseph Anthony of South River & Rhoda Moorman published their intentions of marriage. He is requested to produce a certificate of his clearness.

9/4/1791. Minutes of disunion against Sarah Harris, Edith Stanley & Judith Crew were produced and approved.

9/4/1791. A minute of disunion against Lucy Chiles was produced & approved.

9/4/1791. Soloman Stanley (son of Wm) hath married contrary to the dicipline. Micajah Crew appointed to prepare a minute of disunion against him.

9/4/1791. Cary Pleasants hath removed within the limits of Henrico meeting without a certificate. Thomas Pleasants & Samuel Parsons appointed to make necessary enquiry & prepared one.

172

14/5/1791. Representatives appointed by the preparative meetings: for Cedar Creek Joshua Stanley & Peter Fitz Garrald, for Caroline Thos Terrell & Clark T. Moorman, for Jenito John Johnson & Saml Parsons, for Camp Creek Jno Wilson Maddox, who were present.

14/5/1791. Thos Terrell & Catlet Jones appointed to attend the marriage of Joseph Anthony & Rhoda Moorman.

14/5/1791. Robert Bell of Camp Creek hath joined in marriage contrary to the dicipline. Micajah Crew appointed to prepare a minute of disunion against him.

14/5/1791. Thos Terrell, Jno Harris Catlet Jones, Clark T. Moorman Micajah Crew, Saml Parsons & Thos Stanley appointed to attend Quarterly meeting.

14/5/1791. James Hunnicutt a member & elder of Jenito meeting (who frequently appeared in the ministerial line) departed this life the [blank] last year.

11/6/1791. Representatives appointed by the preparative meetings: for Caroline Catlet Jones & Thos Terrell, for Cedar Creek Thos Hatton & Micajah Crew, for Jenito Thos Pleasants & Saml Parsons, who were present.

11/6/1791. A minute of disunion against Robert Bell was produced & approved.

11/6/1791. Wm Johnson (son of Wm) had left his fathers house in a disorderly manner at the time of the families obtaining certificates, now sent a satisfactory damnation for his conduct. Saml Parsons appointed to prepare a certificate for him to join South River meeting.

9/7/1791. Representatives appointed by the preparative meetings: for Cedar Creek Peter Fitz Garrald & Maddy Stanley, for Caroline Jonathan Terrell & John Peatross, for Jenito Thos Pleasants & Joseph Hunnicutt, who were present.

9/7/1791. Rhoda Anthony (formerly Moorman) requested our certificate to join her to South River meeting where she has removed by marriage. Pleasants Terrell & Catlet Jones appointed to assist the women to make the needful enquiry and prepare one.

9/7/1791. Benjamin Bates Junr gave in a certificate from Whiteoak Swamp meeting & being received.

27/8/1791. Representatives appointed by the preparative meetings: for Caroline Catlet Jones & Clark T. Moorman, for Cedar Creek Wm E. Harris & Ben Bates

Junr, for Jenito Benjamin Johnson & Saml Parsons, for Camp Creek Elijah Johnson & Jno W. Maddox, who were present.

27/8/1791. George Bell of Camp Creek hath frequented places of deversion & has been guilty of fighting. Robert Douglas, Clark T. Moorman & Catlet Jones appointed to visit him.

27/8/1791. Jane Johnson who some time since removed to Deep River, NC by marriage hath no certificate. Saml Parsons & Benjamin Johnson appointed to assist the women to make necessary enquiry and prepare one.

27/8/1791. A certificate from Burleigh meeting for Benjamin Russell & his two daughters, Sophia & Rebecca, was produced & is received.

27/8/1791. Saml Parsons, Thos Terrell & Thos Stanley appointed to attend Quarterly meeting.

10/9/1791. Representatives appointed by the preparative meetings: for Cedar Creek Thos Harris Senr & Thos Stanley, for Caroline Pleasant Terrell & Clark T. Moorman, for Jenito Benjn Russell & Danl Clark, for Camp Creek Elijah Johnson, who were present.

10/9/1791. James Brook of MD & Elizabeth Pleasants published their intentions of marriage. He is requested to produce a certificate of his clearness.

10/9/1791. The women report that Melicent Hargrave condemned her conduct fully to their satisfaction. A certificate to be prepared to join her to South River meeting where she has removed by marriage.

10/9/1791. Thos S. Pleasants of Jenito requests our certificate for himself & wife to join them to Henrico meeting. Micajah Crew & Benjn Watkins appointed to make necessary enquiry and prepare one.

10/9/1791. Danl Clark requests our certificate to join him to Center, Gilford Co, NC meeting. Benjn Watkins & Micajah Crew appointed to inquire into his affairs & prepare one.

10/9/1791. Nicholas Crew sent a condemnation which with a written recommendation from several friends where he now lives are satisfactory. He is reinstated as a member. Saml Parsons & Thos Stanley appointed to prepare a certificate for him to join South River meeting.

8/10/1791. Representatives appointed by the preparative meetings: for Cedar Creek Peter Fitz Garrald & Thos Harris Senr, for Camp Creek Elijah Johnson, for Caroline Catlet Jones & Pleasants Cobbs, for Jenito Benjamin Russell & Saml Parsons, who were present.

8/10/1791. A memorial from South River meeting of Elleanor Ballard was read.

8/10/1791. Elizabeth Pleasants who published her intentions of marriage with James Brooks is since deceased.

12/11/1791. Representatives appointed by the preparative meetings: for Cedar Creek Benjn Bates & Waddy Stanley, for Caroline Pleasant Cobbs & Matthew P. Terrell, for Jenito Benjn Russell & Saml Parsons, for Camp Creek Jno W. Maddox, who were present.

10/12/1791. Representatives appointed by the preparative meetings: for Cedar Creek Thos Stanley & Thos Harris Senr, for Caroline Jonathan Terrell & Pleasant Terrell, for Genito Benjamin Russell & Saml Parsons, for Camp Creek Elijah Johnson, who were present except Benjn Russel.

14/1/1792. Representatives appointed by the preparative meetings: for Cedar Creek Peter Fitz Garrald & Benjamin Bates, for Caroline Catlet Jones & John Peatross, who were present except John Peatross.

14/1/1792. A condemnation from Elizabeth Moorman (formerly Johnson) and a recommendation from several friends where she now resides was produced, which was received. Pleasant Terrell & Micajah Crew appointed to assist the women in preparing a certificate for her to join to South River meeting.

25/2/1792. Representatives appointed by the preparative meetings: for Caroline Jonathan Terrell & Matthew P. Terrell, for Cedar Creek Peter Fitz Garrald & Thos Harris Senr, for Jenito Thos Pleasants & Saml Parsons, for Camp Creek Elijah Johnson, who were present.

25/2/1792. Thos Pleasants, Clark T. Moorman, Pleasants Terrell, Thos Stanley & Jesse Johnson appointed to attend Quarterly meeting.

10/3/1792. Representatives appointed by the preparative meetings: for Cedar Creek Thomas Harris Senr & Benjn Bates, for Caroline Clark T. Moorman & Pleasant Terrell, for Jenito Benjamin Vaughan & Saml Parsons, who were present.

14/4/1792. Representatives appointed by the preparative meetings: for Caroline Matthew P. Terrell, Clark T. Moorman, for Jenito Benjamin Russell & Saml Parsons, for Cedar Creek Thos Harris Senr & Benjamin Bates, who were present.

14/4/1792. Douglas Barksdale of Caroline requests to be joined in membership with friends. Thos Harris Junr, Micajah Crew, Thos Stanley & Clark T. Moorman appointed to visit him.

14/4/1792. Our esteemed friend John Simpson attended this meeting on a religious visit & produced a certificate from Wrights Town with an endorsement from a Quarterly meeting held at Bucks Town, Bucks Co, PA.

12/5/1792. Representatives appointed by the preparative meetings: for Caroline Jonathan Terrell & Catlet Jones, for Cedar Creek Waddy Stanley & Peter Fitz Garrald, for Jenito Thos Pleasants & Benjamin Russell, who were present.

12/5/1792. Sophia Harris (daughter of Moses Harris) hath married out of the unity of friends. Micajah Crew & Thos Stanley appointed to join the women on a visit to her and assist them to prepare a minute of disunion against her.

12/5/1792. Pleasant Terrell, Clark T. Moorman, Saml Parsons & Micajah Crew appointed to attend Quarterly meeting.

12/5/1792. Isaac Stanley requested a certificate to the militia officers of Goochland of his right of membership. The clerk to furnish him one.

9/6/1792. Representatives appointed by the preparative meetings: for Caroline Pleasant Cobbs & Clark T. Moorman, for Cedar Creek Thos Stanley & Micajah Crew, for Jenito Benjamin Russell, who were present.

9/6/1792. A minute of disunion against Sophia Harris was produced & approved.

9/6/1792. A certificate for Thos Stanley Junr from Wrights Burrough meeting was laid before the meeting. He has not since his return appeared as a friend & has married inconsistent with our dicipline.

14/7/1792. Representatives appointed by the preparative meetings: for Caroline Catlet Jones, Matthew P. Terrell, for Cedar Creek Thos Harris Junr & Ben Bates, for Jenito Benjamin Russell & Saml Parsons, who were present.

14/7/1792. Ashley Johnson requested our certificate for himself, his wife & his children Ashley, Watkins, Drusilla, Anna & Edith, to join them to South River meeting. Thos Pleasants & Saml Parsons appointed to make the needful enquirey & prepare one.

25/8/1792. Representatives appointed by the preparative meetings: for Caroline Catlet Jones & Clark T. Morman, for Jenito Isaac Stanley & Benjamin Russell, for Cedar Creek Thos Harris Senr & Micajah Crew, for Camp Creek Elijah Johnson, who were present.

25/8/1792. Judith Douglas of Camp Creek hath married contrary to our dicipline. Elijah Johnson & Micajah Crew appointed to join the women on a visit to her and prepare a testimony of disunion against her.

25/8/1792. A condemnation was offered from Pattey Jones who stands disowned for marrying contrary to our dicipline. Thos Harris Junr, Clark T. Morman & Micajah Crew appointed to unite with the women on a visit to her.

25/8/1792. Jno Winston & Thos Exum Pleasants have removed within the limits of Henrico meeting. Thos Pleasants & Benjamin Russell appointed to enquire into their situation & prepare certificates for them.

25/8/1792. Jesse Crew has for some time neglected to attend our religious meetings and has practiced vain sports, such as gaming & his general conduct is not consistant with our dicipline. Thos Terrell & Jonathan Terrell appointed to visit him.

9/9/1792. Representatives appointed by the preparative meetings: for Caroline Pleasant Terrell & Matthew P. Terrell, for Cedar Creek Thos Harris Junr & Ben Bates, for Jenito Thos Pleasants & Benjamin Russell, who were present except Thos Pleasants.

9/9/1792. Pleasant Terrell is added to that committee appointed to join the women in a visit to Judith Douglas.

13/10/1792. Representatives appointed by the preparative meetings: for Cedar Creek Thos Stanley & Wm E. Harris, for Caroline Pleasant Terrell & Pleasant Cobbs, for Genito Benjamin Watkins & Thos Pleasants, for Camp Creek Jno W. Maddox, who were present except Pleasant Cobbs.

13/10/1792. A testimony of disunion was produced against Judith Douglas & approved.

13/10/1792. Pattey Jones is reinstated a member.

13/10/1792. Benjamin Johnson requests our certificate for himself & wife to join them to … River meeting. Thomas Pleasants & Benjamin Russell appointed to enquire into the state of their affairs, & prepare one.

13/10/1792. Arthanetious Barnett requests our certificate to the commanding officer of the militia of Goochland for himself and his son Thos Barnett certifying their right of membership.

13/10/1792. Thos Pleasants, Thos Harris & Rachel Moorman have a desire to attend the yearly meeting in NC. They being members & elders in good standing it was approved.

13/10/1792. Thos Stanley requested leave to turn a road leading through his land to this meeting house. Thos Pleasants, Pleasant Terrell, Saml Parsons & Benjn Russell appointed to inquire into the true state of the matter & give such council as may be right.

10/11/1792. Representatives appointed by the preparative meetings: for Caroline Jonathan Terrell & Matthew P. Terrell, for Cedar Creek Waddy Stanley & Peter Fitz Garrald, for Genito Benjamin Vaughan & Benjamin Russell, for Camp Creek Elijah Johnson, who were present.

10/11/1792. Friends appointed to visit Jesse Crew reported that he should not be disowned at present.

10/11/1792. Pleasant Terrell, Catlet Jones, Saml Parsons, Thos Harris Junr & Thos Harris Senr appointed to attend the Quarterly meeting.

8/12/1792. Representatives appointed by the preparative meetings: for Caroline Catlet Jones & Pleasant Terrell, for Cedar Creek Thos Stanley & Thos Harris Senr, for Genito Isaac Stanley & Saml Parsons, who were present.

8/12/1792. Douglas Barksdale of Caroline received as a member.

8/12/1792. A certificate for Cary Pleasants given by this meeting 5th mo 1791 was returned by Henrico meeting. He removed within the limits of this meeting.

8/12/1792. Benjamin Bates requests our certificate to join him to Henrico meeting. Thos Harris Junr & Micajah Crew appointed to make the necessary enquiry and prepare one.

12/1/1793. Representatives appointed by the preparative meetings: for Caroline Catlet Jones & Matthew P. Terrell, for Cedar Creek Thos Harris Junr & Obadiah Crew, for Genito Saml Parsons & Joseph Hunnicutt, who were present.

12/1/1793. David Terrell & Patty Johnson published their intentions of marriage. He is requested to produce a certificate of clearness.

12/1/1793. A certificate granted to Thos Exum Pleasants to join him to Henrico now returned. He had removed within the limits of this meeting.

23/2/1793. Representatives appointed by the preparative meetings: for Caroline Catlet Jones & Clark T. Moorman, for Cedar Creek Thos Harris Senr & Micajah Crew, for Genito Benjamin Russell & Saml Parsons, who were present.

23/2/1793. Thos Harris Junr & Micajah Crew appointed to attend the marriage of David Terrell & Patty Johnson.

23/2/1793. Catlet Jones recommended to be a minister.

23/2/1793. Ann Jones appointed an elder.

23/2/1793. John Harris (son of Jeremiah) hath run in the practice of overseeing slaves and manifested a disposition to continue it. Pleasant Terrell, Micajah Crew & Thos Terrell appointed to visit him.

23/2/1793. Lewis Cobbs requested to be received a member in our religious society but it appearing that there was not that clearness and unanimity of judgment which is best in such cases. Thos Stanley, Saml Parsons, Micajah Crew & Thos Harris Junr appointed to visit with him.

23/2/1793. Pleasant Terrell, Thos Harris Junr, Saml Parsons & Thos Harris Senr appointed to attend the Quarterly meeting.

9/3/1793. Representatives appointed by the preparative meetings: for Caroline Catlet Jones & Pleasant Terrell, for Cedar Creek Thos Hatton & Waddy Stanley, for Genito John Johnson & Benjamin Russell, who were present.

9/3/1793. Elijah Johnson & Betsey Watkins published their intentions of marriage. Micajah Crew & Thos Hatton appointed to inquire into his clearness.

9/3/1793. Thos Johnson married contrary to our dicipline. Saml Parsons & John Johnson appointed to prepare a minute of disunion against him.

13/4/1793. Representatives appointed by the preparative meetings: for Thos Terrell & Pleasant Cobbs, for Jenito Benjamin Russell & Saml Parsons, for Cedar Creek Thos Stanley & Thos Harris Senr, who were present.

13/4/1793. William Jackson produced a satisfactory certificate from New Garden, Chester Co, PA meeting which is directed to be recorded.

13/4/1793. ... Stanley & Benjamin Russell appointed to attend the marriage of Elijah Johnson & Betsey Watkins.

13/4/1793. Jesse Crew's condemnation read and received.

13/4/1793. Thos Stanley & Micajah Crew appointed to prepare a testimony of disunion against Jno Harris (son of Jeremiah).

11/5/1793. Representatives appointed by the preparative meetings: for Cedar Creek Joshua Stanley & Thos Stanley, for Caroline Catlet Jones & Clark T. Moorman, for Jenito Thos Pleasants & Saml Parsons, who were present, except Thos Pleasants who was hindered by indisposion of body.

11/5/1793. Catlet Jones, Saml Parsons, Micajah Crew, Thos Stanley, Thos Harris Junr & Thos Harris Senr appointed to attend Quarterly meeting.

8/6/1793. Representatives appointed by the preparative meetings: for Cedar Creek Wm Jackson & Waddy Stanley, for Caroline Catlet Jones & Pleasant Cobbs, for Jenito Thos Pleasants & Issac Stanley, who were present.

13/7/1793. Representatives appointed by the preparative meetings: for Cedar Creek Joshua Stanley & Thomas Hatton, for Genito Benjamin Russell & Saml Parsons, for Caroline Jonathan Terrell & Matthew Terrell, who were present.

13/7/1793. Shadrack Vaughan who has removed within the limits of this meeting produced a certificate from Henrico meeting which is recorded.

13/7/1793. Clark T. Moorman, Micajah Crew, Saml Parsons & John Harris appointed to consider the matter of alterations and repairs to this meeting house.

24/8/1793. Representatives appointed by the preparative meetings: for Caroline Jonathan Terrell & Thos Terrell, for Genito Wm Henry Pleasants & Joseph Hunnicutt, for Cedar Creek Micajah Crew & Jesse Crew, who were present.

24/8/1793. Thomas Stanley & Unity his wife recommended to the Quarterly meeting as sutable friends for elders.

24/8/1793. Thos Exum Pleasants of Genito has removed within the limits of Henrico meeting. Thomas Harris Junr & Micajah Crew appointed to inquire into his situation & prepare a certificate.

24/8/1793. Thos Terrell, Thos Stanley, Elijah Johnson, Saml Parsons & John Harris appointed to attend Quarterly meeting.

14/9/1793. Representatives appointed by the preparative meetings: for Cedar Creek Thos Hatton & Joshua Stanley, for Genito Benjamin Vaughan & Saml Parsons, for Caroline Catlet Jones & Pleasant Terrell, who were present.

180

14/9/1793. Moses Harris of Cedar Creek sent a condemnation of his disorderly marriage. Catlet Jones, Saml Parsons, Pleasant Terrell & Clark T. Moorman appointed to visit with him.

14/9/1793. Andrew Moorman who many years ago became a member by a certificate from South River has since married disorderly & has never been disowned. Micajah Crew & Thos Harris Senr appointed to examine the records.

12/10/1793. Representatives appointed by the preparative meetings: for Cedar Creek Thos Harris Junr & Littlebury Stanley, for Caroline Pleasant Cobbs & Matthew Terrell, for Genito Thomas Pleasants & Isaac Stanley, who were present except Thos Pleasants & Issac Stanley.

12/10/1793. Our beloved friends Margaret Elgar from Monallen, PA meeting and her companions Mary Brooks & Isaiah Boone of Indian Spring, MD meeting, attended this meeting on a religious visit.

12/10/1793. Miriam Pleasants of Jenito is in the practice of holding slaves and manifested a disposition to continue it. Thos Stanley, Pleasant Terrell & Micajah Crew appointed to join the women to visit her.

12/10/1793. Elizabeth Tucker Pleasants (widow of Thos Snowdon Pleasants) sent information that the certificate granted them in her husbands life was never given in, but was since lost, and she having returned within the limits of this meeting & the meeting satisfied, she is acknowledged with her infant child members of this meeting.

9/11/1793. Representatives appointed by the preparative meetings: for Cedar Creek Thos Harris Junr & Thos Stanley, for Caroline Thos Terrell & Clark T. Moorman, for Genito Thos Pleasants & Isaac Stanley.

9/11/1793. Benjamin Bates Junr & Tace Crew published their intentions of marriage. He is requested to produce a certificate of clearness.

9/11/1793. Peter Fitz Garrald hath been in the practice of drinking spirits to excess & using ill words, also of neglecting meetings. Pleasant Terrell, Jonathan Terrell & Clark T. Moorman appointed to visit with him.

9/11/1793. Pleasant Terrell, Thos Stanley, John Harris & Thos Harris Junr appointed to attend Quarterly meeting.

14/12/1793. Representatives appointed by the preparative meetings: for Cedar Creek Thos Harris Senr & Littlebury Stanley, for Caroline Pleasant Terrell &

Clark T. Moorman, for Genito Saml Parsons & Benjamin Vaughan, who were present.

14/12/1793. Thos Harris Junr & Thos Stanley appointed to attend the marriage of Benjamin Bates Junr & Tace Crew.

14/12/1793. Edward Stabler of Fairfax and Mary Pleasants published their intentions of marriage. He is requested to produce a certificate of clearness.

11/1/1794. Representatives appointed by the preparative meetings: for Cedar Creek Littlebury Stanley & Moses Jackson, for Caroline Catlet Jones & Matthew Terrell.

11/1/1794. A testimony of disunion against Peter Fitz Garald produced and approved.

11/1/1794. Sarah Winston (daughter of Nathl Winston deceased) had married contrary to the dicipline. Matthew Terrell & Pleasant Stanley appointed to join the women on a visit to her and assist them to prepare a minute of disunion against her.

11/1/1794. Our beloved friend Richd Jourdan & his companion Jeremiah Outland from Rich Square, NC meeting attended this meeting on a religious visit.

22/2/1794. Representatives appointed by the preparative meetings: for Cedar Creek Joshua Stanley & Thos Hatton, for Caroline Catlet Jones & Matthew Terrell, for Jenito Isaac Stanley & Saml Parsons, who were present.

22/2/1794. Saml Parsons & Micajah Crew appointed to attend the marriage of Edward Stabler & Mary Pleasants.

22/2/1794. Rhoda Terrell (daughter of Thos Terrell) married contrary to the discipline. Thos Stanley appointed to assist the women to prepare a minute of disunion against her.

22/2//1793. A testimony of disunion against Miriam Pleasants was produced & approved.

22/2/1793. Saml Parsons appointed to the state of overseer of Jenito meeting in room of Benjamin Watkins deceased.

22/2/1793. A certificate from South River meeting for Jno Johnson (son of Jos) was received.

22/2/1793. A certificate from White Oak Swamp for Jas Ca...han was received.

22/2/1793. Jesse Terrell of Caroline requests a certificate to Whiteoak Swamp meeting from clearness of marriage engagements. Jonathan Terrell & Clark T. Moorman appointed to make the necessary enquiry.

22/2/1793. Pleasant Winston hath married contrary to the dicipline. Pleasant Terrell & Matthew Terrell appointed to visit him and prepare paper of disunion.

22/2/1793. Thos Pleasants, Pleasant Terrell, Micajah Crew & Jonathan Terrell appointed to attend Quarterly meeting.

ABELL, Richard, 45
ADDOMS, Anne, 107; Moring, 107
ALBEMARLE (County), 2, 9, 10, 17,
 26, 45, 46, 56, 124, 163
ALEXANDRIA, Town of, 24
PETERSBURG, Town of, 24
ALLINSON, William, 30
ALVIS, Mary, 13
AMELIA (County) 1, 4, 8, 9, 18, 20,
 35, 42, 50, 53, 55, 62, 63, 74, 76,
 78, 88, 93, 97, 99, 112, 113, 114,
 115, 116, 117, 118, 120, 121,
 123, 124, 126, 127, 128, 129,
 130, 131, 132, 133, 134, 136,
 139, 141, 143, 144, 145, 146,
 152, 153, 154, 155, 156, 157,
 158, 160, 162, 165, 166, 167,
 168
ANDERSON, John, 12
ANTHONY, Joseph, 12, 21, 150,
 156, 157, 171, 172; Rhoda, 22,
 30, 172
ANTONEY, Christopher, 99
ANTONY, Christa, 93
AUSTIN, Dorothy, 13
BAILEY, Anselm, 109
BALLARD, Amos, 2, 9; Ann, 56;
 Barcklay, 113; Barckly, 113;
 Barksley, 18; Bartlett, 111;
 Bettey, 9; Betty, 2; Byram, 2, 99,
 102; Byrom, 2, 9, 72, 112, 114,
 117, 119, 120, 122, 123, 124,
 125, 131, 132, 134, 135, 136,
 137, 139, 142, 163; Byron, 10;
 Byrum, 9, 10; David, 2, 97, 102,
 112; Delphin, 2, 102; Eleanor 2,
 9, 10, 142; Elleanor, 174;
 Frances, 2, 102; Francis, 62;
 Judith, 2, 9; Mary, 2, 9, 10, 34,
 35, 95, 101, 102; Moorman, 2,
 97, 102, 120; Mouring, 2;
 Mourning, 9; Richard, 33, 34, 35,
 36, 37, 38, 41, 44; Sarah, 35, 37,
 38, 42, 43, 53, 102; Thomas, 2,
 41, 61, 74, 102, 116; William, 2,
 9, 18, 52, 56, 72, 73, 74, 86, 87,
 95, 101, 102, 106, 107, 111, 113
BALLORD, Richard, 40, 45; Sara,
 40; William, 40
BALTIMORE, 29, 171
BARDIN, Arther, 102
BARKESDALE, Douglass, 28
BARKSDALE, Achillis, 20; Ann, 11,
 16, 161; Douglas, 175, 177;
 Nancy, 152
BARNARD, John, 115, 119
BARNART, John, 66
BARNAT, John, 72, 75
BARNET, John, 58, 72, 75, 115, 116,
 118, 119
BARNETT, Anna, 83; Arlanashoush,
 85; Arthanasious, 26, 27;
 Arthanatious, 145, 148, 166, 167,
 169; Arthanetious, 176;
 Arthanitious, 168; Athanasius,
 163; Athanathous, 84;
 Athnatious, 83; Elizabeth, 27, 87;
 Hutchins, 26; Jane, 27; Jesse, 27;
 John (Jno.), 27, 46, 83, 84, 85,
 86, 87, 89, 92, 93, 99, 101, 110,
 112, 121, 138, 140, 142, 150,
 163; Martha, 83; Mary, 27;
 Milicent, 27; Nancy, 27;
 Obedience, 149; Thomas, 27,
 176
BATES, Ann, 20, 127; Anne, 168;
 Benjamin, 2, 21, 23, 24, 25, 28,
 29, 172, 174, 175, 176, 177, 180,
 181; Caroline Matilda, 14, 157,
 158; Elizabeth, 98; Fleming, 2,
 24 28, 29, 30, 33; Hannah, 24;
 James, 12, 20, 127, 152, 157;
 Lucy, 2; Macajah, 2; Martha, 2;
 Nancy, 12, 158; Tace, 2, 28;
 Tace Crew, 2; William Savery, 2
BAUGHMAN, Mary, 16
BAYLEY, 65
BEAVERDAM, 10, 11, 16

184

BEDFORD, 116
BEDFORD COUNTY, 18, 27, 28,
29, 50, 51, 53, 71, 72, 74, 78, 90,
96, 113, 164
BELL, Anthony, 2, 8; Ashley, 2, 8,
28; Cicily, 2, 8; Cisley, 19; Cisly,
87; George, 2, 8, 10, 18, 19, 21,
22, 28, 41, 49, 50, 51, 56, 58, 62,
63, 72, 73, 87, 95, 97, 112, 115,
118, 119, 130, 133, 139, 148,
154, 163, 173; Moore, 57;
Nathan, 2, 8, 16, 23; Pleasants, 2,
8; Robert, 2, 8, 17, 21, 116, 121,
131, 133, 145, 147, 149, 166,
172; Samuel, 112, 163; Sarah, 23
BELLEVILLE, 10
BENEGATS, Antony, 99
BENFORD, James, 51; John, 32
BENNET, Dorcus, 135
BLACKWATER, 96, 109
BLOCKSOM, Ann, 91; Richard, 84,
89, 90, 91, 92, 93, 96, 97, 98, 99
BLONSOM, Richard, 94
BLOOMER, Nehemiah, 19
BLOSSOM, Ann, 8; Cuzaveth, 8;
Gregory, 8; Mary, 8; Obadiah, 8;
Richard, 8; Sarah, 8; William, 8
BLOXOM, Ann, 1; Elizabeth, 1;
Gideon, 1; Gregory, 1; Mary, 1;
Obediah, 1; Richard, 1, 132, 133,
135, 136, 138, 139, 140, 141;
Sarah, 1; William, 1
BLOXSOM, Ann, 22; Richard, 22,
108, 116, 119
BOOCKEN, Edward, 74
BOONE, Isaiah, 180
BRADFORD, 141, 142
BRAME, 36
BRANSON, Thomas, 44
BRIME, Kesenhappuck, 33; Richard,
33
BROOCKES, David, 79
BROOCKS, David, 77; S R, 71;
Samuel R, 71; Samuel Robert,
69, 70
BROOK, James, 173

BROOKES, David, 85; Mary, 23, 29
BROOKS, David, 17, 111, 129, 137,
166; Elizabeth, 151; James, 136,
174; Mary, 20, 96, 151, 180
BRUNSWICK COUNTY, 116
BUCH, Samuel, 78
BUCHANNAN, James, 37
BUCKS COUNTY, PA, 105, 175
BUCKS TOWN, 175
BULLARD, Richard, 39
BULLORD, Richard, 33; Sarah, 39;
William, 39
BUNCH, Ann, 16, 162; Charles, 143,
166; Elizabeth, 97, 98; George,
139, 165; Hannah, 116; James,
14, 16, 50, 106, 108, 109, 111,
117, 119, 156, 162, 163;
Margery, 14, 156; Mary, 10, 16,
17, 56, 107, 139, 154, 162;
Nancy, 12, 161; Priscilla, 130;
Rebeckar, 78; Samual, 102, 106,
107; Samuel, 17, 78, 118, 125,
127, 154, 164, 166; Sarah, 130
BURCH, Ben, 14; Hannah, 33; John,
12
BURLEIGH, 22, 173
BURLEY, 95, 97
BURLINGTON, NJ, 30
BURRUS, Henry, 19; William, 19
BURRUSS, Rachel, 18
BUSH RIVER, SC, 136
BUTLER, Joseph, 31, 32; Richard,
34
BYRD, 169
CAIN CREEK, 44, 88, 94, 107
CAINE CREEK, 45, 46
CALLARD, William, 102
CALLIHAM, June, 13; Rachel, 13
CAMP CREEK, 2, 8, 10, 59, 70, 72,
75, 78, 85, 90, 91, 97, 99, 100,
101, 108, 111, 113, 114, 115,
116, 117, 118, 119, 120, 121,
122, 123, 124, 125, 126, 127,
128, 129, 130, 131, 132, 133,
134, 135, 136, 137, 138, 139,
140, 141, 142, 143, 144, 145,

146, 148, 152, 153, 154, 155,
156, 157, 158, 159, 160, 162,
166, 168, 169, 170, 171, 172,
173, 174, 176, 177
CAMPBELL COUNTY, 12, 14, 18,
19, 21, 22, 23, 26, 142, 156, 162
CAMRON, Catherine, 13; Elizabeth,
13; Lucy, 13
CANDLE, William, 53
CANDLER, Agness, 156; David, 52;
James, 18, 148; John, 18;
William, 50, 54
CANE CREEK, 49, 50, 52, 53, 57, 70
CANE CREEK, NC, 155
CAROLINA, 104, 105
CAROLINE (County), 1, 3-7, 9, 10-
15, 17-21, 25-27, 29, 30, 32-43,
45, 46, 50, 51, 53, 54, 56, 59, 62,
65, 69, 72, 80, 84, 90, 93, 103,
107, 111-129, 131-162, 164-182
CEDAR CREEK, 6, 7, 9, 11, 12, 13,
21, 22, 28, 30, 31, 37, 70, 72, 87,
92, 111, 112, 113, 114, 115, 116,
117, 118, 119, 120, 121, 122,
123, 124, 125, 126, 127, 128,
129, 130, 131, 132, 133, 134,
135, 136, 137, 138, 139, 140,
141, 142, 143, 144, 145, 146,
147, 148, 149, 150, 151, 152,
153, 154, 156, 157, 158, 159,
160, 161, 162, 166, 167, 168,
169, 170, 171, 172, 173, 174,
175, 176, 177, 178, 179, 180,
181
CENTER, 22, 173
CHARLES CITY COUNTY, 26, 34,
64, 76
CHARLES FOREST, 11
CHEADELS, John, 81
CHEADLE, Anne, 33; Eliza, 12, 56,
63; Elizabeth, 10, 11, 14, 17, 19,
43, 80, 158; George, 1, 93, 100,
101; Isaac, 55; Jacob, 20, 144,
165; John (Jno.), 1, 31, 32, 33,
34, 35, 36, 38, 39, 40, 41, 42, 43,
45, 47, 48, 49, 51, 52, 53, 54, 55,

58, 60, 61, 62, 63, 64, 65, 66, 67,
68, 69, 71, 73, 75, 77, 78, 79, 89,
93, 130, 133; Joseph, 31; Joshua,
35; Judeath, 80; Judith, 1, 11, 15,
18, 22, 51, 135, 158, 160;
Lettice, 35; Lucy, 11, 18; Martha,
42; Mary, 35, 36, 93; Melicent,
31; Milason, 31; Molley, 80;
Molly, 1; Salley, 93; Sarah, 93,
96; Stanley, 34; Thomas, 1, 17,
31, 35, 36, 37, 38, 39, 40, 42, 43,
44, 45, 46, 47, 49, 51, 52, 53, 55,
56, 57, 58, 59, 60, 65, 67, 68, 69,
70, 93, 124, 135; Ursla, 11, 15,
158, 160; Ursla F, 12, 14, 19, 21;
William, 52
CHEADLES, Elizabeth, 80; John
(Jno.), 32, 78, 81, 84; Judeth, 80;
Mary, 91
CHESTER CO, PA, 141
CHESTER COUNTY, 24
CHESTER COUNTY, PA, 142, 178
CHEWING, Jemima, 80
CHEWMING, Joseph, 85
CHEWNING, Jamima, 82; Jemima,
80; Jemime, 84; Joseph, 80, 82
CHEWNINS, Jameme, 84
CHIELS, Ann, 93; John (Jno.), 93
CHILDES, Henry, 97
CHILDS, Henry, 111
CHILES, Agness, 35; Ann, 27, 37,
42, 43, 45, 50, 63, 69, 79, 80;
Anne, 1, 33, 34; Elizabeth, 40,
41; Henry, 1, 14, 33, 93, 96, 113;
John (Jno.), 1, 20, 21, 27, 80, 81,
91, 124, 125, 164, 171; Lucy, 21,
171; Manoak, 33, 34, 35, 36, 37,
42, 50, 51, 52, 56, 58, 59, 79, 80;
Manock, 58; Mary, 27, 54, 55,
56; Menoah, 11 Menoak, 39, 40,
41, 164; Molly, 18; Patte, 100;
Patty, 1; Salley, 11, 14, 18, 22;
Sally, 26; Samuel, 1, 19, 20, 159,
160; Susanna, 50; Sushannah, 48;
Thomas, 18; Walter, 33
CHOUNING, Jamima, 64; Jemimah,

115, 117; Joseph, 59, 62
CLARK, Adward, 49; Benjamin, 49,
53, 54, 79, 80, 81, 82; Benjmin,
106; Betty, 101; Boling, 101,
103, 104, 106, 107, 108; Bonler,
52; Bowlen, 49, 50; Bowler, 52;
Charles, 102, 107; Christania,
106; Christopher (See also
Expher, Xper, Xpher), 2, 43, 47,
49, 55, 56, 58, 65, 66, 67, 71,
101, 103, 104, 106, 107;
Cristion, 43; Daniel, 20, 22, 160,
169, 170, 173; Edmond, 90, 93;
Edward, 2, 49, 50, 52, 101, 102,
103; Elizabeth, 80, 81, 101;
Expher, 104; Francis, 37, 43, 46,
48, 49, 53, 79, 80, 88, 89, 90,
101, 102, 103, 104, 105, 106,
107, 108; Isaac, 52, 53; John
(Jno.), 2, 49, 52, 53, 62, 88, 89,
92, 94, 101; Joseph, 54, 80;
Judith, 2, 101; Lucy, 53, 54;
Micajah, 2, 56, 101, 103; Milley,
80; Moley, 101; Mourning, 2, 50,
56, 101; Nicklous, 101;
Penelope, 103; Robert, 2, 52,
101; Tabitha, 106; Thomas, 46,
47, 53, 60, 62, 72, 80, 87, 91, 92,
93, 94, 100, 101, 102, 103, 104,
108; Ursula, 43, 54, 95; Ursule,
106; Winiford, 105; Winifred,
105; Xper, 106; Xpher, 103, 108
CLARKE, Anne, 2; Benjamin, 37;
Betty, 2; Boling, 2; Christiana, 2;
Christopher, 2; Elizabeth, 2;
Frances, 2; Francis, 2, 37, 46;
John (Jno.), 2; Molley, 2;
Nicholas, 2; Thomas, 2;
Winifred, 2
CLERK, Daniel, 16
COBBS, Abigal, 2, 9; Aggatha, 12;
Amey, 14, 19, 30; Amy, 2, 9, 26;
Anselm, 3; David, 165; Davis,
131; Elizabeth, 3, 9; Joanna, 3;
Joseph, 3; Lealey, 19; Lewis, 12,
178; Mary, 2, 9; Phoebe, 9;

Pleasant, 2, 3, 9, 12, 14, 19, 21,
24, 26, 29, 30, 146, 153, 158,
162, 167, 171, 175, 176, 178,
179, 180; Pleasants, 174;
Rebecca, 2, 9; Rhoda, 2; Robert,
3, 12, 50, 52, 53, 78, 79, 83, 84,
165; Samuel, 12; Thomas, 2;
Thomas Pleasants, 12
COLEMAN, Daniell, 33; Jno, 38, 41
COLLER, Thomas, 79
COLLEY, Edmond, 102
COOK, Charity, 136
COPAGE, Thomas, 145
COPPAGE, Thomas, 29, 132, 150
COPPEDGE, Thomas, 145
CORK, IRELAND, 94
CORNWALL, NY, 28
COUCH, Ann, 3; Rebecca, 3;
Samuel, 3, 26, 29
COWGILL, Abigail, 3; Charlotte, 3;
James, 3; John (Jno.), 3; Rachael,
3
CRAWFORD, Peter, 19
CREW, Aggy, 1; Agnes, 1; Agness,
155; Andrew, 32, 34, 42, 64;
Armesby, 1; Armsbe, 84, 96;
Armsbee, 134, 135, 146, 155;
Armsby, 119, 120; Armslee, 81;
Armsley, 80; Benjamin, 2, 3, 8,
16, 26, 64, 78; David, 32;
Deborah, 2; Dorathy, 8; Dorothy,
2, 28; Elizabeth, 31; Frances,
155; Huldah, 3; James, 2, 3, 8,
11, 12, 13, 16, 21, 28, 30, 62, 64,
75, 76, 77, 78, 79, 80, 81, 82, 83,
84, 85, 86, 87, 88, 89, 91, 92, 95,
98, 109, 111, 112, 113, 114, 115,
116, 117, 118, 120, 121, 122,
123, 124, 132, 138, 140, 141,
143, 149, 150, 162, 163; Jesse, 2,
8, 24, 28, 29, 30, 176, 177, 178,
179; John (Jno.), 3, 23, 31, 38,
40, 44, 50, 57, 62; Joseph, 1, 34,
39, 41, 42, 43, 44, 51, 52, 57, 88,
94, 106; Judeth, 79; Judith, 2, 8,
13, 16, 21, 23, 24, 28, 29, 30, 78,

171; Lemuel, 2, 23, 24, 28, 29, 30; Littleberry, 27, 28, 30; Littlebury, 2, 3, 8, 29, 149; Macajah, 1; Margaret, 2, 16, 23, 24, 26, 28, 30; Margreat, 114; Mary, 1, 2, 8, 24, 28, 30; Micah, 2; Micajah, 12, 13, 16, 23, 24, 25, 28, 29, 30, 110, 115, 118, 119, 121, 122, 123, 124, 125, 126, 127, 129, 130, 131, 132, 133, 134, 135, 137, 138, 139, 140, 141, 142, 143, 144, 146, 147, 148, 149, 150, 151, 152, 153, 154, 155, 156, 157, 158, 159, 160, 161, 162, 166, 167, 169, 170, 171, 172, 173, 174, 175, 176, 177, 178, 179, 180, 181, 182; Milly, 3; Nicholas, 22, 127, 130, 135, 165, 173; Obadiah, 28, 29, 30, 166, 169, 171, 177; Obediah, 2, 8, 19, 20; Ro: H, 23; Robert, 26; Sarah, 2, 8, 16, 162; Sucky, 1; Susanna, 2; Tace, 2, 23, 24, 180, 181; Tallitha, 2; Unity, 2, 8, 11, 28, 29, 30, 128, 129; Walter, 2; William, 26, 32, 151, 153, 154, 160, 161, 162, 166, 169

CREWS, James, 78, 83; Joseph, 51, 57

CROASDALL, Grace, 64

CULPEPER, 3

CUMBERLAND, 63

CUMBERLAND COUNTY, 64, 65, 77, 98, 112

CUMINGS, David, 24

CUNCH, James, 48

CURLEE, 10

DARBY, Deborah, 24

DAVID, John (Jno.), 56, 85, 90; Robert, 105

DAVIS, John (Jno.), 47, 49, 54, 55, 56, 58, 59, 61, 62, 63, 64, 65, 68, 70, 71, 72, 73, 74, 75, 77, 78, 79, 81, 84, 85, 86, 87, 88, 89, 91, 92, 93, 94, 95, 96, 97, 98, 99, 100, 105, 106, 108; Jon, 107; Martha, 3, 8; Mary, 3, 8, 111, 117; Micajah, 3, 22, 93, 96, 109, 110, 111, 112, 113, 114, 115, 116, 117, 118, 119, 121, 122, 123, 125, 126, 127, 131, 163; Micayah, 8; Richard, 106; Samuel, 25; Susanah, 8; Susanna, 3, 28; William, 22, 117, 120, 121, 122, 123, 124, 125, 126, 127, 128, 131

DAVISE, John (Jno.), 85, 88

DAVISS, John (Jno.), 47, 48

DEAR (Deer) CREEK, MD, 79, 80

DEEP CREEK, 19, 26, 27, 28

DEEP CREEK, NC, 126, 143

DEEP RIVER, 17

DEEP RIVER, NC, 128, 129, 130, 131, 133, 135, 137, 138, 139, 141, 143, 145, 147, 148, 149, 150, 166, 173

DICKS, Nathon, 83

DICKSON, Joshua, 52

DIGGS, Agness, 88; Judeth, 88; Marshall, 63, 88; Pleasant, 88; Rebacer, 88; Sarah, 88; William, 46, 60, 61, 62, 63, 88, 107

DIGS, William, 47

DIXON, Edward, 61

DOSWELL, Thomas, 23

DOUGHLESS, Archillss, 102; Charles, 47; Thomas, 90

DOUGLAS, Acchilles, 132; Acchillis, 14, 126, 129, 131; Accillias, 130; Accillis, 133, 135, 136, 137; Achillas, 109; Achillis, 110, 111, 119; Anne, 3; Archilas, 11; Archillis, 16; Betsey, 13; Charles, 3, 13, 15, 23, 159; Elizaboth, 3; John (Jno.), 3, 11, 158, 159; Judith, 3, 23, 170; Mary, 13; Milley, 11; Polly, 3; Robert, 13, 29, 153, 156, 158, 159, 160, 161, 171, 173; Sarah, 162; Thomas, 3, 129, 136

DOUGLASS, Acchillis, 116, 118,

124, 125, 127, 128, 163; Accillis, 119; Achilles, 112, 115; Achillis, 123; Archillis, 114; Arcillis, 117; Charles, 17, 116, 119, 121, 163; John (Jno.), 71, 122, 123; Robert, 123, 154, 155, 163; Sarah, 17; Thomas, 69, 165
DOUGLESS, Charles, 102, 107; Elizabeth, 102; John (Jno.), 102; Judeth, 102
DOUGLISH, Charles, 95; Elizabeth, 95; Judeth, 98
DRINK, Henry, 30
DUFF, Eliza, 61; Ellizabeth, 43; Widow, 56
DUGHLISS, Darkass, 102
DUGLASS, Thomas, 90
DUGLESH, Arcchillas, 112
DUGLESS, Charles, 103, 107; John (Jno.), 86, 105; Thomas, 86
DUGLISH, Ann, 98; Charles, 95; John (Jno.), 96; Judeth, 97; Thomas, 96, 98
DUGLISS, John (Jno.), 102; Polly, 102; Thomas, 86, 102
DUGLLESS, Anne, 102
EAST JERSEY, 83
EASTIN, Charles, 12, 135, 145, 160; Elizabeth, 11
EASTING, Elizabeth, 131
EDMOND, Elizabeth, 129
ELGAR, Margaret, 180
ELLESON, Garrard, 63; Garrat, 55; Robert, 55
ELLESS, George, 82; William, 39
ELLIS, Catharine, 19
ELLISON, Garrard, 66; Garrat, 47, 54; Garratt, 68; Robert, 32
ELLMORD, Archelious, 54
ELLMORE, Archillus, 55
ELLOSON, Matthew, 34
ELLWOOD, Thomas, 96
ELLYSON, Benjamin, 44; Gidion, 43, 44; Susanah, 44; William, 44
ELMOND, Ceslah, 57
ELMORE, Archelaus, 44; Archilius,

54; Cisley, 61, 63; Elizabeth, 138, 143, 150; Gerard, 54; John (Jno.), 31; Mary, 31; Thomas, 63, 80
EMLEN, Samuel, 64
EMLIN, Samuell, 44
ENGLAND, 24, 70
ENOUGH, Stanlus, 74
FAIRFAX, 16, 17, 25, 28, 29, 45, 60, 63, 68, 75, 76, 100, 147, 154, 170, 181
FARISH, Robert, 18; Stephen, 18
FARMER, Thomas, 68
FERRELL, William, 68
FILLIP, Richard, 99
FINE CREEK, 98
FITZ GARALD, Peter, 181
FITZ GARRALD, Peter, 114, 135, 142, 146, 155, 157, 159, 160, 161, 166, 168, 169, 172, 173, 174, 175, 177, 180
FITZGERALD, Peter, 24
FORK CREEK, 2, 37, 49, 59, 60, 86, 87, 88, 89, 90, 105, 108
FO, XGeorge, 83
FREDERICKSBURG, 30
FREDRICKSBURG TOWNSHIP, SC, 68
FULCHER, Joseph, 37; William, 36, 37, 38, 42, 60
FULIKER, William, 36
FULSHER, William, 60, 61
GARLAND, David, 1, 33, 35, 36, 39; Edward, 36; Elizabeth, 1; Mary, 1, 42
GELSUN, Alban, 28
GENELO, 11, 29
GENETO, 72, 111, 120
GENITO, 20, 139, 140, 145, 146, 174, 176, 177, 178, 179, 180, 181
GENOLOCREEK, 10
GILFORD CO, NC, 173
GILFORD COUNTY, 17, 22
GLASS, Thomas, 34
GLISTINE, Sarah, 38

GOFFIN, Seth, 129
GOING, Agness, 59; Agnis, 58
GOOCH, Mary, 93
GOOCHLAND, 175, 176
GOOCHLAND COUNTY, 3, 4, 5, 9,
    10, 11, 17, 20, 23, 24, 29, 30, 42,
    47, 50, 51, 53, 59, 93, 112, 164
GOOS(E) CREEK, 12, 27, 160, 170
GOWING, Agnis, 58
GREAT BRITTON, (Britain) 105
GREATH, Thomas, 38
GREEN SPRING CREEK, 38
GREEN SPRINGS, 39
GREENE SPRING, 37
GRIFFITH, Abraham, 122
GRISCOM, John (Jno.), 30
GUINEDD, PA, 169
GUTTERY, Henry, 36
GUTTREY, Henry, 35
HADDENFIELD, 41
HADLY, Bridget, 19; Simon, 19
HAGGITT, Anthony, 46; Jane, 45, 46
HAINES, Casper Wister, 168
HALE, William, 103
HALEY, Bartlett, 93; Bartlitt, 89;
    Esom, 49; John (Jno.), 55, 59,
    60, 63, 88, 90, 93, 95; Judith, 61,
    63; Ursule, 95; William, 37, 46,
    47, 48, 49, 52, 53, 103, 104, 105,
    106, 107, 108
HALLEY, William, 46
HAMBLER, Stephen, 65
HANOVER, 37
HANOVER COUNTY, 1, 2, 3, 4, 5,
    6, 7, 8, 11, 12, 13, 15, 16, 19, 21,
    24, 27, 28, 29, 30, 32, 33, 34, 35,
    36, 38, 39, 40, 41, 44, 47, 51, 55,
    56, 64, 65, 67, 69, 74, 78, 79, 80,
    93, 103, 165
HARDGROVE, Samuel, 79
HARDING, Obdiance, 111;
    Obedience, 26
HARFORD, Isaac, 80
HARGRAVE, Elizabeth, 1, 3, 18;
    Garland, 4; Garlend, 9; Jesse, 1,
    3, 14, 15, 18, 19, 26, 131, 158,

159; Jessee, 109, 114; John
(Jno.), 1, 3, 19, 20, 168, 169;
Joseph, 4, 9, 14, 19, 26, 28, 167,
168, 170; Lucy, 4, 9, 19, 26;
Martha, 1, 3, 11, 12, 14, 50, 156;
Mary, 1, 3, 14, 18, 122, 132,
133; Melicent, 22, 171, 173;
Milecent, 170; Millicent, 19;
Rachael, 4, 9; Rachel, 26; Sally,
9; Samual, 83, 84, 85; Samuel, 1,
3, 9, 12, 14, 15, 18, 19, 20, 26,
42, 47, 51, 53, 55, 58, 59, 60, 61,
62, 63, 64, 65, 66, 67, 68, 69, 70,
71, 72, 73, 75, 76, 77, 78, 79,
109, 110, 112, 113, 115, 116,
117, 118, 121, 122, 123, 124,
158, 159, 163, 165; Samuell, 57;
Sarah, 1, 3, 12, 140, 141; Susana,
19; Thomas, 1, 3, 12, 14, 15, 19,
158, 159
HARGROVE, Jesse, 93; Martha, 80,
81, 93; Mary, 11; Salley, 11;
Samual, 85, 86, 88, 89, 91, 93,
94, 96, 99, 100; Samuel, 78, 79,
80, 81, 82, 83, 84, 87
HARLOW, Thomas, 116, 118
HARRIS, Ann, 3, 17, 166; Benjamin,
4, 18, 41, 42, 43, 44, 45, 46, 47,
48, 50, 51, 53, 54, 56, 57, 58, 59,
65, 68, 69, 79, 93, 167; Chatilda,
4; Cheadle, 3, 27; Chlotilda, 16,
17, 24, 28, 29, 157; Cornelius, 3,
47; Daniel, 1, 3, 79, 81, 82, 85,
89, 90, 92, 93; Daniell, 32, 33,
37, 41; Deanel, 85; Deborah, 4;
E:De, 47; Ede, 59, Edeth, 79, 81,
93; Edith, 1, 3, 13, 16, 23, 24,
29, 149; Elizabeth, 3, 12, 18, 31,
167; Isabella, 4; James, 18, 81,
82, 83, 90, 91, 93, 94, 115, 117,
122, 125, 132, 133, 138, 140,
147, 166, 167; Jeremiah, 3, 17,
20, 21, 24, 26, 27, 79, 80, 81, 85,
120, 142, 143, 144, 165, 178,
179; Jerimiah, 116; John (Jno.),
1, 3, 12, 13, 16, 20, 23, 24, 29,

36, 41, 47, 51, 57, 59, 72, 78, 79,
80, 81, 82, 83, 84, 85, 86, 87, 88,
89, 90, 91, 92, 93, 94, 95, 96, 97,
98, 99, 100, 101, 121, 122, 124,
125, 126, 127, 128, 129, 130,
134, 135, 136, 137, 138, 139,
140, 141, 142, 143, 144, 145,
146, 147, 148, 149, 150, 151,
152, 154, 155, 156, 157, 158,
160, 163, 166, 167, 170, 172,
178, 179, 180; Joseph, 34, 36,
44, 53, 80; Judith, 16, 18, 19,
167; Lucy, 3, 18, 26, 167; Mary,
1, 3, 18, 31, 33, 35, 38, 46, 81,
167; Moses, 1, 3, 12, 23, 28, 59,
65, 82, 83, 84, 85, 86, 88, 89, 90,
91, 92, 93, 94, 95, 96, 97, 98, 99,
100, 101, 116, 117, 118, 120,
121, 122, 123, 125, 126, 127,
129, 130, 131, 132, 133, 134,
135, 136, 137, 138, 140, 141,
142, 143, 144, 145, 146, 147,
163, 165, 175, 180; Nicholas, 3;
Obadiah, 80, 141; Obediah, 78;
Pleasant, 97; Plummer, 28;
Priscilla Lowes, 3; Rachael, 29;
Rachal, 66, 79, 81, 93, 94;
Rachel, 13, 16, 23, 24, 53;
Rebackeh, 41; Rebeca, 59;
Rebecca, 4; Rebeccah, 47;
Rebeckah, 44; Remley, 32;
Richard, 27, 145; Sally, 3; Sally
Lowes, 3; Samuel, 13, 144, 161,
166; Sarah, 3, 4, 12, 13, 21, 23,
24, 29, 30, 41, 46, 56, 63, 80, 81,
93, 106, 118, 171; Sarah Ann, 4;
Sophia, 23, 89, 175; Sopphia, 3;
Standley, 59; Standly, 59, 64;
Stanley, 31, 32, 33, 34, 35, 36,
37, 38, 39, 40, 41, 42, 43, 44, 45,
141; Stanly, 110; Susanah, 13;
Susannah, 23; Thomas, 3, 4, 16,
18, 20, 23, 24, 28, 29, 30, 79, 81,
85, 88, 91, 92, 93, 94, 114, 116,
119, 120, 121, 122, 126, 127,
128, 130, 131, 140, 142, 144,

146, 147, 148, 149, 150, 151,
152, 153, 155, 156, 157, 158,
159, 160, 161, 162, 163, 166,
167, 168, 169, 170, 171, 173,
174, 175, 176, 177, 178, 179,
180, 181; Unity, 4; William E,
28, 169, 170, 172, 176; William
Eley, 3, 161, 168
HARRISON, Benjamin, 67
HARRISS, Ann, 8; Benjamin, 39, 46,
47, 49, 50, 55, 58, 59, 60, 61, 62,
63, 64, 66, 70, 78; Cheadle, 8;
Cornelious, 64, 65; Cornelis, 57;
Daniel, 46, 47, 63, 64, 109, 110;
Daniell, 33; Ede, 78; Elizabeth,
8; James, 78, 112, 113; Jeremiah,
8, 113; Jerimiah, 112; John
(Jno.), 8, 47, 48, 58, 64, 65, 66,
67, 69, 70, 71, 72, 73, 74, 75, 76,
77, 78, 109, 110; Judith, 62, 64;
Lucy, 8; Mary, 47, 78; Moses,
69, 70, 109, 110, 112, 113;
Nicholas, 78; Obediah, 69, 76,
111; Rachall, 78; Rebecca, 78;
Sally, 8; Standle, 63; Standley,
62; Standly, 64; Stanley, 65;
Stanly, 79, 109; Thomas, 110,
116; Unity, 77, 78; William, 53
HART, Elizabeth, 3, 102; Henary,
103; Henery, 50; Henry, 107;
Henry Philip, 108; Henry Philips,
3; Henry Phillip, 49; Henry
Philups, 102; James Philips, 3;
James Philups, 102; Jane, 30;
John (Jno.), 3, 82, 102; Joseph, 3,
102; Judith, 28, 30; Malcolin, 28;
Malcolm, 30; Mary, 3, 102;
William, 3, 102
HATTON, Edward, 13; Jesse, 13;
Mary, 13, 23, 24, 29; Pleasants,
13; Sarah, 13, 16, 24, 161;
Susana, 13; Susanna, 29;
Susannah, 28, 29; Thomas, 13,
16, 23, 24, 28, 29, 161, 162, 170,
171, 172, 178, 179, 181
HAWFIELD, 44

HEIRST, John (Jno.), 170
HENDERSON, Richard, 102, 105
HENRICO (County), 16, 17, 18, 20,
   21-27, 32-45, 47, 49, 51, 57, 64,
   65, 68, 69, 71, 75, 77, 79, 87, 91,
   96, 109, 110, 111, 112, 114, 118,
   120, 126, 128, 152, 157, 161,
   171, 176, 177, 179
HEWLET, Millicent, 19; Polly, 19
HEWLETT, Polley, 14
HIATT, Christopher, 12
HIGGASON, Jno, 41
HOGGAT, Joseph, 51
HOGGATT, Antoney, 47; Jane, 47;
   Joseph, 47
HOGGETT, Jane, 49; Phillip, 48
HOGGIT, Jane, 104; Phillup, 105
HOGGITT, Anthony, 46; Antoney,
   48; Antony, 53; Anttony, 108;
   Jane, 46, 102, 106, 108; Philip,
   51, 108; Philup, 107; Phylys, 45;
   William, 102, 105, 106, 108
HOGGITTS, Jane, 49
HOPEWELL, VA, 77
HOPKINS, Gerrard, 25
HUBBARD, George, 31, 33, 34, 35,
   36, 37, 38, 39; John (Jno.), 32,
   33, 34, 35, 36; Judeth, 35; Judith,
   37; Peter, 35, 39, 41
HUCHANS, Strangman, 39
HUCHENS, Ede, 51; Elizabeth, 59;
   Nichlious, 101; Nichlous, 92;
   Strangeman, 54, 55, 57, 81;
   Strangman, 41
HUCHING, Strangmon, 91
HUCHINGS, Cedey, 92; Edey, 48;
   Eliza, 47; Nicholas, 75;
   Strangeman, 48, 50, 68, 72, 75
HUCHINS, Nichlous, 92,
   Strangeman, 66
HUFF, Daniel, 19; Elizabeth, 19
HUGHENS, Strangeman, 82
HUGINGS, Leda, 92; Strangeman,
   55, 59, 69, 73, 75, 76, 77, 78
HUGINS, Strangeman, 57, 63
HUNICUTT, Ann, 98; James, 96,
   135, 136; Joseph, 98; Margit, 98
HUNNICUTT, Ann, 4, 29; James, 4,
   16, 17, 29, 95, 112, 114, 116,
   119, 120, 124, 125, 126, 127,
   128, 129, 131, 134, 136, 137,
   138, 139, 140, 141, 142, 143,
   144, 145, 147, 148, 149, 150,
   154, 155, 156, 157, 158, 159,
   160, 161, 162, 165, 166, 167,
   172; John (Jno.), 15, 20, 29, 112,
   158, 160; John (Jno.) Murdaugh,
   4; Joseph, 12, 20, 112, 169, 170,
   171, 172, 177, 179; Margreat,
   113, 114; Milley M, 25; Miriam
   Murdaugh, 4; Miriam Murdock,
   29; Nancy, 12, 20, 23, 170;
   Rebecca, 4, 17, 25; Thomas, 25;
   Thomas Pretlow, 4
HUNT, William, 44, 70
HUSBAND, John (Jno.), 58
HUTCHASON, Strangman, 32
HUTCHENS, Elizabeth, 85; Jane, 84,
   85; John (Jno.), 58, 59; Mary, 51,
   59; Nichlous, 99; Sarah, 93;
   Strangeman, 51, 59, 79, 81, 82,
   84, 85; Strangemon, 93;
   Strangman, 82; Strangmon, 86,
   96, 97; Thomas, 100
HUTCHIN, Strageman, 47
HUTCHING, Strangman, 123
HUTCHINGS, Agatha, 9; Alce, 9;
   Benjamin, 108; Eliza Cobbs, 42;
   Elizabeth, 9; Jane, 35; John
   (Jno.), 9, 19; Jonathan, 9, 165;
   Marthy, 34; Mary, 9, 70; Milley,
   164; Nicholas, 115, 120, 121,
   122, 123, 125, 126, 127, 132;
   Nicholass, 124; Nicholus, 120;
   Patrick, 9; Strangeman, 34, 38,
   42, 45, 46, 129, 140; Strangman,
   9, 39, 40, 113, 114, 115, 116,
   118, 121, 122, 123, 124, 125,
   126, 127, 163, 164; Susanah, 9;
   Thomas, 9, 112, 126; William, 9
HUTCHINS, Agatha, 3; Alice, 3;
   Benjamin, 147; Cedia, 93;

Elizabeth, 3, 147; John (Jno.), 3, 137; Jonathan, 3, 137, 138; Mary, 3; Nicholas, 19, 128, 129, 131, 133, 135, 136, 138; Patrick, 3; Sarah, 19; Strangeman, 45, 51, 130, 132; Strangman, 3, 133, 134, 135, 136, 137, 142, 143, 146, 147; Susana, 129; Susanna, 3; Thomas, 142, 146, 147; Thomass, 3; William, 3

HUTHENS, Elizabeth, 84

INDIAN SPRING, 16

INDIAN SPRING, MD, 162, 180

IRELAND, 168

ISLE OF WHITE COUNTY, 42, 85, 89

ISLESHILL COUNTY, 40

JACKSON, Mary, 44, 46; Moses, 181; William, 24, 28, 178, 179

JAMES, Edm, 28; Edmund, 28; Fanny, 13

JARSEYS, 41

JENATO, 75, 79

JENETO, 72, 86, 92, 109, 112, 114, 115, 116, 118, 119, 121, 123, 125, 126, 127, 137, 140

JENETOE, 99, 101

JENITO, 123, 124, 128, 129, 130, 133, 134, 135, 136, 138, 139, 141, 142, 143, 146, 147, 148, 149, 150, 151, 152, 153, 154, 155, 156, 157, 158, 159, 160, 161, 162, 166, 167, 168, 169, 170, 171, 172, 173, 174, 175, 176, 178, 179, 180, 181

JERITO, 169

JOHNSON (See also Johson.), Agatha, 1, 4, 8, 18, 22; Aggatha, 86; Agnes, 4; Agness, 18, 59, 98, 102, 103, 105, 106, 148, 156; And, 131; Andrew, 4; Anna, 175; Anne, 1, 18; Ashley, 18, 19, 24, 34, 42, 43, 44, 46, 48, 53, 55, 56, 58, 61, 62, 63, 68, 76, 80, 81, 84, 88, 90, 95, 96, 107, 108, 111, 114, 115, 126, 129, 130, 131,

134, 139, 140, 141, 147, 148, 149, 154, 156, 165, 175; Ashly, 1, 4, 20, 23, 37, 66, 73, 74, 75, 79, 93, 104, 113, 116, 128; Ben, 18; Benjamin, 1, 4, 5, 16, 19, 23, 38, 54, 59, 60, 61, 62, 63, 74, 78, 93, 98, 100, 102, 103, 104, 106, 107, 108, 111, 113, 115, 120, 128, 132, 133, 139, 140, 142, 147, 148, 150, 156, 162, 165, 166, 173, 176; Benjmon, 102, 103; Betsey, 4, 19, 24; Charles, 4, 8, 31, 35, 36, 43, 47, 53, 55, 62, 63, 68, 71, 81, 82, 88, 89, 90; Christopher, 4, 12, 14, 16, 90, 102, 107, 128, 140, 141; Cicily, 27; Cisley, 62; Collass, 69; Collings, 4, 102; David, 4, 19, 126; Deborah, 5; Dorothy, 5, 30; Drusilia, 18; Drusilla, 18, 175; Drusylla, 1; Edith, 1, 175; Edward, 4, 102; Elerah, 4; Elijah, 11, 16, 18, 24, 29, 119, 121, 122, 125, 129, 130, 131, 132, 133, 134, 135, 136, 137, 139, 141, 142, 143, 145, 146, 147, 148, 149, 150, 151, 152, 153, 154, 155, 156, 157, 158, 159, 160, 161, 162, 166, 167, 168, 169, 170, 171, 173, 174, 176, 177, 178, 179; Elisha, 18, 22, 145; Elizabeth, 1, 4, 8, 9, 12, 18, 19, 28, 38, 86, 89, 90, 92, 113, 161, 174; Garrard, 18, 151, 153, 155, 156, 162, 166, 168; Garratt, 68; Garret, 65; Gerard, 1, 4, 19; Gerrad, 113; Gerrard, 22, 23, 149; Gidion, 61, 63, 64; Gidron, 38; James, 4, 5, 8, 18, 22, 25, 27, 28, 58, 59, 61, 62, 63, 64, 65, 66, 75, 76, 90, 95, 98, 102, 103, 104, 105, 108, 113, 118, 120, 126, 127, 128, 130, 158, 159, 164; Jane, 1, 4, 9, 18, 19, 22, 145, 173; Jarrad, 117; Jesse, 1, 9, 18, 20, 24, 27, 38, 42, 55, 61, 63, 66,

68, 74, 75, 80, 88, 89, 90, 93,
113, 114, 115, 116, 117, 118,
120, 123, 124, 125, 127, 128,
129, 132, 133, 134, 135, 136,
137, 139, 140, 143, 144, 145,
146, 147, 148, 150, 154, 156,
158, 165, 167, 168, 174; Jessee,
118; John (Jno.), 1, 4, 5, 8, 16,
18, 19, 20, 25, 26, 28, 29, 30, 31,
32, 36, 37, 38, 42, 43, 47, 48, 50,
53, 57, 62, 63, 74, 75, 76, 80, 86,
92, 93, 112, 113, 114, 116, 118,
120, 121, 122, 123, 124, 126,
127, 128, 130, 132, 133, 134,
135, 136, 139, 152, 156, 157,
160, 162, 170, 172, 178, 181;
John (Jno.) Watkins, 4; Jonathan,
4; Joseph, 4, 8, 18, 22, 134, 139,
145, 181; Judith, 4, 5, 8, 18, 19,
111, 113; Lidia, 16, 18, 19;
Lorana, 95; Lucy, 19, 98; Lydia,
4, 8, 18, 113; Margaret, 4;
Martha, 19, 23, 24, 107, 159;
Mary, 1, 4, 5, 16, 18, 19, 43, 62,
96, 98, 103, 106, 113, 135, 139,
140, 142, 150, 165; Massey, 19;
Mathew, 47; Matthew, 107;
Melicent, 22; Micajah, 118;
Milley, 4, 18, 134; Moorman,
128, 132, 164; Moreman, 4;
Nicholas, 14; Nicholus, 156;
Nyorid, 9; Patsey, 4; Patte, 103;
Patty, 19, 23, 177, 178;
Penelope, 4, 5, 102; Pleasant, 8;
Pleasants, 4; Rachael, 4; Rachal,
8; Robert, 4, 18, 61, 63, 79, 90,
102; Sally, 4; Samuel, 4, 8, 18,
19, 22, 145; Sara, 18; Sarah, 1, 4,
5, 18, 88, 90, 102, 103; Squire,
33, 38; Strangeman, 4; Susana,
16, 18; Susanah, 8, 18, 51, 52;
Susanar, 106; Susanna, 4; Talton,
75; Thomas, 1, 4, 8, 16, 18, 24,
88, 89, 90, 92, 95, 126, 141, 170,
171, 178; Thomas Garland, 4;
Thomas Watkins, 1; Unity, 5;

Watkins, 1, 20, 175; William, 1,
4, 8, 16, 18, 21, 22, 23, 27, 51,
52, 74, 75, 80, 86, 101, 102, 113,
123, 143, 145, 146, 154, 161,
162, 172; Zachariah, 4; Zachreas,
101
JOHNSTONE, Micah, 34
JOHSON, Anna, 23; Ashley, 23;
Drusila, 23; Edith, 23; Mary, 23;
Thomas, 23; Watkins, 23
JONES, Ann, 23, 24, 26, 28, 30, 178;
Catlet, 11, 16, 18, 21, 24, 26,
130, 134, 135, 136, 137, 138,
139, 140, 141, 142, 143, 146,
147, 148, 149, 150, 151, 152,
153, 154, 155, 156, 157, 158,
159, 160, 161, 162, 166, 167,
168, 169, 170, 171, 172, 173,
174, 175, 177, 178, 179, 180,
181; Catlett, 28, 29, 132, 145;
Catlit, 23; Catlitt, 29, 30; Father,
30; Humphry, 33; Pattey, 26,
176; Patty, 23; William, 33
JONSON, Agness, 54; John (Jno.), 54
JONSONS, Jno, 57
JORDAN, Elizabeth, 38
JOURDAN, Richard, 25, 181
JUDI, Nancy, 20
KERBY, Mary, 64
KING GEORGE COUNTY, 43
LADD, Ann, 16; Isabell, 16; James,
16, 17, 27, 62, 74, 78; James D,
26; John (Jno.), 77, 78; Joshua,
41; Mary, 23; Priscilla, 16;
Rachel, 23; Salley, 23; Sarah, 74;
Thomas, 20, 23, 24, 25; Unity,
17; William, 32, 78
LAIN, Ann, 97; Margry, 97;
Mordicai, 97; Thomas, 58, 97;
William, 31
LAINE, Daniell, 34; William, 32, 34
LALLEY, Edmond, 104
LAME, Thomas, 31
LANCASTER, Aron, 143
LANE, Jno, 38; William, 37, 41, 76
LAVERY, William, 30

LAY, Gideon, 132
LEWIS, Richard, 13, 69, 88, 100, 154, 155
LIGHTFOOT, Mical, 108; Michal, 44
LILLY, Edmond, 105
LITTLEBURY, Maddox, 128
LOGAN, Charles, 10; James, 138; Mary, 15, 138, 157, 158; Sarah, 138
LONDON, 82
LOUDOUN COUNTY, 17, 25, 60, 100, 147
LOUISA COUNTY, 1, 3, 4, 5, 6, 8, 10, 13, 14, 17, 18, 21, 22, 23, 24, 27, 28, 35, 37, 39, 40, 41, 43, 50, 51, 54, 56, 59, 61, 62, 63, 64, 69, 73, 76, 77, 79, 80, 81, 88, 89, 93, 94, 95, 98, 103, 106
LUNCH, Sarah, 46, 56
LYLLEY, Edmon, 104
LYNCH, Charles, 46, 49, 50, 51, 52, 56; Sarah, 45, 46, 49, 51, 103, 104, 105
MCGEEHEE, Ann, 14; Elizabeth, 12; Joseph, 14; Milisant, 12; Milley, 15
MCGEHEE, Ann, 80; Cair, 67
MCGEHEE, Cair, 68
MCGEHEE, Cair, 80; Judith, 108; Mary, 80
MACHGEEHEE, Ann, 15; Milley, 158
MACKELBOROUGH, Robert, 33
MACKGEE, Ann, 18
MACKGEEHEE, Ann, 158, 160; Joseph, 54, 55; Milley, 160
MACKGEHE, Benjamin, 56; Joseph, 56
MADDO, XGriffin, 133; John (Jno.), 5, 8, 9, 30; Jno (John) P, 169; John (Jno.) W, 10, 13, 142, 143, 146, 149, 150, 151, 152, 153, 155, 156, 160, 170, 173, 174, 176; John (Jno.) Wilson, 5, 8, 27, 132, 133, 138, 140, 141, 143,

144, 147, 148, 172; Mildred, 5, 9, 10, 13, 133; Nelson, 9; Thomas, 5, 8, 27, 30, 133; William, 133; William Griffin, 5, 8; Wilson, 5, 8, 10, 133
MADO, XMildred, 127
MAEGEY, Nancy, 12
MAGEHEE, Ann, 81
MALLORY, Priscilla, 28; Thomas, 28
MARYLAND (State), 16, 28, 64, 104, 153, 173
MASSEY, Thomas, 143
MATHEWS, Daniell, 45, 46; George, 57; William, 46
MATO, XWilliam, 50
MATTHEWS, Daniell, 43; George, 70
MEADER, Jason, 34; Joel, 35; Jonas, 34
MEADOR, Janoh, 38; Joel, 37, 38; Jonas, 37
MILES, Manoak, 33
MONALLEN, PA, 180
MOOR, Ann, 103, 107, 159; Anne, 10; John (Jno.), 107
MOORE, Ann, 103, 148, 155, 160; Anne, 41, 45, 46; Gamm, 121; James, 16; John (Jno.), 40, 41, 57, 59, 60, 66, 90, 102, 103, 104, 105, 106, 107, 118, 121, 127, 136; William, 104, 106
MOOREMAN, Accallus, 77; Acculas, 74; Achillas, 61; Aggatha, 74, 75; Andrew, 113; Charles, 47, 48, 49, 50, 54, 58, 59, 61, 62, 63, 64, 65, 66, 72, 74, 75, 76, 77, 78, 113; Clark T, 113, 167; Judeth, 78; Micajah, 48; Mildred, 61, 62; Rachal, 62, 63; Rachall, 47, 78; Rilley, 50; Robert, 108; Thomas, 47, 48, 58, 59, 60, 61, 62, 63, 64, 66, 68, 71, 72, 74, 78; Zacariah, 49; Zachariah, 63, 69, 74
MOOREMAND, Thomas, 58

MOORMAN, Acchillis, 115, 120,
163; Achillis, 14; Aggy, 5;
Andrew, 18, 112, 180; Archilles,
112; Betty, 22; Charles, 5, 45,
46, 81, 84, 88, 89, 90, 99, 114,
115, 124; Clark, 29, 30, 110;
Clark T, 12, 14, 16, 21, 24, 114,
115, 140, 141, 142, 147, 148,
149, 150, 152, 153, 154, 155,
156, 157, 158, 159, 160, 161,
162, 163, 166, 168, 169, 170,
171, 172, 173, 174, 175, 176,
178, 179, 180, 181, 182; Clark
Terrel, 117; Clark Terrell, 110,
112, 116, 124, 141, 145, 146;
Clark Terrill, 111, 118, 119;
Clarke Terrell, 167; Dosha, 22;
Elizabeth, 5, 10, 12, 22, 174;
Frances, 14; James, 119, 121,
124, 163; Jude, 5; Judith, 5;
Lucy, 5; Mary, 5; Micajah, 5, 22,
110, 111, 112, 116, 162;
Mildred, 5; Molley, 5; Nancy,
22; Pleasant, 5; Rachael, 5, 10,
28, 29; Rachel, 11, 12, 14, 16,
18, 19, 22, 23, 24, 30, 149, 177;
Rhoda, 14, 16, 19, 21, 171, 172;
Robert, 5; Salley, 14, 156, 157;
Susanah, 114; Thomas, 5, 10, 46,
111, 119, 128, 162, 163;
Zachariah, 5
MOORMEN, John (Jno.), 106
MOORMON, Achillias, 102; Agge,
101; Benjmon, 106; Bettey, 107;
Charles, 87, 92, 93, 95, 96, 97,
98, 99, 101, 102, 103, 104, 105,
106, 107, 108; Clark, 94; Clarke,
100; Elizabeth, 101, 103; John
(Jno.), 106, 108; Jude, 101;
Lucey, 101; Mary, 95, 98, 101,
103, 106; Micajah, 101; Mildred,
101; Molley, 101; Pleasant, 101;
Rachael, 101; Rachal, 103, 105,
106; Robert, 101; Thomas, 101,
103, 104, 105, 106, 108;
Zacariah, 101

MOORS, William, 42
MORE, Ann, 56
MORELAND, Charles, 55; Thomas,
50, 55
MOREMAN, Charles, 52, 54, 55, 56,
57; Clark T, 23; John (Jno.), 51;
Lucy, 54; Mary, 45; Rachel, 23;
Thomas, 36, 37, 52, 54, 55, 56,
57, 64
MORMAN, Charles, 35, 51, 52, 54,
56; Clark T, 19; Elizabeth, 54;
Mary, 54; Micajah, 50; Rachel,
50, 51, 54; Thomas, 35, 51, 52,
54, 58; Zachariah, 51; Zacharias,
56
MOSBY, Ursley, 114; Ursly, 114,
115, 117
"Mountains, The" 103
MUCDANALD, John (Jno.), 102
MUDDY CREEK, 148
NANSEMOND (County), 31, 38
NEAL, 94
NELSON, Jemima, 14
NEW, Anthony, 21, 30; Nancy, 30
NEW GARDEN, 12, 17, 48, 49, 51,
70, 71, 74, 75, 76, 79, 80, 81, 83,
84, 85, 86, 88, 89, 90, 94, 95, 96,
97, 98, 111, 118, 120, 121, 122,
140, 161, 178
NEW GARDIAN (Garden), NC, 54
NEW JERSEY, 56
NEW KENT COUNTY, 44, 55
NEW YORK, 143
NEWBY, Jno, 50; Joseph, 54, 66
NICLESON, Thomas, 57
NORTH CAROLINA, 12, 17, 18, 19,
22, 23, 25, 26, 42, 44, 45, 46, 47,
48, 49, 50, 51, 52, 53, 54, 55, 56,
58, 60, 66, 70, 71, 74, 75, 76, 79,
80, 83, 84, 85, 86, 88, 89, 90, 94,
95, 96, 97, 98, 106, 108, 118,
119, 120, 121, 125, 139, 140,
141, 143, 144, 161, 177
NORTH CAROLINE, 27
NORWICK, ENGLAND, 94
OLD ENGLAND, 52, 59, 60

OPECKIN, 45
OPERKON, 64
ORANGE/ORRANGE (County), 11,
    15, 16, 23, 29, 44, 61, 88, 147,
    149, 159, 165
OSLEY, Joseph, 94
OUTLAND, Jeremiah, 25, 181
PAGAN (Pagin) CREEK, 40, 42
PAGGIT, Jerimiah, 46
PARSONS, Lane, 20; Margaret, 30;
    Margaret P, 29; Samuel, 10, 16,
    17, 20, 23, 24, 25, 29, 30, 139,
    140, 142, 143, 145, 146, 147,
    148, 149, 150, 151, 152, 153,
    154, 155, 156, 157, 158, 159,
    160, 161, 162, 166, 167, 168,
    169, 170, 171, 172, 173, 174,
    175, 177, 178, 179, 180, 181;
    Samuel P, 25; Sarah, 10, 16, 17,
    20, 24, 25, 29, 30; Sarah
    Pleasants, 10, 139; Thomas, 63
PATTON, Catherine, 46
PAYN, John (Jno.), 77, 78; Mary, 77,
    78
PAYNE, Christopher, 79; Dolley, 12,
    89; John (Jno.), 21, 79, 89, 91,
    92, 93, 96, 97, 98, 100, 109, 110,
    111, 114, 115, 117, 118, 119,
    120, 121, 122, 124, 125, 126,
    127, 128, 129, 130, 133, 136,
    137, 138, 162, 163, 164; Mary,
    12, 79, 114, 129, 164; Mordecai,
    135; Temple, 89; Walter, 89,
    125; Williams, 89
PAYTON, Catheran, 47
PEARSON, Mary, 136
PEASLEY, Mary, 46, 47
PEATROS, John (Jno.), 26
PEATROSS, Amey, 5, 9; Amy, 29;
    Anna, 5, 9, 30; Elizabeth, 5, 9,
    29, 30; James, 14; John (Jno.), 5,
    9, 10, 19, 21, 30, 117, 118, 131,
    134, 150, 154, 156, 157, 158,
    160, 172, 174; Mary, 5, 9, 14,
    29, 30; Nelson, 5, 9, 10; Rhoda,
    5, 9; Richard, 30; Sarah, 5, 10,

14, 30; Tar, 9; Thomas, 30;
    William, 14, 30
PEATRUS, John (Jno.), 167, 168
PEATRUSS, John (Jno.), 135, 136,
    137, 143, 167
PECKOVER, Edmond, 33
PENNSYLVANIA (Pensylvany), 13,
    24, 80, 108, 143, 171
PERQUIMANS, PEQUAMMANS,
    Pirquimons, etc. (County), NC,
    49, 54, 68, 104, 106
PERSONS, Samuel, 93
PETERSBURG, 17
PETROSS, John (Jno.), 125
PETTROSS, John (Jno.), 14, 124,
    125, 126
PHILADELPHIA, 30, 44, 105, 122,
    125, 129, 137, 138, 143, 147,
    168
PHILADELPHIA COUNTY, 122
PIKE, Abigail, 44
PILLAR, Elizabeth, 18
PILLER, Milley, 18
PIPE CREEK, 30
PIPE CREEK, MD, 118
PITTRUS, Sarah, 14
PLEASANT, James, 77; John (Jno.),
    51; Samuel, 65; Thomas, 31, 57
PLEASANTS, Archabald, 111, 162;
    Archable, 87; Bary, 17; Cary, 20,
    27, 171, 177; Deborah, 16, 17,
    25, 162; Eliza, 17, 20, 33; Eliza
    T, 17; Elizabeth, 10, 17, 20, 24,
    29, 114, 117, 132, 173, 174;
    Elizabeth Snowden, 5, 10;
    Elizabeth T, 20, 25, 170;
    Elizabeth Tucker, 5, 20, 22, 30,
    139, 180; Gary, 21; Henrietta M,
    29; Isaac, 124, 125, 164; Jacob,
    20; James, 17, 20; James B, 16,
    24, 153, 154, 160, 162; James
    Brook, 152; Jane, 25; John
    (Jno.), 25, 33, 48, 50, 51, 63, 64,
    65, 77; John (Jno.) S, 20, 27;
    John (Jno.) Scott, 139, 147, 154;
    Joseph Jordan, 5; JW, 25;

Margaret, 11; Mariam, 25; Mary, 5, 10, 11, 16, 24, 27, 29, 33, 136, 181; Miriam, 114, 125, 180, 181; Mirim, 98; Philip, 20, 25; Polley, 20; Polly, 17; Robert, 10, 16, 25, 33, 50, 64, 66, 67; Ruben, 20, 25; Samuel, 122, 125, 164; Sarah, 17, 20, 24, 25, 27; Susanah, 109; Thomas, 10, 11, 16, 17, 20, 23, 24, 48, 50, 51, 63, 64, 66, 72, 79, 82, 84, 85, 87, 92, 99, 100, 111, 113, 114, 117, 118, 119, 121, 123, 127, 128, 129, 130, 133, 136, 137, 139, 140, 145, 146, 147, 148, 150, 154, 155, 157, 158, 160, 161, 166, 167, 168, 169, 170, 171, 172, 174, 175, 176, 177, 179, 180, 182; Thomas E, 17, 20; Thomas Exum, 23, 139, 176, 177, 179; Thomas S, 20, 156, 158, 162, 168, 169, 170, 173; Thomas Snowden, 5, 10, 20, 22; Thomas Snowdon, 180; Thomas T, 17; Thomas W, 17, 20; Thomas Willing, 10; William A, 17; William H, 11, 24, 25, 29; William Henry, 5, 26, 154, 179
POSPATANK COUNTY, 104
POTTS, Joseph, 171
POWHATAN COUNTY, 10, 15, 20, 25, 164
PRICE, Elizabeth, 57, 79, 80
PRINCE GEORGE COUNTY, 22, 95, 97
RAILEY, Abagail, 34; Elizabeth, 33; Rachel, 33
RATCLIFF, Elizabeth, 5; Gideon, 5; Harrison, 5; John (Jno.), 5; Mary, 5; William, 5
RATLIFF, Elizabeth, 86, 91; Gedion, 91; Harrison, 91; John (Jno.), 91; Mary, 91; William, 86, 87, 91, 93
RATLIVE, William, 89
RATTIKIN, James, 170
RAY, Joseph, 77, 81, 83
RAYS MEETING, England, County

of Durhanm, 50, 52
READ, Hugh, 32; Judeth, 32
RED, Hugh, 31, 32; Judeth, 31, 32
REDD, Elizabeth, 14
REDNOR, 122
REDSTONE QUARTERLY MEETING, 30
REDSTONE QUARTERS, 29
RETLIFF, Gidion, 90; Harrison, 90; John (Jno.), 90; Mary, 90; William, 90
RICH SQUARE, NC, 181
RICHMOND, 5, 10, 27
RICHSQUARE MONTHLY MEETING, 25
RIDELL, Thomas, 100, 101
RIDGEWAY, Mary, 168
RIGBIE, Anne, 79; James, 80; Sarah, 79
RISTOLE, Janey, 24
ROBBERTS, John (Jno.), 106
ROBENSON, George, 45, 63
ROBERDS, John (Jno.), 107
ROBERTS, John (Jno.), 49, 50
ROBESSON, George, 48
ROBINSON, George, 62, 63, 64
ROGERS, Salley, 14
ROSS, Robert H, 20
ROWAN (Roan) COUNTY, NC, 74
ROYNOLDS, Agness, 74
ROYSTER, Agness, 20; Frances, 17; Joel, 17
RUNALDS, Agness, 76
RUSEL, Benjamin, 97; Sara, 12
RUSSEL, Benjamin, 22, 24, 25; Rebecca, 22; Sophia, 22
RUSSELL, Benjamin, 100, 101, 144, 145, 173, 174, 175, 176, 177, 178, 179; Rebecca, 173; Sophia, 173
SANDARS, Jno, 39
SANDERS, Catron, 37; Elizabeth, 40, 41; Hezakiah, 59; Hezekiah, 44, 60, 62, 80; Jane, 34, 37, 38, 44, 46, 47, 74, 75; Jesse, 38; Joel, 75; John (Jno.), 31, 32, 33,

198

34, 35, 36, 37, 38, 39, 40, 41, 42,
43, 45, 49, 52, 54, 55, 56, 59, 60,
61, 62, 63, 64, 65, 66, 67, 68, 69,
70, 71, 72, 73, 74, 75, 76, 79, 84,
106; Joseph, 34; Sarah, 66, 67;
Susannah, 57
SANDORS, John (Jno.), 39, 40, 41,
46, 52, 63, 71
SAUNDERS, Hezikiah, 57; Jane, 46;
Jean, 56; Joel, 137; John (Jno.),
46, 47, 48, 53, 54, 55, 56, 57, 58,
59, 62, 63
SCOTT, Stephen, 104
SHELTON, John (Jno.), 12; Nancy,
12
SIMPSON, John (Jno.), 175
SMITH, John (Jno.), 58
SOUTH CAROLINA, 83
SOUTH PINE, 82
SOUTH RIVER, 12, 16, 19, 21, 22,
23, 25, 26, 30, 70, 74, 78, 87, 90,
94, 96, 97, 98, 99, 100, 110, 111,
112, 120, 123, 126, 127, 128,
130, 131, 132, 133, 134, 135,
137, 140, 141, 142, 145, 148,
150, 156, 157, 159, 160, 162,
166, 169, 170, 171, 172, 173,
174, 175, 180, 181
SOUTH RIVER MONTHLY
MEETING, 14
SOUTHWORTH, James, 33
STABLER, Deborah, 17; Edward, 24,
66, 82, 85, 181; Mary, 17, 24,
25; William, 16, 17, 23, 162
STABLERS, Edward, 64
STANDLE, Archales, 59; John
(Jno.), 49, 56
STANDLEY, Alce, 58, 59; Archileus,
53; Catherine, 63; Elee, 53;
Eliza, 63; Elizabeth, 63; John
(Jno.), 33, 47, 48, 51, 54, 56, 57,
59, 60, 63; Madox, 47, 53; Mary,
58; Pleasant, 47, 57; Thomas, 47,
50, 51, 56, 57; William, 47, 51,
56, 57, 58, 59, 60, 61, 62, 63, 64
STANDLY, Archilon, 65; James, 47;

John (Jno.), 59, 65, 68; Martha,
59; Micajah, 68; Nichelaus, 58;
Pleasant, 47, 65; Shadrack, 66,
79, 84; Shadrick, 67; Shardrick,
69; William, 47, 64, 65, 66, 67,
69, 73; Zacariah, 67
STANLEY, Abigal, 6, 11, 155;
Abraham, 6, 155; Achilles, 6;
Agatha, 37; Aggatha, 13, 152;
Agnes, 6; Agness, 6, 12, 28;
Angess, 79; Ann, 44, 45; Anne,
5, 6, 45; Archaldous, 83;
Archalus, 82; Ben, 170;
Benjamin, 6, 9, 20; Bulah, 141;
Caleb, 5, 8; Catharine, 5;
Cathren, 41, 42; Cathron, 31, 40,
43; Dadely, 29; Edith, 6, 13, 21,
28, 29, 171; Edmund, 6; Elijah,
6; Eliza, 12; Elizabeth, 1, 5, 6, 8,
11, 21, 25, 29, 31, 34, 35, 96,
141, 169; Fanney, 13; Frances, 6;
Hannah, 1, 6; HG, 31; Hulda, 11,
28, 41; Huldah, 12, 13, 142;
Hulday, 1, 6; Isaac, 6, 13, 21, 23,
151, 169, 175, 177, 179, 180,
181; James, 5, 6, 8, 9, 13, 31, 32,
34, 36, 37, 38, 39, 40, 41, 43;
Jesse, 6; Joel, 6; John (Jno.), 1, 5,
6, 11, 12, 13, 15, 19, 21, 28, 29,
30, 31, 34, 38, 40, 41, 42, 43, 44,
45, 46, 85, 96, 128, 141, 142,
158, 159, 169; Jonathan, 28, 29,
30, 164; Joseph, 5, 6, 9; Joshua,
11, 12, 13, 23, 24, 28, 29, 30,
139, 140, 141, 147, 148, 153,
155, 158, 168, 172, 179, 181;
Judith, 6, 11; Littlbury, 12;
Littleberry, 13, 134; Littlebury,
6, 152, 180, 181; Lucy, 6;
Maddox, 1, 5, 6, 11, 15, 31, 144;
Maddy, 6, 172; Madox, 35, 36;
Margaret, 12, 16, 161; Margery,
5; Margory, 43; Margrey, 44;
Martha, 5, 6, 11, 13, 40, 43;
Mary, 1, 5, 6, 46, 47; Micajah, 5;
Milley, 19, 166, 168; Milly, 6,

28; Moses, 6, 30; Nancy, 13;
Nathan, 5; Obediah, 1, 6; Peggey,
13; Pleasant, 5, 181; Priscilla, 6;
Rachael, 1, 6; Rachel, 30;
Rebecca, 12, 13, 26, 28;
Rebecka, 29; Rebekah, 6;
Samuel, 1, 6; Sarah, 5, 6, 65,
155; Shadrack, 12, 15, 17, 44,
81, 82, 83, 85, 109, 129, 130,
131, 133, 134, 135, 136, 138,
139, 140, 141, 142, 152, 154,
160; Soloman, 158, 171;
Solomon, 6, 21, 159;
Strangeman, 6; Susanah, 12, 13,
155; Susaner, 96; Susanna, 6;
Temperance, 6, 11; Thomas, 5, 6,
9, 11, 13, 16, 20, 24, 28, 29, 30,
31, 32, 33, 34, 40, 41, 44, 128,
129, 132, 137, 138, 140, 141,
142, 144, 145, 146, 148, 149,
150, 151, 152, 153, 154, 155,
156, 157, 158, 159, 160, 161,
162, 166, 167, 168, 169, 170,
171, 172, 173, 174, 175, 176,
177, 178, 179, 180, 181; Thomas
Binford, 6; Unity, 6, 9, 11, 24,
28, 29, 30, 179; Ursla, 12;
Ursley, 13; Waddey, 136, 148;
Waddy, 13, 23, 26, 28, 29, 30,
151, 154, 155, 166, 167, 170,
174, 175, 177, 178, 179;
William, 1, 5, 6, 12, 21, 34, 38,
41, 43, 45, 54, 66, 70, 158, 159,
170, 171; Zacariah, 66;
Zachariah, 5, 6, 13, 130, 131,
132, 134, 135, 138, 141, 142,
143, 144, 146, 153, 155
STANLY, Agness, 79, 81; Ann, 73,
74; Archaldas, 92; Archaldes, 79;
Archaldious, 89; Archaldous, 79,
84; Archaldus, 95, 96, 99, 100;
Archalious, 98; Archalus, 94;
Archelaus, 93; Archeldas, 81;
Archelous, 113; Archiles, 109;
Archilous, 111; Bettey, 98;
Cathrine, 74; Eliza, 65;

Elizabeth, 79, 97; Hulda, 81;
James, 103; John (Jno.), 51, 69,
71, 74, 78, 79, 81, 93, 113, 122,
123, 162; Jonathan, 126; Joshua,
79, 93, 98, 99, 113, 120, 125,
126, 127, 136; Maddox, 78, 79,
80, 81, 99, 100; Madox, 74, 101,
109, 115, 163, 165; Micajah, 75,
76; Milley, 79; Milly, 74, 78;
Moses, 8; Nathan, 74, 75, 94;
Obediah, 115, 163; Pleasant, 73,
74, 75, 76, 79, 81, 84, 85;
Pleasants, 83; Sarah, 74;
Shadrack, 71, 79, 81, 86, 87, 88,
89, 92, 93, 94, 95, 98, 99, 110,
117, 118, 119, 121, 123, 124,
126, 127, 128, 137, 163;
Shadrick, 73, 74, 75, 77, 78;
Soloman, 111, 113, 115, 162;
Stanley, 128; Strangeman, 74;
Susanah, 93; Thomas, 8, 71, 74,
127; Unity, 8; Ursley, 91; Ursula,
74, 78, 79; Waddy, 128; William,
65, 69, 70, 71, 72, 73, 74, 75, 76,
77, 91; Zacariah, 65, 66; Zacha,
97; Zachariah, 69, 74, 76, 119,
124, 126; Zachriah, 88; Zacky,
93
START, Jahu, 98
STATLER, Edward, 82
STEADHAM, Henry, 136
STEPHENSON, John (Jno.), 70
STEVENS, Ann, 21
STEWART, Jahu, 96
STOCKDON, Thomas, 38, 39, 41
STOCKTON, Daniel, 96; Newbery,
67, 68; Prudence, 45, 46;
Thomas, 43, 44, 45, 46, 53, 55,
58, 65, 67, 68, 69, 70, 71
STOCKTON, COUNTY OF
DURHAM, England, 70
STOCTON, Thomas, 52, 64, 65
STONE, Agness, 34; Angness, 34;
Christian, 35; Christion, 37;
Elizabeth, 37, 43; John (Jno.),
43, 51, 53, 54, 55; Joshua, 72,

82; Lucy, 63, 80; Luse, 96; Mary,
31, 33, 35, 37, 38, 42; Michall,
46; Nichlos, 62; Nichlous, 81,
82, 83, 85, 86, 87, 88, 90;
Nicholas, 37, 38, 39, 41, 42, 43,
45, 48, 50, 52, 53, 54, 55, 56, 60,
63, 64, 65, 66, 68, 70, 71, 72, 73,
75, 76, 77, 78, 112, 134;
Nicholus, 40; Nicklas, 47;
Niclios, 94; Nicolas, 32, 33, 34,
35, 45, 51, 54, 57, 58; Richard,
48, 58, 64; Susanah, 44, 45, 72;
Sushannah, 73
STRONG, Ann, 46; Elizabeth, 12, 13;
George, 13; John (Jno.), 13;
Mary, 12, 51, 79; Sara, 12
SUGERLOFE MOUNTAIN, 104
SURRY (Surre) COUNTY, 18, 19,.
26, 96
SURRY (Surre) County, NC, 116,
148
SYDNOR, Worth, 13
TAKE, James, 105
TATE, James, 104, 105, 106
TAYLOR, George, 53, 61, 63, 103,
106; Jno, 35
TEMPLE, Fanney, 14; Lu, 19
TERREL, Agatha, 11; Amey, 12;
Amy, 12; Caty, 14; David, 93,
116; Deborah, 12; Elizabeth, 11;
Henery, 70; Henry, 91; Jesse, 12;
Jonathan, 12, 14, 171; Margaret,
14; Mary, 12, 17; Matthew, 12;
Matthew P, 12, 14; Micajah, 11;
Pleasant, 11, 12, 14, 16;
Pleasants, 129; Rebecca, 11, 12,
14, 16; Rhoda, 12, 14; Robert,
14; Salley, 16; Sarah, 11;
Thomas, 12, 14, 16
TERRELL, Abagail, 7; Abigail, 6;
Agatha, 33, 34, 37, 43, 46, 51,
53, 136; Agga, 6; Aggatha, 56;
Amy, 7, 146; Ann, 136; Anna,
31, 49, 51; Anne, 6, 7, 51, 54;
Benjamin, 6, 96; Betty, 6, 7, 51;
Caleb, 7; Catherine, 7; Caty, 7,

26, 30, 49; Charles, 6, 7; Charles
Linch, 124, 129, 131, 133;
Charles Lynch, 124, 132; Chiles,
7, 9, 138; Christian, 19; Clark, 7;
Daniel, 34; David, 6, 8, 18, 22,
23, 26, 31, 32, 33, 34, 35, 36, 37,
38, 39, 40, 41, 42, 43, 44, 45, 46,
47, 48, 49, 50, 51, 53, 54, 55, 56,
57, 58, 59, 60, 61, 62, 63, 70, 71,
72, 83, 84, 86, 87, 89, 90, 93, 94,
103, 113, 116, 117, 118, 119,
120, 132, 177, 178; Deborah, 18,
121; Edward, 6, 8, 108; Eliza
Ann, 7; Elizabeth, 7, 9, 18, 125;
George, 6, 7; Henary, 88;
Henery, 47, 48, 53, 55, 57, 59,
60, 61, 63, 65, 66, 67, 70, 71, 86;
Henry, 6, 7, 23, 31, 32, 33, 34,
35, 36, 37, 38, 39, 41, 42, 43, 45,
46, 47, 50, 51, 52, 53, 54, 56, 58,
62, 87, 89, 91, 92, 110, 114, 115,
163; Jesse, 7, 25, 152, 182;
Jessee, 11; Joanna, 7, 9, 22, 30;
John (Jno.), 7, 9; Jonathan, 7, 9,
19, 21, 23, 26, 29, 113, 114, 135,
136, 137, 138, 140, 142, 143,
144, 146, 149, 150, 151, 152,
153, 154, 155, 156, 158, 159,
166, 167, 168, 169, 170, 172,
174, 175, 176, 177, 179, 180,
182; Joseph, 7, 9, 29; Judith, 6,
7; Katherine, 8; Lucy, 7, 18, 122,
123; Mahala, 7, 9; Mahion, 7;
Margaret, 7, 19, 26; Margret, 9;
Maria, 7; Mary, 6, 7, 8, 11, 51,
52, 53, 119, 120, 136, 157; Mary
Bailey, 26; Mathew P, 19, 155;
Mathew Peatross, 9; Matilda, 7;
Matthew, 7, 21, 23, 26, 29, 30,
179, 180, 181, 182; Matthew P,
153, 156, 157, 159, 166, 167,
168, 169, 170, 174, 175, 176,
177; Matthew Peatross, 7;
Micajah, 18, 42, 45, 46, 51, 56,
67, 71, 109, 110, 111, 112, 114,
115, 116, 117, 118, 119, 121,

122, 123, 125, 126, 127, 128,
130, 131, 132, 133, 134, 135,
136, 163; Milla, 51, 56; Miriam,
7; Molly, 19; Nancy, 19, 26;
Nanny, 7, 9; Parmelia, 7; Pattey,
26; Pleasant, 8, 18, 19, 26, 30,
51, 56, 72, 86, 87, 89, 90, 91, 94,
95, 115, 116, 129, 131, 133, 134,
135, 136, 138, 139, 140, 141,
142, 143, 144, 145, 146, 148,
149, 150, 151, 152, 153, 154,
155, 156, 157, 158, 159, 160,
161, 162, 163, 167, 168, 169,
170, 171, 173, 174, 175, 176,
177, 178, 179, 180, 182;
Pleasants, 7, 29, 109, 110, 111,
112, 114, 117, 118, 119, 120,
121, 122, 123, 124, 126, 127,
128, 129, 130, 148, 166, 172;
Rachael, 7; Rachal, 167; Rachel,
19, 168; Rebecak, 114; Rebecca,
7, 9, 19, 22, 30; Rebeccah, 11;
Rebekah, 9, 10; Rhoda, 7, 19, 22,
25, 181; Robert, 7, 19, 26, 114,
119; Salley, 9, 19, 21, 22, 26;
Sally, 7, 30; Samuel, 6, 7, 19, 23,
24, 26; Sarah, 6, 7, 8, 19, 35, 51,
56, 63, 83, 136; Tarlton, 6, 7;
Thomas, 6, 7, 9, 10, 11, 18, 19,
21, 25, 29, 30, 51, 53, 63, 64, 65,
109, 110, 111, 112, 113, 114,
115, 117, 118, 119, 120, 121,
122, 123, 124, 125, 126, 127,
128, 129, 130, 131, 132, 133,
134, 135, 136, 137, 138, 139,
140, 141, 142, 143, 144, 145,
147, 148, 149, 150, 151, 153,
154, 155, 156, 158, 159, 160,
161, 166, 167, 168, 169, 170,
171, 172, 173, 176, 178, 179,
180, 181; Timothy, 7, 9, 29, 30;
Ursula, 6, 7; William, 49;
Winifred, 6
TERRILL, Aggatha, 103; Benjamin,
96; David, 90, 93, 94, 95, 97, 98,
99, 103, 111, 121, 123; Edward,

96, 98; Henery, 110; Henry, 90,
91, 93, 94, 95, 97, 98, 99, 100;
Micajah, 93, 99, 119, 120;
Pleasant, 86, 90, 91, 93, 94, 95,
96, 97, 98, 100, 113; Pleasants,
117, 120; Rebeccak, 117;
Rebeck, 100; Sarah, 98; Thomas,
100, 117, 120
THOMAS, Charles, 169; William, 33
THOMPSON, Jno, 28
THORNBURG, Thomas, 12
THORNBURGH, Martha, 12
THORNTON, Martha, 44; William,
38
TILLESS, Richard, 100
TOATHER, Armiges, 31, 32
TOMS CREEK, 116
TOMS CREEK, NC, 120
TOWNSEND, Joseph, 30
TURNER, James, 33; R, 25; Thomas,
43, 56
UNTHANK, Allen, 12
VAUGHAN, Anna Ladd, 7;
Benjamin, 7, 20, 25, 171, 174,
177, 179, 181; Bowling, 7;
James, 25, 27; John (Jno.) Ladd,
7; Joseph, 7; Lucy Dabney, 7;
Margaret, 7, 26, 28, 29, 30;
Margaretta B, 7; Mary M, 7;
Matilda, 7; Samuel, 7; Shadrack,
24, 26, 29, 179
WADKINS, Benjamin, 32, 35, 41,
46; Elizabeth, 42; Ledy, 48
WAITE, Mary, 57
WALKER, Elizabeth, 144, 145, 146
WARD, Sarah, 99
WARDELL, Charles, 30
WATKINS, B, 17, 20; Ben, 20, 168;
Benjamin, 11, 24, 26, 27, 39, 42,
44, 48, 50, 51, 53, 58, 68, 96,
101, 111, 114, 116, 118, 125,
126, 127, 128, 130, 149, 156,
173, 176, 181; Betsey, 24, 178;
Betsy, 23; Edeth, 93; Eliza, 17;
Elizabeth, 20, 42, 53; Jane, 51,
98; Joseph, 128, 129; Judeth, 51;

Judith, 68; Ledy, 47; Lydia, 50;
Mary, 20, 27, 53; Nicholas, 12;
Polley, 24, 25; Prissilla, 24;
Robert, 16, 167; Salley, 20, 23;
Susanah, 99; Thomas, 20, 26, 98
WATSON, Jno P, 25; June, 168
WATTS, Susana, 16
WEST, Jane, 100; Jean, 123
WEST RIVER, MD, 57, 65, 66, 69
WESTERN BRANCH, 85, 89, 108
WESTMORELAND, 38
WHITE, Easter, 105; Joseph, 105
WHITE OAK, 37, 49, 64
WHITE OAK (Oke) SWAMP, 16,
17, 18, 20, 21, 22, 24, 25, 26, 27,
28, 29, 30, 32-36, 38-45, 47, 51,
57, 62, 65, 68, 75, 77, 79, 82, 91,
98, 110, 114, 118, 122, 129, 132,
139, 152, 157, 161, 167, 172,
181, 182
WHITESWAMP, 18
WILD, Thomas, 41
WILDING, Cagiah, 93
WILLIS, Robert, 83
WILSON, James, 28, 29; John (Jno.),
128
WILSON and NIXON, 82, 85
WINSOR, Pleasants, 20
WINSTON, Anthony, 1, 7, 18, 124,
126, 164; Christian, 18; Edmond,
18; Elizabeth, 29, 114, 127;
George, 1, 7, 18; Isaac, 22, 127;
Jemima, 13, 43, 80, 153, 155;
Jemimah, 1, 7; John (Jno.), 23,
28, 127, 176; Lucy, 18, 22;
Martha, 12, 14, 157; Mary, 1, 7,
91; Molley, 80, 93; Nanthanual,
90; Nathan, 12, 19, 167, 168;
Nathanial, 85; Nathaniel, 1, 7,
13, 14, 15, 41, 43, 47, 48, 51, 55,
58, 63, 65, 67, 70, 77, 80, 81, 84,
144, 148, 150, 157, 158, 164,
181; Nathanual, 84, 86, 87, 92,
93, 94, 103, 104; Pleasant, 182;
Rebecca, 7, 12, 15, 18, 158;
Rebeccah, 1; Samual, 93, 94;

Samuel, 1, 7, 12, 13, 14, 111,
113, 114, 115, 120, 127, 132,
133, 144, 145, 148, 150; Sarah,
181; William, 33
WINSTONE, Edmond, 167; George,
158, 167; Nathaniel, 25;
Pleasant, 25; Samuel, 133; Sarah,
25
WODSON, Jacob, 50; Talton, 50
WOODSON, Ann, 87, 123, 129, 152;
Charles, 33, 73, 87, 123, 124,
125, 126, 164; Jacob, 48; Joseph,
17, 48, 50; Mary, 53, 56; Talton,
48, 72, 73; Tarlton, 33; Thomas,
53
WOOLMAN, John (Jno.), 56
WRIGHT, Rachall, 46; Rachell, 44,
46
WRIGHT(S) BOROUGH
(Bourough), GA, 27, 30, 149,
151, 175
WRIGHTS TOWN, 175
YARMO, 70
YORK COUNTY, 20, 24
YORK, GREAT BRITAIN, 57
YOUNG, Rebecca, 24
YOUNGHUSBAND, Mary, 17, 20,
25; Mary P, 24, 25, 29; Polly T,
17
ZACHARY, Jemima, 130

Heritage Books by Mary Marshall Brewer:

Abstracts of Administrations of Montgomery County, Pennsylvania, 1822–1850

Abstracts of Land Records of King George County, Virginia, 1752–1783

Abstracts of Land Records of Richmond County, Virginia, 1692–1704

Abstracts of the Wills of Montgomery County, Pennsylvania, 1824–1850

Early Union County, New Jersey Church Records, 1750–1800

Essex County, Virginia Land Records, 1752–1761

Essex County, Virginia Land Records 1761–1772

Essex County, Virginia Land Records 1772–1786

Kent County, Delaware Guardian Accounts: Aaron to Carty, 1752–1849

Kent County, Delaware Guardian Accounts: Caton to Edinfield, 1753–1849

Kent County, Delaware Guardian Accounts: Edmondson to Hopkins, 1744–1855

Kent County, Delaware Guardian Accounts: Houston to McBride, 1739–1856

Kent County, Delaware Guardian Accounts: McBride to Savin, 1739–1851

Kent County, Delaware Guardian Accounts: Savin to Truax, 1754–1852

Kent County, Delaware Guardian Accounts: Truitt to Young, 1755–1849

Kent County, Delaware Land Records, 1776–1783

Kent County, Delaware Land Records, 1782–1785

Kent County, Delaware Land Records, 1785–1789

Kent County, Delaware Land Records, 1788–1792

King George County, Virginia Court Orders, 1746–1751

King George County, Virginia Court Orders, 1751–1754

Land Records of Sussex County, Delaware, 1681–1725

Land Records of Sussex County, Delaware, 1753–1763

Land Records of Sussex County, Delaware, 1763–1769

Land Records of Sussex County, Delaware: Various Dates: 1693–1698, 1715–1717, 1782–1792, 1802–1805

Land Records of York County, Pennsylvania, Libers A and B, 1746–1764

Land Records of York County, Pennsylvania, Libers C and D, 1764–1771

Land Records of York County, Pennsylvania, Libers E and F, 1771–1775

Land Records of York County, Pennsylvania, Libers G and H, 1775–1793

New Castle County, Delaware Wills, 1800–1813

Northumberland County, Virginia: Deeds, Wills, Inventories, etc., 1737–1743

Northumberland County, Virginia: Deeds, Wills, Inventories, etc., 1743–1749

Probate Records of Kent County, Delaware, Volume 1: 1801–1812

Probate Records of Kent County, Delaware, Volume 2: 1812–1822

Probate Records of Kent County, Delaware, Volume 3: 1822–1833

Quaker Records of Cedar Creek Monthly Meeting: Virginia, 1739–1793

Spotsylvania County, Virginia Deed Books, 1722–1734

Spotsylvania County, Virginia Deed Books, 1734–1751

York County, Virginia Deeds, Orders, Wills, Etc., 1698–1700

York County, Virginia Deeds, Orders, Wills, Etc., 1700–1702

York County, Virginia Deeds, Orders, Wills, Etc., 1705–1706

York County, Virginia Deeds, Orders, Wills, Etc., 1714–1716

York County, Virginia Deeds, Orders, Wills, Etc., 1716–1718

York County, Virginia Deeds, Orders, Wills, Etc., 1718–1720

York County, Virginia Deeds, Orders, Wills, Etc., 1728–1732

York County, Virginia Land Records: 1694–1713

York County, Virginia Land Records:1713–1729

York County, Virginia Land Records: 1729–1763

York County, Virginia Land Records: 1763–1777

York County, Virginia Wills, Inventories and Court Orders, 1702–1704

York County, Virginia Wills, Inventories and Court Orders, 1732–1737

York County, Virginia Wills, Inventories and Court Orders, 1737–1740

York County, Virginia Wills, Inventories and Court Orders, 1740–1743

York County, Virginia Wills, Inventories and Court Orders, 1745–1759

www.ingramcontent.com/pod-product-compliance
Lightning Source LLC
Chambersburg PA
CBHW070910270326
41927CB00011B/2518